Invited

Invited

Simple Prayer Exercises for Solitude and Community

Written and compiled by Lorie Martin

Fresh Wind Press

Editing: Ed Strauss Inkwell Writing Services - inkwell@shaw.ca.
Cover photo and design by Tiffany Martin: her_thoughts@hotmail.com
http://www.flickr.com/photos/tiffanyalisemartin
Interior Layout by Jon Paul Vooys: www.vooys.ca

Printed in Canada by Friesens Corporation, Altona, MB Canada.
To contact the author: Email Lorie Martin at invitedin@telus.net

ISBN: 978-0-9780174-4-6

Library Archives of Canada Cataloguing in Publication
available on request
2nd printing 2011

To order copies of *Invited*, visit:
www.freshwindpress.com

Fresh Wind Press
2170 Maywood Crt.,
Abbotsford, BC Canada V2S 4Z1

This book is dedicated to God,

the One who loves me completely, sets me free,
and never leaves.

My deepest thanks

to those who have shared their lives and prayer journeys with me:

To Dwight, my devoted husband,
you are wise and strong, you make me laugh, you hold me up,
and you always do the dirty dishes. You're the best.

To our children, Cam, Jessica and Chris, Tiffany, Brady, and Adri.
Each of you is extraordinary, unique and a brilliant individual. I
celebrate our family, our memories, our love and acceptance; let
us continue to receive each other as we are, forgive faults, trust
each other with our hearts, and free one another to fly with God
wherever we are led. I love you beyond all words.

To each of my family members, whom I cherish,
You are a well established place of love and joy. Years of life
with you have shaped and blessed me. May our care and prayer
for each other continue to surround and strengthen each of us.
Mom, thanks for the many blessings including sewing pretty
dresses for me for Sunday School.
Dad, I believe that you always love me, no matter what – xo

To my life friends:
Eden, Jodi, Herta, Karin, Cathy, Diane, Deb, and Bev: You are
perfect! You are irreplaceable in my life. You are "pure" love.

To my Fresh Wind church family:
You are my ministry anchor. Your faith, love, trust, and acceptance are a solid support that I've known through many days
and nights, trips and battles, fears and losses. You give grace,
strength, and laughter.
Our committed Leadership Team: Eden, Bill and Jamie, and
Charles; and to our mighty intercessor group: Fiona, Anne,
Barb, Nicole, Lora, and Desiree, who pray without ceasing for
Fresh Wind, every area of my life, and for those we serve; and
to my cherished friends and ministry companions: Brad, Diane
and John, Jenn, Trish and Bruce, Corinne and Jon Paul, Catherine and Lyle, Lara, Doreen and Heinz, Barb and Tony, Jacquie,
Tracey and Greg, Rose, Phyllis, and Nicole and Eric.

Thanks also to:

SoulStream: My contemplative community and peer supervision
group from whom I learn deep and lasting things of God.

MARK Centre friends and Steve & Evy who meet God together
and share the Good News.

To those who meet with me for spiritual direction, Your hearts
are precious; when we are together I learn much about our God
who walks with us.

To those who helped this book to become a reality:
Tiffany Martin: Cover photography and design.
Brad Jersak: Fresh Wind Press; Jon Paul Vooys: layout.
Dwight, Irene, Sue, Cathy, Eden, Fiona, Kevin & Heidi,
Herta, Catherine, and Ed Strauss, editor,
Jessa: Hugs for the sticky note that helped me believe;
'Go for it Mom! All the way!'
And to you, Julie: 'Auntie Lorie, you should write a book!'

Contents

Invited to Scripture

Invited to Rest

Invited to Solitude

Invited to Community

Invited to Healing

Invited to Action

Invocation

 ## Prayer
Soul of Christ

Jesus, may all that is you flow into me.
May your body and blood
be my food and drink.
May your passion and death
be my strength and life.
Jesus, with you by my side
Enough has been given.
May the shelter I seek
Be the shadow of your cross.
Let me not run from the love
Which you offer,
But hold me safe from the forces of evil.
On each of my dyings,
Shed your light and your love.
Keep calling me until that day comes,
When, with your saints,
I may praise you forever. Amen

David Fleming, SJ
A paraphrase of the *Anima Christi*
a favourite prayer of St. Ignatius.

Foreword

Receiving an invitation is much like being given a gift. The gift of invitation communicates a sense of worth—in being recognized as a person, wanted, accepted, one who belongs. Every meditation in this book is God's invitation, sealed for you personally. Each one has your name on it, announcing your arrival at the King's banquet.

This labour of love is no mere compilation. Lorie didn't simply research and catalogue as many prayer encounters as she could collect like so many recipes for a cookbook. No, she's taste-tested God's goodness in every dish and offers this spiritual feast as a joyful and thankful serving participant. Lorie first accepted and embraced the invitations herein long before any thought of a book was considered. Her love for Jesus, her desire to drink deeply at the well of spirituality, and the fruit of time spent with Jesus are evident throughout.

Lorie has practiced these encounters personally, but is also inspired to bring them to as many others as possible. She has led numerous prayer encounters with the House of Prayer at Fresh Wind Christian Fellowship. She has brought these gifts to WILD Retreats (Women in Leadership Day-Retreat) and to the Sacred Space at the Mark Centre in Abbotsford, BC. She has walked countless people in recovery through such exercises—broken people fresh off the streets and looking for a better meal than that which the world had poisoned them. She has shared them at conferences from the UK to North America and into Asia. As personal witnesses, we can say that the fruit of this ministry—from this generous giving—has been so very sweet.

Those who enter into these encounters with Christ will inevitably see how extremely vital contemplative prayer is for a healthy Christian community. These exercises will equip and develop the spiritual eyes and ears of anyone who partakes, rather than leaving the depths of spirituality to vocational 'Super Christians.' The simplicity of what Lorie presents allows even the newest and youngest believers to enter in. Never has the 'prophethood of all believers' been so necessary to the health of the church and her members. So come in, find your seat at the Lord's table, and dig in!

Eden and Brad Jersak
Fresh Wind Christian Fellowship
Authors and Speakers

Your Invitation Has Arrived

"As for me, I shall behold your face in righteousness; I will be satisfied with your likeness when I awake."
Psalm 17:15 NASB

It is my desire and prayer that this book of simple exercises and stories be a series of invitations that draw you near to God – and more than near; close enough to hear the voice of the Most High God, to see the face of the Good Shepherd gazing at you, and to know the heart of the One who created you out of love.

God constantly takes the initiative in love toward us. God's endless presence and our encounters are active and interactive, as well as quiet and still. We have been created to drink deeply of God's love, kindness, wisdom, peace, and freedom. We've been designed to encounter the Divine; we will not be satisfied with anything other than to experience the beautiful oneness of life with God.

There are so many ways to be present to God. May the variety of exercises in this book be helpful for you to begin or to continue connecting with The One Who loves you most.

My long-time friend, Herta, gave me this definition that describes well one of my hopes for this book; "*Invited* is a verb...living, active, something that I move into. In reading your book I feel invited to participate in it, I'm moved by the words, I'm drawn into it. It is so full of life and action."

In a recent email from my daughter, Tiffany, she says something very profound: "Since, well, no one knows what God looks like, nature is the best representation for me...and "OPEN" space is always inviting..."

May these exercises lead you to open spaces where you will be aware of the nearness of God and experience being deeply loved with a profound sense of belonging. From these encounters may you enjoy inner freedom, be encouraged to remain true to the way of Jesus, and carry God's loving presence to others and into all that you have been given to do.

It is also my hope that you will share these when you gather together as a family, at prayer times, retreats, or church gatherings. People are hungry to encounter God. My daughter, Jessica, and son-in-law, Chris, asked me to come to their home group to share some prayer invitations with their friends. It was remarkable how well these young adults entered into experiencing God, hearing words of encouragement for each other, and receiving pictures to guide them and build their faith. There seems to be a strong desire for intimacy with God among all ages and people groups in these days, what joy!

Escaping the hurried life is not always easy. We live with much noise, action, busyness, and often chaos. Our time, personal space, and energy are highly contended for. We may battle fears and inse-curities in approaching God. We may face lies such as, *it's all up to me* or *God couldn't possibly love or desire me.* Regardless of what may be going on for you, you are invited in. Our Creator and Friend adores us and desires to be with us vastly beyond our understanding. God wants to meet with us even if we are bringing our anger, indif-ference, judgements, or endless needs.

Teresa of Avila (1515-1582), whom I count as my friend, taught me in her writings (*Interior Castle)* to see that my receiving from God is to be different than a laborious act of tying together a series of pipes to bring some distant water from the source to me. Rather, it is to simply look up and be open to the rain of Heaven, God's glori-ous presence, coming upon me and within me.

I remember a time when I felt a nudge to turn on a CD and spend some moments in worship adoring God. I wanted to focus for this one whole song on the One who has set me free and made me whole. It seemed like an easy aspiration. After three attempts, and three re-starts, I wept in despair over my inability to give my attention to God for these very few moments. I turned my tear filled gaze to God with my many apologies. Instead of huge disappointment I received comfort, joy and delight. God was pleased with my deep longing and sincere effort to connect and to bring my adoration. How kind God is.

Some things may be dreadfully out of place in our hearts or lives or perhaps only slightly off. At times we can struggle or strive for God to come near, and at other times our beautiful longing and genuine desire for our Living God can turn to disappointment or apathy. I believe whatever state our soul is in that one of these prayer exercises can be used to fill the cup of your being, perhaps even to overflowing. May you hear the heart of Jesus longing for you.

Let us hold in a healthy tension the grand encounters we may have with God along with the little whispers of love, knowing all that we are given whether plenty or want is beautiful. St. Therese of Lisieux (1873-1897) makes this point well, "Let us remain very remote from all that glitters. Let us love our littleness; let us love to feel nothing. Then we shall be poor in spirit, and Jesus will come seeking us, however far away we are. He will transform us into flames of love!"

I invite you to dedicate some time to meet with God in both intentional ways, and in the ordinary moments of the day. May you *clear the table* of the clutter that sits before you, *clear the dance floor* of your life of all that wants to engage you, and take hold of your schedule to make some space and find a place to meet with God. I hope you will lay down any sense of performance or obligation toward God and simply respond by moving as you feel led toward the invitations that are before you.

My heart has heard you say, "Come and talk with me."
And my heart responds, "LORD, I am coming."

Wait for the LORD;
Be strong and let your heart take courage;
Yes, wait for the LORD.
Psalm 27: 8 NLT; 14 NASB

User's Guide

There are many ways this book can be of value in your life. Here are some suggestions:

1. **Follow the Sections** If you can, you are invited to participate in all of the exercises as you go through the book, whether you do so daily or once a week. Stay in each section or exercise as long as you are receiving life from it, before going on. Simply begin at the beginning and journey page by page with God into all that is for you. Keep a journal if possible. You need not record each thing God shows you, or write at length; a simple word, sentence, or sketch can remind you of the powerful essence of what you will want to remember.

2. **Topical Guide** Read or skim the various topics or scriptures in the Contents at the front of the book, or in the Topical Guide at the back to see where you sense the Spirit is inviting you at this time. There may be a certain type of exercise that is best for you right now. Follow what your heart feels Jesus is drawing you to. Linger there as long as you are able and move on when you sense a completion to what God is saying or giving to you.

3. **Time Guide** ⏳ Some exercises work well for a short few minutes of connection time with God, some approximately a half an hour sitting, others are designed for a longer time period – perhaps as a Sabbath devotional or for a spiritual retreat. Each exercise has an hour-glass shape beside it. One hour-glass signifies the short exercises, two hour-glasses are for medium length exercises, and three are for the longer, more involved exercises.

⏳ Short exercise	approximately		10 – 20 minutes
⏳⏳ Medium length	"		20 – 30 minutes
⏳⏳⏳ Longer exercise	"		30 – 60 minutes

Invited to Listen

I Give You My Heart

Hush Listen
I hear Him coming
Hush Listen
Now He is here

O what can I bring Him?
What can I offer?
How can I show Him?
I'll give Him my heart

All of my dreams (give Him)
All of my hopes (give Him)
All that I am (give Him)
I give Him my heart

Stop Listen
I behold you
You are beloved
I sing for you

Rise up O daughter/son (beautiful one)
Lift up your head (there is no shame)
Return my gaze (show me your face)
For I give you my heart

You are mine (Beloved)
From before time (Beloved)
I give all that I am (Beloved)
I give you my heart

How Do You Hear the Lord?
Let us Count the Ways

Isaiah 55:3
"Incline your ear and come to me. Listen that you may live." NIV
"Pay attention, come close now, listen carefully to my life-giving,
life-nourishing words." The Message
"Come to me with your ears wide open.
Listen and you will find life." NLT

I can still remember when I started recognizing the voice of the Lord speaking to me personally. Such joy filled my heart as I began to trust the voice of the One I love. My relationship with God had been established over the years, yet it changed drastically from being distant-like and effort-filled, to doing life together like having the best room-mate ever.

"For God does speak—now one way, now another—"
(Job 33:13 TNIV)

PRAYER EXERCISE **1**

LET US COUNT THE WAYS   **XX**

1 Make a list of many of the ways that we hear God speaking to us. What is the first thing that comes to mind? Think of your day, your night, as well as your times in quietness, in community, and in nature. The list can get quite long, can't it? Here are a few: Scripture   Preaching   Songs or Music   Nature   A friend   A child   Movies   A parent   A circumstance   An object or symbol   A book, story or poem   An event   A dream   In community interaction   A stirring or prompting   In silence …

2 Do you have a common or favourite way you hear the Lord? Do you seem open to one way more than others? Why do you think that is? Are you open to other ways?

3

3 Do you seem to hear an inner voice? Do you see pictures or visualize what you are hearing, thinking, or experiencing? Do you tend to simply know in your innermost being what God is saying or showing you?

4 Ask Jesus a question, as you would a friend, and take time to simply listen. Choose one of the following questions and journal what you hear or what is made known to you. I hope you feel free to interact with Our Beloved Friend.

a.) Jesus, how do you want to be with me right now? What shall we do together?

b.) Jesus, how do you want me to know and experience you at this time? Why?

c.) Jesus, how do you see me today? Why did I need to know that?

d.) Jesus, what gift do you have for me today? Why?

e.) Jesus, what can I do for you today?

Hearing God – Imagine That!
Using our Imagination

"That is what the Scriptures mean when they say,
'No eye has seen, no ear has heard, and no mind has imagined
what God has prepared for those who love him.'
But it was to us that God revealed these things by his Spirit.
For his Spirit searches out everything and shows us God's deep
secrets."
(1 Corinthians 2:9-10 NLT)

Using our imagination as a way to visit and spend time with God is probably one of the prime reasons God gave us an imagination in the first place. God does command us not only to love Him with all our heart, but also with our entire mind (Matthew 22:37 NIV). When we use our mind and our imagination in our interactions with God we are able to have an inward connection with the Holy One, experience the actual reality of God's presence, hear the life-giving voice, and receive what we are being shown or what is being imparted to us. God sends healing and transformation to us this way. Leanne Payne, a trusted teacher and author on listening prayer for decades refers to our "sanctified" imagination. I highly recommend her book, *Restoring the Christian Soul*, where she explains and clarifies the use of the imagination in Christian healing. Other words that we may use when referring to the use of our imagination would be to picture, to envision, visualize, think of, conceive of, or to see in our mind's eye.

My friend Brad Jersak teaches this in an easy-to-understand way. He describes our imagination as the screen upon which the mind and heart project and ponders images. It is not a voice. The flesh and the spirit are the films that compete to fill the soul with thoughts and images. The soul loads and then projects these onto the screen. The will of a person is like the projectionist who chooses what he or she will engage with.

5

Brad goes on to explain that the flesh will allow us to escape into dangerous dream worlds, rather than refreshment or recreation. These fantasies capture us in delusion and lure us away from reality. He suggests we test the effects of the uses of our imagination to see if they are constructive and helping us to face life, marriage, spiritual life, etc —something that listening prayer for inner healing or meditating on God, does. If our thoughts are causing dissatisfaction, discontent, fear, paranoia, escapism or distraction from life in this world and in God's kingdom, then he says, you're likely gazing through the wrong spiritual window. For further study and clear explanations on this I highly recommend, *Can You Hear Me?* By Brad Jersak <www.freshwindpress.com>.

Isn't it almost impossible to read Psalm 23 or sing "I Come to the Garden Alone," without images coming to our minds? Using our imagination can connect our heart, mind and body to what God is making known to us and to what is actually happening in the unseen places within us.

This is what I have experienced for myself and with others for many years. I am thankful for God's power over darkness and deception and His perfect ability and grace to lead us close to Himself. I invite us all to keep the "baby" (meeting with God and receiving what He shows us) while we throw out the "bath water" (confusion, fear, other things popping up on our screens, etc.)—or better yet, we should bring the fear or other distractions to the Lord and receive His touch, truth or healing.

It is God's kind and great idea for us to test, weigh and discern everything we are receiving from Him and others (1 Thessalonians 5:21; 1 Corinthians 14:29), especially as it relates to connecting with Him and being sanctified. We are to use Scripture, the Church community (past and present), and our spirits within us to bear witness to discern what we are hearing, Once again I highly recommend Brad's teaching and insights in *Can You Hear Me?* for a thorough look at testing what we hear.

Let's remember that God created our humanity and that we are loved as we are and with all the ways that we were made to function.

The Holy One has made many ways to speak to us and make His heart of love known to us. I'd like to share these words from a song that I've known for years, using it as an invitation.

Turn your eyes upon Jesus.
Look full in His wonderful face.
And the things of earth will grow strangely dim,
In the light of His glory and grace.

PRAYER EXERCISE 2

THE VOICE OF THE ONE I LOVE

1 Choose one of the following three invitations:

a.) The words of the song written above: *Turn your eyes upon Jesus.*

b.) This scripture:

*"That is what the Scriptures mean when they say,
'No eye has seen, no ear has heard, and no mind has imagined
what God has prepared for those who love him.'
But it was to us that God revealed these things by his Spirit.
For his Spirit searches out everything and shows us
God's deep secrets."* (1 Cor. 2:9-10 NLT)

c.) Ask God a question such as: What is Your love like? What promise do You have for me today? How do You see me today? What do You want me to do today?

2 Set aside some quiet listening space to read, ponder, and open your heart and mind to receive what the Lord wants to tell you. You may engage your imagination if thoughts or pictures come to mind that will add to your listening time. Not everyone "sees" when they meditate on the Lord; some hear, some feel, and some simply have a profound sense of knowing deep in their spirits. However you connect with our Living God is valuable. It is best for us to be content with what we receive regardless of how little it may seem, yet letting God know what we would like is good, and to ask for all that we are able to receive.

THE ROLE OF IMAGINATION IN PRAYER:

Imagination is the power of our memory and recall which enables us to enter into the experiences that come to mind. Through images we are able to touch the center of who we are and to surface and give life and expression to the innermost levels of our being. Images simultaneously reveal multiple levels of meaning and are therefore symbolic of our deeper reality. Through the sanctified & structured use of active imagination, we release the hidden energy, the truth of God, and the potential for wholeness which is already present within us by God's Spirit. When we use active imagination in the context of prayer, and with an attitude of faith, we open ourselves to the power and mystery of the truth of what God is doing in our lives and His transforming presence within us.

A STORY FROM THE JOURNEY...

Eden Jersak, my dear friend and ministry companion, and I were at a retreat facilitating a group of people to listen and hear God. They were with a missions organization called TREK and were preparing for a missionary trip. The leaders of TREK asked us to teach the many ways that we all hear God, and to discover and explore some new ways. The groups have their questions, which are excellent, and are usually open to this kind of listening and praying. We've seen wonderful visitations of the Holy Spirit as He makes His voice known to many hearts.

At one session, a young woman said, "Oh, I've heard of Listening Prayer. I've heard of churches that do that. But, not ours, we wouldn't do that. I wasn't sure if what you were suggesting is okay to do. So I prayed and asked God if it was okay to do this. As I waited for an answer to know what to do about this, I saw a picture of a garden and God taking me to the garden. We went to this very fragrant flower that was in the corner of the garden."

She went on to describe the garden and this particular flower. It seemed to be a garden of prayer, full of many flowers that represented the various ways of prayer. The Lord showed her this fragrant flower and told her that Listening Prayer was like this flower—that it was one of many ways to pray, and that it was very beautiful and that its fragrance filled the garden and drew her in.

I asked her how she felt about Listening Prayer after those things had come to her heart and mind. She told us that she had total peace with it now, for God had made this truth known to her within her own heart and mind.

This is one of my favourite Listening Prayer encounters of all time. God used Listening Prayer to show this young woman that Listening Prayer was okay. How did God do that? Why did God do that? It's because we are loved, because God wants to have intimacy with us, and because God's heart for us is to hear the Voice of Life.

"For the eyes of the Lord move to and fro throughout the earth
that He may strongly support those whose heart is
completely His"
(2 Chron. 16:9 NASB).

Trek is a program of MBMSI (Mennonite Brethren Missions and Services International) <www.mbmsi.org/trek/overivew/>; <www.markcentre.org>.

RECOMMENDED READING:

Rivers from Eden – 40 days of intimate conversation with God by Eden & Brad Jersak

I Can't Hear God!
Now What?

"If only I knew where to find him;
if only I could go to his dwelling!"
(Job 23:3 NIV)

Can you identify with one of these statements: "I can't hear God." Or "Where did God go?" What is going on in your life? Have you heard God in your heart before or is this a new longing emerging from somewhere inside you?

This point in our spiritual journey is a well-known part of the road that none of us like to travel. It can be dark, lonely, confusing, cold, scary, or crazy-making. All manner of descriptive words tell us about it. What words describe this "place" for you?

We may find ourselves believing or thinking that for some known or unknown reason, we are unable to hear God. Or perhaps we have had a season of great intimacy with God when we heard from him clearly and it now seems to have vanished or faded away. First, let's consider His voice "disappearing."

I experienced a dark night of the soul recently and it truly was like someone started dimming the lights and didn't stop until it was completely black. I lost my bearings and was drawn into a time where I wondered what on earth had happened. My faith was challenged and my trust and love for God was severely tested. Losing our known sense of God, being unable to hear His voice or connect with Him in ways that have previously been familiar, safe or life-giving, takes us into uncharted territory and feels far from good. Drowning might well describe it.

I could genuinely understand David pouring out his heart in the Psalms (and the experience of Christ on the cross) "My God, my God, why have You forsaken me? Far from my deliverance are the words of my groaning. O my God, I cry by day, but You do not answer; And by night, but I have no rest. Yet you are holy" (Psalm 22:1-2 NASB). "Jesus cried out with a loud voice, saying, 'My God, my God, why have you forsaken me?' (Matthew 27:46 NASB)

Both David and Christ show us that God never did leave, but that there is sometimes a very real sense of God's absence. Here is David's conclusion and his experience a few verses later in Psalm 22, verse 24: "He has not hidden his face, but has listened to the cry for help." The NLT says, "He has not turned and walked away." Jesus was given a real sense of knowing God's presence while experiencing great darkness, and said, "Father, into your hands I commit my spirit" (Luke 23:46 NASB).

Father Thomas Keating, a Benedictine Monk for the past sixty years, describes Spiritual Formation as an archaeological dig with the Holy Spirit, going into the layers of our lives. It's not a ladder going upwards, or a circle going around, it is more like a spiral staircase where we take steps down and we take steps going up. We go down in humility to the depths of our limitations and to all that is not yet developed within us and up to the heights of our love and inner resurrection experience with God. During such times of transformation by the Spirit of God our lives can become very chaotic. Things we were really interested in like books, music, and church, things we knew to be stable, enjoyable, and fresh from God, become stale, empty, and old. It's like the honeymoon is over and things fall flat. At the onset of our spiritual journey we think that this emotional fervour, or spring-like sense of newness, will go on forever—or we sure hope it will.

When God knows we are ready for the next level in our spiritual growth we will experience a challenging time called the "night of sense" or the "dark night of the soul." This is when our "spring" seems to turn to "winter." We wonder, question, anguish, and fear this time when everything seems to be going all wrong. Blame, doubt, or anger at God can appear, or a low sense of self worth can surface, and nothing seems to bring us much joy. Strong sensations of loss, rejection, loneliness, temptation, and depression can come up. Some bad attitudes that we thought for sure were gone, reappear for more transformation.

I love Father Keating's humour when he laughs and, in the midst of describing this very intense time, says that the Holy Spirit is relentless and assumes we actually like the process of transformation and want more! Each stage and level is important for us to journey. Habits or possessions that we hold onto could have damaging or denying affects and we need to visit these dark places even if it seems that we are getting worse. It can be a real detriment to ourselves, families, relationships, and ministries if we do not deal with these issues. As we are healed we are able to give ourselves to others more freely and to serve them well. Jesus is our "Divine Therapist."

We will eventually "plateau," Keating teaches. We will reach a place where our relationship with Jesus will appear like a dawning as the chaos settles. We will accept our weakness and our love for God will be more pure, deep, and strong even when we don't know what is happening within us. The Holy Spirit continues to move deeply taking us to deeper rest, and we learn to trust that God loves us no matter what. As we feel worse, sometimes raw or primitive places coming to our awareness, we can rejoice knowing that we are getting to the bottom of things, and can enter what is called, "divine union with God." Here we find that we are being freed from obstacles and that we don't care anymore what comes up – we know who we are and that God is right with us. We actually will welcome brokenness with an open mind; it will no longer hold as much fear, and we can even have the faith to let others experience this journey without fearing for them. The outcome of these transitional periods is Perfect Love.

I highly recommend reading *The Dark Night of the Soul* by Gerald G. May, M.D. He takes the profound teaching of St. John of the Cross and Theresa of Avila—both of whom deeply understood and taught us about the Dark Night. Their primary goal was to help us not despair in these times. May has powerfully described this process, the signs, the outcome, and the journey as it relates to us today. He uses wisdom to help us in the midst of a dark night or to understand what others may be experiencing.

He says in *The Dark Night of the Soul*, "Each experience of the dark night gives its gifts, leaving us freer than we were before, more available, more responsive, and more grateful. Like not knowing and lack of control, freedom and gratitude are abiding characteristics of the dark night. But they don't arrive until the darkness passes. They come with the dawn." He encourages us to enter these mysteries with God as, "there is something wonderful at the heart of our existence, and it is about nothing other than love: love for God, love for one another, love for creation, love for life itself."

How kind of God to give us journey-mates like St. John, St. Teresa, Father Keating, and Dr. May who put words and wisdom to our spiritual experiences and help us through the dark tunnels we must pass through.

When we lead listening prayer seminars, workshops, or private sessions, we occasionally meet a dear soul who is or has been struggling with hearing God. There are usually very good reasons why this is happening. It is an impasse that I believe our loving God longs to come to. We have seen the Spirit come countless times to this spot that very good Christian men and women encounter. Sometimes our rational thinking gets in the way of the language of our heart. Sometimes we have fear of what we might hear, or that we might not hear, and this can block what we actually have been hearing all along. Occasionally a wrong belief about being worthy to hear, or special enough, can delay an encounter with God. It can also be that we do not feel safe in the room or with the person we are praying with, so it is best to settle these things before going on. Whatever the predicament, I know Jesus has an answer and will extend his hand to lead us on.

I am confident in God always being with us and sharing messages of powerful, yet tender love in a variety of ways to us. I invite you to keep waiting upon the One that embraces all that you are.

Here are two exercises for each of the dilemmas that are described above.

> *"Your kingdom come. Your will be done,*
> *on earth as it is in heaven."*
> (Matthew 6:10 NASB)
> Now, here, with you.

PRAYER EXERCISE 3

A DARK NIGHT   XX

1 Picture your heart as a room or building where God dwells.

2 See what it might look like in the full light of day.

3 Picture the lights going out. Feel. Listen. Experience God with you.

4 Receive the real presence of God as much as you are able. Rest, trust, and be loved.

5 Share your present experience and feelings with God, He can handle it. Job shared his authentic feelings (Job 23), which weren't always nice, and he also said, "When he has tested me, I will come forth as gold" (Job 23:10 NIV). (The life of King David in the scriptures, especially the Psalms, shows us much about the freedom and reality of sharing what we feel.)

6 Do only what you are responsible to do, or that which presents itself as needing attention, in each hour or day. Try not to make things change or happen. Be open to things unfolding as you obey God in each little step of the way.

7 Be vulnerable with people who are safe and whom you trust. Share truthfully what you are able to articulate. Continue to put your trust in God as you are able.

"All shall be well, and all shall be well." Julian of Norwich

PRAYER EXERCISE **4**

"I CAN'T HEAR"   XX

1 Open your Bible to Psalm 23.

2 Picture God, or Jesus, as the Good Shepherd and you as one of His sheep or lambs.

3 Slowly read or move through the psalm asking God these questions:

a.) What does the pasture, water, and shadow of death look like in my life?

b.) Where would Jesus be if He was in this picture? How would you view Him? What would He look like?

c.) Where are you (the reader) as His lamb? What condition are you in?

d.) How would Jesus feel when He saw you? How would you feel when you saw Him? Can this be an inward picture of your present situation?

e.) How do you think Jesus would want to come to you? Is that okay with you?

f.) What would He say to you? What gifts or promises would He give you?

g.) What would you want to say to Him? How would you like to respond?

h.) Continue looking at the verses, the scenes, the images, the truths of God, and how He might want to walk with you through each verse.

i.) Trust that you have heard God – it's what He is saying to you or wanting to make known to you at this time. If it felt too simple, try to receive the essence of His heart to you and take time to let it sink in. He may have other pieces of this message that are still to come, you'll know them when you see or hear them.

j.) Continue to take time to practice this way of listening and conversing with God. Test what you hear by comparing it to Scripture and sharing it with godly people whom you trust. Does this sound like God? If so, then it likely IS Him.

Listening to Your Heart
Symbols & Seasons

"Above all else, guard your heart, for it is the wellspring of life."
(Prov. 4:23 NIV)

My long-time friend and journey-mate, Jodi Krahn, taught me this prayer exercise and so much more! Every week I would sit fascinated by Jodi leading our small group. Her authenticity, message, and delivery were so life-giving. We listened, we laughed, we cried, and always she would take us right into our hearts.

We were deeply impacted this one week when she asked us to do a simple assignment and then share with the group what happened for us personally. We were to look at a table that was covered with items that Jodi had brought from home. Spread out before us were items such as a lantern, a rock, a bowl, a flower in a vase, a man's well worn running shoe, a tea pot, etc. We were to watch how our heart would be drawn to one of them in particular. The question was, "If one of these objects represents your heart today, which one would it be, and why?" We spent time pondering and meeting with God. Jodi led us on: "Be mindful of God with you and your heart that is symbolized by this object. How does God want to be for you? How does God see you? What is being given to you?"

After some time to ponder and reflect on these questions, we went around the room to share what we were feeling and hearing. To our amazement God had spoken to each of the nearly twenty participants in a very personal way. Something significant happened when we were able to identify with a symbol. The symbol was able to depict more than words and described what was going on within us at that particular time. The symbol became a focal point from which God could speak to us with more clarity.

A symbol is a tangible thing (noun) or action (verb) that we use to represent an intangible concept because of something the thing and the action have in common. God often uses a physical reality to

17

illustrate a spiritual reality. This is why some have called symbolism "the language of God." Others identify symbols as the language of the heart.

Scripture is saturated with symbols that are pregnant with meaning. Entire books have been dedicated to cataloguing and defining the types and symbols of the Bible. (Suggested reading: *Interpreting the Symbols and Types* by Kevin J. Conner.) The images and pictures that God draws for us throughout Scripture function to simplify, explain, obscure, create wonder, and even to terrify. They convey information and evoke strong emotion much more than plain words would. They lure us closer for a better look and trigger new questions in our minds. God also uses symbols to get important truths past our rational defences and in behind faulty paradigms. Most of all, much of God's character is revealed through symbols in order to help us know more about our Creator. Here are some examples: The Rock, The Root of Jesse, Branch, Great Physician, Counsellor, King of Kings, Shepherd of the sheep, Great High Priest, Chief Cornerstone, Judge, Fire, Water, Light, Dove, etc.

Jesus enjoyed using symbolism when He was trying to teach His followers. His parables were simple spiritual lessons taken from common life occurrences. He created a parable by stringing symbols together to make a point. For example, Jesus loved to use wedding symbols (i.e. bride and bridegroom, invitations, the banquet, etc.) to teach us about God's kingdom. (See Matthew 22:1–14.)

The heart is an inner place. It is our physical, emotional and moral centre. It is where union and conflict with God occur. It is the place that tells us what is happening with us and where our responses will begin. It is where detachment (freedom) is. The heart is a meeting place with God where we relate to God with all that we are. It is where we are transformed by the Holy Spirit. It is good to pay attention to the movement or stirrings of our hearts. There is a difference between movement of the heart and emotions. When we have an experience, our heart is moved; this is the first feeling. The second thing that happens is that we experience thoughts about what just happened. Third, after our thoughts have come through our mental grid (how we see or believe things to be), we then feel emotions. Our emotions are not our reality; they are simply how we feel. It is very important to listen to God as to what is really going on inside us and to be attentive to God who is there offering comfort, wisdom and truth. "Let me not run from Your love that You offer," St. Ignatius prayed, most likely in both difficult and delightful times.

Vital to our wellbeing is the state of our receptivity, our core posture of the heart. Are we open, resting, and trusting as we bring our hearts before God? The will of God is for us to receive. God's voice and presence bring unexplainable joy, peace, certainty, energy, interest, longing, and passion. The Most High God truly is the wellspring of life within us. We may want to grab, grasp, and do whatever we feel like, as it is in all of us to want to own that which we love. The invitation is to let go of this propensity to grab and to simply be receptive or open to receive whatever God gives.

Solitude is the furnace of transformation rather than an escape from busyness. Times of solitude develop sensitivity to God and allow us to savour intimate moments, to let them fill us and satisfy us. Prayer is our response to what is going on in life. These movements of our heart turn us to God.

Let us live with an awareness of our heart's movements, but not follow our hearts, rather meet God in our hearts and move in The Way of Jesus. Prayer: "Lord, let us not fear our hearts, but rather love them as You do, and enter deeply within to experience all that You have for us. Amen."

PRAYER EXERCISE 5

WHAT SYMBOL REPRESENTS MY HEART TODAY?   ☒☒

In Solitude: Gather a few of your favourite things or things that seem to grab your attention today.

In a Group: Provide an array of objects that symbolize or that hold meaning – bits of nature, containers, etc.

1 After identifying an object that you seem drawn to, hold it if possible, examine it, and use all your senses to discover things about it. Return it as soon as possible to the table if this is a group activity.

2 Go into prayer and listening. Some questions you may want to ask:

a.) Jesus, why does this object symbolize my heart today?

b.) Is there any particular facet of this object or symbol that You want to speak to me about? Can You tell me why this is important?

c.) What truth about my heart do You want to speak to me using this symbol?

d.) How do You want me to experience You with my heart in this state?

e.) How do You see me? What do I need to know about Your love and power?

f.) Let the things that Jesus shared with you enter into your heart. Hold onto them, continue to enjoy and receive from these truths and His loving presence with you.

Prayer Exercise 6

Additional Focus Questions XX

1. What season is my heart in at this time? Spring, winter, Christmas, etc.

2. What weather condition is my heart today? Calm, stormy, raining, unsettled, etc.

3. What kind of container represents my heart? Large, small, full, cracked, open, etc

4. What would the title of my heart be today if it were a book? Why? Which character?

5. What song comes to mind when I think of my heart today? Why this one? Listen closely to all the words, there may be a lot more in this than just the title.

6. What outfit would I wear today as a symbol of my heart condition? Why?

7. What food or spice or flavour represents my life at this time? Why?

8. What kind of water source represents my present state of being? Why?

Questions to take into each of the above exercises:

1. Why is my heart in this condition? Explore this state of my heart using my senses: What does it look like, feel like, or smell like? What colors are predominant? Is there any activity going on? Does it remind me of something?

2. Where are You, God, in the midst of my current heart condition? God, what do you want to show or tell me about this?

3. What do I need to know about You in this situation?

4   Am I able to accept this, or embrace it? Do I want to exit or fight it?

5   How long have I been here? Have I felt God with me? Why or why not? Am I stuck here? How might God want to help me get unstuck and move forward?

6   What does God have for me here? What have I already been given that I may need to be reminded of? How does God respond to my need?

7   Can I trust that I'll be okay without it changing quickly or getting fixed? Why or why not?

8   Be loved in the circumstances that brought me pain or loss without trying to fix or change them.

9   What symbol or item do I have that I could put out as a reminder of what God is saying to me or doing in my life at this time? Keep it front and centre for awhile.

You Show Me the Path of Life

"You have made known to me the path of life;
you will fill me with joy in your presence,
with eternal pleasures at your right hand."
(Psalm 16:11)

"Keep me O God
For I trust in you
You show me the path of life
In you there's fullness of joy"
A prayer/song from the community of Taize.

Re-read the above words imagining them being sung to the Lord by a clear melodious, yet powerful voice up in the hills of Mission, B.C. at Westminster Abbey. This heavenly sound permeated the air of this vast room, and filled our hearts to a rich fullness. My friend, Cathy Hardy (and a Taize team) shared this gift of song with us .

Cathy's passion is to create sacred space through music for the healing of the heart and for deep connection with God. Her main training and vocation has been in the area of music. She has a music studio with 30 students and has recorded two CDs with original music and prayer songs from the Taizé community in France. The first CD is called *REST ... inspirations from Taizé*, and the second is called *TRUST ... inspirations from Taizé* (the song mentioned above is on this CD.) Both of these projects have been done in collaboration with harpist Karin Dart (also a very dear friend of mine.) Cathy has been involved in leading many community events including ecumenical Taize services in the Fraser Valley, leading contemplative retreats, guiding people with spiritual direction and teaching about stillness and rest. Cathy lives in Mission, B.C. with her husband and 2 teen daughters. For information on recordings please visit: <www.cathyajhardy.com>.

Each December 31st, on the last day of that year, Cathy, Eden and I head up to the Abbey to ponder the past year, and to listen silently while being together for the year to come. These afternoon treks to the simple beauty and stillness of this place have been filled with wonder, guidance, clarity, songs, pictures, and encouragement.

Here are a couple of prayer exercises you may want to consider as you head into a new year, another school year, or the beginning of something new.

PRAYER EXERCISE 7

LETTING GO – HOLDING ON   **XXX**

1 Do a personal inventory: What are your responsibilities, jobs, areas of overseeing, dreams, goals, etc... (I.e. Personal, Job, Ministries, Finances, Home, Children, A musical production, etc.) You may want to journal these. Listen on one or a few areas of your life.

2 Ask God to show you anything you may be invited to let go of as you enter this new season in your life. Receive strength to say "Yes" to this invitation. If this is difficult, it may be helpful to ask, "Why?" As you listen to your heart and what God is making known to you, receive care and comfort to any loss that may be happening.

3 Ask God to show you what you are to hold onto and take with you into this new season. You may want to ask, "Why is this important to hold onto?

4 Ask God to make known to you what He may be inviting you toward. What is a promise for this next season? Perhaps there is a word or phrase that will be valuable or helpful for the time to come.

PRAYER EXERCISE 8

SIGN POST (FROM CATHY HARDY)   XXX

Supplies needed: A piece of paper (nice art paper if possible) and some felt pens

1 Enter into Silence. Where are you on the path of your life right now? Perhaps the desert, the woods, a meadow, a busy roadway, a mountain, alone, with others, etc.

2 Imagine where you are on this path.

3 Take time to draw what the path looks like and yourself on it. (Stick men are fine!) Use simple lines and circles if you are uncomfortable with drawing.

4 In the place where you are presently on the path draw a 'signpost' and leave it blank.

5 Take time with the drawing as your thoughts and feelings emerge.

6 Stay in silence and ask God to reveal to you what the word is for the signpost. Often there has been one word that has come to me that has sustained me for an entire year – a word that I can go back to and anchor myself with – or a word that calls for me to know in a deeper way and allows for greater understanding and growth. Some of the words in the past 10 years have been: wait, courage, trust, rest, hope.

Listen for the word for you. It may come now, or later, but it will come as you listen. When you are ready, place that word on your picture.

7 If you are able to, reinforce the significance of this word given to you by creating something such as a string of beads with symbolic colors or the letters of this word. We are called to 'remember' the words that God brings us and to honor them, to let them soak into our beings and change us.

8 Go back and re-read the words to the Taize Community Song, Keep Me O God. Entrust yourself and this next season into God's hands.

As God gives you gifts that significantly impact you, you may want to put something tangible in your view (on a table, in your car, around your neck, etc.) to continue to be mindful of what God is giving and doing in your life. In a sense, you are allowing this gift (a promise, a word, a healing, etc.) to be ongoing for some time to come. There is no need to quickly put it away, like you would put something into a cupboard, or up on a shelf; rather set it out to honor and delight in what God is offering and bestowing to you. Keep this in mind as you move through the many prayer exercises in this book.

Listening in All of Life

The following few prayer exercises show us that life is full of prayer encounters in all of our regular daily moments. You are invited to enter this exercise using only one item – a cup, next you are invited to enter more deeply into the prayers we read, and then you may want to experience what God has for you in the regular songs we sing as we go through the regular seasons of life.

PRAYER EXERCISE 9

HOLDING YOUR CUP   XX

It was John's turn to lead our class in a prayer exercise that morning. We settled and quieted our greetings and shifted our thoughts to intentionally receive this time of focused prayer. John has created a unique prayer exercise which I have found very helpful. The exercise may appear very simple, as well as quite short, but it is most powerful. This is an excellent example of the principle that having a very meaningful time with God can be uncomplicated yet very satisfying. You need only one item – a cup.

(Use any cup for this exercise, or choose one that represents your life at this time.)

WELCOME to your solitary prayer.

Please take a moment to re-center yourself in God's embracing presence as you say this breath prayer silently or out loud. Say the first line as you breathe in, and the second line as you breathe out, continuing slowly through the prayer. Repeat until you come to a place of quiet stillness and feel led to go on.

"Breath Prayer"
Breathe In – "Held in Your mercy."
Breathe Out – "Held in Your love."
Breathe In – "You are here, Lord."
Breathe Out – "I am listening."

HOLD YOUR CUP in both hands.

Notice its style, shape, color, size, etc.
Be aware of yourself as a cup held in God's hands.
Accept your uniqueness and God's acceptance.
Thank God for creating you as you are.

> Fear Not, I have called you by name;
> you are Mine, you are precious
> and honoured in My sight..
> I love you

HOLDING YOUR CUP in your hand:

Recognize your cup as a container.
Lift up your cup and acknowledge any thirsting you hold.

> O God, you are my God, earnestly I seek you;
> my soul thirsts for you,
> my body longs for you.

Now simply read this poem or listen to it being read. Allow
yourself to be attentive to God's presence. Receive whatever
God desires to offer.

> Generous God,
> so many times I've come with my empty cup,
> a beggar of the heart,
> devoid of nourishment,
> depleted of energy,
> and you have filled.
> Generous God,
> so many times I've come afraid of unknowns,
> full of negatives and no's,
> fighting the challenges,
> closed and resistant to growth,
>
> and you have opened.

Generous God,
so many times I've come,
a stranger to my spirit,
crammed with cultural noise,
caught in endless clutter
crowding my inner space,

and you have emptied.

Generous God,
I come to you again,
holding out my waiting cup,
begging that it first be emptied
of all that blocks the way
then asking for its filling
with love that tastes like you.

Joyce Rupp, 1997

SET YOUR CUP back a ways from you, near yet alone.

Clear the spot around your cup.
Let this solitary cup lead your prayer:
"God, You are enough for me."

A STORY FROM THE JOURNEY...

We were out in the middle of the lawn, with the sun and lotion. I shared this prayer exercise with my friend, Eden. We were just quietly resting as I read it aloud. She was moved deeply as the Spirit came close to both empty and fill her cup. It was a special moment in her day, perhaps her week. A few minutes later she shared with me a song that came to her on her IPOD. Below are the lyrics. You may want to incorporate this song or its words into your prayer time now.

You Are by **Brian Doerksen**

My soul is yearning for Your living stream.
My heart is aching for You.
All that I long for is found in Your heart.
You are
Everything I need.

You are the thirst, You are the stream,
You are the hunger living deep inside of me.

You are the food that satisfies,
provision for the journey of our lives.
YOU are everything.
YOU ARE.

FURTHER QUESTIONS FOR MEDITATION AND REFLECTION:

1 Is there something you thirst for? Something that is empty in you?

Share that with Jesus.

2 How do you sense Jesus is responding to you?

3 Are there any ways your cup may be closed,? Can you let Jesus come to open your hearts to receive?

If so, do that now.

4 Is there some void He wants to fill in you?

Receive.

5 Is there something that needs to be emptied from you?

Surrender.

6 Pray, "Jesus, You are enough for me." Be at peace.

God's Might to Uphold Me

I arise today
Through a mighty strength, the invocation of the Trinity,
Through the belief in the threeness,
Through confession of the oneness
Of the Creator of Creation.
I arise today
Through God's strength to pilot me:
God's might to uphold me,
God's wisdom to guide me,
God's eye to look before me,
God's ear to hear me,
God's word to speak for me,
God's hand to guard me,
God's way to lie before me,
God's shield to protect me,
God's host to save me
From snares of devils,
From temptations of vices,
From everyone who shall wish me ill,
Afar and anear,
Alone and in multitude.
- from St. Patrick's Prayer

PRAYER EXERCISE 10

GOD'S MIGHT TO UPHOLD ME **XX**

(Reflect on this piece of St. Patrick's Prayer above)

1 What does the strength of the Trinity look like to you? Describe it, feel it, enter into it, arise by it.

2 Which of the ways that the Trinity comes to us impacts you today; pilot, uphold, guide, hear, etc…?

Open your heart, mind and body and receive this way as a gift.

3 Draw a picture in your mind of what this might look like for you; the Trinity actually giving you all of these.

4 As you "Arise" today, be mindful of these truths that have been given to you.

PRAYER EXERCISE **11**

BELONGING   ⌛

1 Take a few deep breaths as if breathing from the bottom of your toes up through your legs, your abdominal muscles, and your chest. Be still before God breathing slowly & deeply.

2 Place your hand on your heart and ask God to bring to your mind a moment in your life when you felt that you really belonged. Let your whole self bask in that moment and breathe in again the sense of belonging.

(Adapted from *Don't Forgive too Soon* by Dennis, Sheila, and Matthew Linn)

What Child is This?
Entering into a Song

Jesus was given a womb, a manger, and Mary's lap. These provisions from God were enough. We too, were given a womb, a crib, and a mother. Could it be that these provisions from God were also enough for us? Could it be that these "safe places" from God were Immanuel "God with us?" Can He be in the weak, the marvellous, the mean estate, the insecure, and the simple?

Do you know this Christmas Song, *What Child is This*?

What child is this,
Who, laid to rest,
On Mary's lap is sleeping,
Whom angels greet with anthems sweet
While shepherds watch are keeping?

This, this is Christ the king,
Whom shepherds guard and angels sing;
Haste, haste to bring Him laud,
The babe, the Son of Mary!

Why lies He in such mean estate
Where ox and ass are feeding?
Good Christian, fear: for sinners here
The silent Word is pleading.

So bring Him incense, gold, and myrrh;
Come, peasant, king, to own Him!
The King of kings salvation brings;
Let loving hearts enthrone Him!
Raise, raise the song on high!

PRAYER EXERCISE 12

WHAT CHILD IS THIS? ⏳

1 What comes to your mind when you take a few moments to revisit the beginning of your physical life? Become aware of these long ago moments and know that God was there with you, as Nurturer, Provision, and Ultimate Love.

2 What might it have been like? What might God, as your Heavenly Mother and Father want to show you or remind you of? How does the awareness of this Divine Presence always having been with you change that time and perhaps some of your understanding?

3 Be mindful of God in all that you have been provided today. Notice what comes to your mind as you go about your normal activities.

4 What have you already been given this Christmas? What might the Loving Creator want you to have?

5 Are you full and carrying Christ who is being born in you? What is being born in you? How does this feel? What do you need to know?

6 Let all that is within you, and that which is going on in your life, be enough for you today remembering, Immanuel – God with you.

7 Look for a symbol to put out on your table, desk, or to have with you in your car to remind you that God is now, and has always been, with you,

"Let loving hearts enthrone Him!"

Discernment and Direction
Which Way?

Do you have a decision to make where both directions are good but you don't know which way to go? Making a decision between good and evil is not usually an issue when we journey with our Holy God, but two good choices can be very difficult to process. We can get stuck or be paralyzed in a double-bind.

The following Ignatian exercise has been so helpful to Dwight and I when we find ourselves in the position of having to make a decision between two good choices. If we are not clear of which way to go, or if we are not hearing the same thing, we are thankful for this prayer exercise to help us listen to God. If we are not in agreement after doing this exercise we will set another time to listen; a couple of days or weeks in the future, depending on the situation. Not knowing which way to choose usually means that the time isn't right for us to move in any way. As we continue to process the decision waiting and checking in with God will usually bring us to hear something new, or one of us will sense to yield to the other.

PRAYER EXERCISE 13

WHICH WAY?   XX

1 Imagine each choice having a path that is laid out in front of you.

2 Begin to walk down one of the paths and see how your heart responds and where God is in this decision or on this path. See if anything comes to your mind that you needed to know. What might this be showing you? What feelings surface? How does God want to meet you with these emotions? Follow the path as far as God wants to take you.

3 Do the same for the other path. Where is the greatest peace? Which one seems to be more inviting and be more filled with light? Test it with God's Word and wait until God leads you to go on. Be aware of any compulsive or obsessive feelings or behaviours, and make sure that you move in peace and rest. (See page   re: Compulsive vs. Contemplative Actions.)

4 Do you have someone that you could go to for co-discernment, or confirmation of your hearing? If so, ask to meet with them. If not, ask God to highlight who might be good to connect with.

5 Move into your decision with confidence that God has spoken, and that you have listened as best as you were able.

Invited to Scripture

Follow Jesus around the Scriptures – be an observer
Watch how He looks
Watch how He touches
Watch how He is present to people
Watch how He prays and takes time out

Let Him look at you
Let Him touch you
Let Him hold you
Let Him heal you
Let Him be present to you

Then become the look
Become the touch
Become the presence

By Doreen Kostynuik

Lectio Divina

"Listen, listen to me, and eat what is good,
and your soul will delight in the richest of fare."
(Isaiah 55:2 TNIV)

One of my very favourite places to meet with God, and one of the easiest ways to hear God's voice is in the Scriptures. These truths are so powerful that probably no amount of books could hold the tales of those who have had God encounters while reading or meditating on Scripture.

The Word of God has a special place in my heart and life. I can still remember receiving my first big black Bible, given to me by my Sunday School teacher, Mrs. Lillian Kuhn. I started going to Church when a Sunday School bus came around the neighbourhood, offering to take "whosoever will." I walked over to the house of Jack Smith (whom I would love to meet again someday), headed off to Sunday School and was returned with a chocolate bar or bag of chips that we'd picked up on the way home from a convenience store en route. I was only seven years old, but the magnet of Jesus drew me to Himself and a place where I could sing, be taught and prayed for faithfully every week.

I still have that Bible and enjoy the memories from my early years of time spent with God and that "dear old book." It was my faithful friend living with me in my bedroom, speaking to me often. I love the touch of it, the smell of it, and the special scriptures that I've underlined. I probably earned it through Sunday school attendance or the Scripture memorization contests that we had back then. Nonetheless, along with the many pretty scripture wall decorations I received over those years, that I hung around my room, I am sure that God's Word was planted within me as I sat at my desk devouring the delicious words and the thirst-quenching Spirit in that Bible.

I was introduced to a prayer exercise, *Lectio Divina*, a few decades later. It is a most delightful scripture encounter, a very old exercise, and very dear to many. I love its invitation to meditate on God's Word where I use my mind and energies to engage with the written words. I also love when I wait upon God and my meditation turns to quiet, non-active contemplation as wondrous love and truths are revealed to me.

My first experience with this group exercise was at a Spiritual Direction course given by SoulStream, a community committed to contemplative living and values <www.soulstream.ca>.

God is very present when two or three people gather in His name (Matthew 18:20), and it can be very rewarding to experience the group dynamics of waiting on the Lord and listening together.

Lectio Divina is an ancient, monastic method of reading the Scriptures, and is Latin for *Divine Reading*. We read a piece of Scripture a few times with pauses in between each reading to think about what has been read or what God is highlighting in the verses. I can still remember Dwight's enthusiasm after the first time he had experienced a *Lectio Divina*. It is still one of his favourite ways to read Scripture and to enter into God's presence and to hear God's voice.

Following are two of the many ways this exercise can be done. The first is the more "proper" way as originally practised by St. Ignatius of Loyola. You may enjoy this when you have some time to spend with a portion of scripture that Jesus is inviting you to. The second format is on the following pages and is meant for group ministry time or for when you have a shorter prayer time available.

PRAYER EXERCISE **14**

LECTIO DIVINA   ⚯

Go through the exercise using the steps below.

Journal what comes to mind as God highlights things for you in the following verses:

Isaiah 50:4-9 NLT

"The Sovereign Lord has given me his words of wisdom, so that I know what to say to all these weary ones. Morning by morning he wakens me and opens my understanding to his will. The Sovereign Lord has spoken to me, and I have listened. I do not rebel or turn away. I give my back to those who beat me and my cheeks to those who pull out my beard. I do not hide from shame, for they mock me and spit in my face. Because the Sovereign Lord helps me, I will not be dismayed. Therefore, I have set my face like a stone, determined to do his will. And I know that I will triumph. He who gives me justice is near. Who will dare to oppose me now? Where are my enemies? Let them appear! See, the Sovereign Lord is on my side! Who will declare me guilty? All my enemies will be destroyed like old clothes that have been eaten by moths."

1 **Find a place of stillness before God.** Embrace His peace. Calm your body, concentrate on breathing slowly, and clear your mind of the busyness of life. Ask God to touch you as you pray.

2 **Read the passage twice, slowly.**

a.) Allow its words to wash over you and sink into your spirit. Picture the scene being described – interact with it. Listen for words that catch your attention, and when they do, savor them.

b.) In the silence that follows the reading, meditate upon what you have heard. Let the verse stir up thoughts and/or memories.

3 If a word or phrase from the passage strikes you, say it out loud and write it down.

a.) Continue to allow it to wash over you. Let its rhythm and repetition flow through you. In the silence that follows, continue to enter into and engage with the scene and the author's words.

b.) What themes emerge for you? How do you and your past experiences connect with what is being read?

4 Read the passage two times more.

a.) Continue to meditate on it.

b.) What action might God be calling you to through this verse?

c.) Let your meditation lead you to silent prayer, thanksgiving, petition, and confession.

d.) Interact with God about what you are thinking; communicate your thoughts.

e.) Write to God as if writing to a dear friend. Go with the flow of your heart.

"Jesus, may all that is You flow into me."
From a paraphrase of the Anima Christi – a favourite prayer of
St. Ignatius.

Lectio Divina
Group Exercise (or Solitude)

This shortened version of *Lectio Divina* works well with a group or when time constraints don't allow for a long period of listening. A few simple components make this exercise easy to facilitate, yet it is very effective as God speaks to our hearts from the written, spoken, and living Word. When this exercise is done and shared in community, it produces much good fruit as we open the Word, our hearts, and lives to each other. When done at a retreat day it is a great way to start the day! The following pages include many such exercises.

PREPARATION FOR GROUP PARTICIPATION:

1 Ask God to direct you to the scripture portion He wants to speak through.

2 Sit in a circle facing each other if the room space allows for this. Sitting at tables or in rows with a larger group works well too.

3 Each person receives a copy of the scripture that is to be read. I usually include a list of the five steps we will move through so others can follow along as well.

4 We read the passage four times. The leader can read all four readings or ask others to read, allowing for different voices and tones to be heard.

5 At the leader's invitation there are appropriate places for the group to share. Invite the participants to keep their words few and succinct to keep the main focus on the Scripture and to give each one a turn. You need to be clear that when you ask for a word, phrase or image, that this means no elaboration at this time. This may be more difficult for groups with whom this kind of sharing is new, so you can model this by sharing first. It is quite interesting and often very beautiful to see what themes emerge. If a person does not want to share publicly I ask them to simply look to the person next to them, so we can move on to the next person. They may have received something very intimate and personal from God, or, as can happen with all of us, perhaps nothing significant has come to mind at that time; either is understandable from time to time.

A main key is to *read slowly* allowing time to listen, feel, and to digest what is being read and/or spoken. Take a moment to be quiet and to still your body, heart and mind. *Sit in a comfortable manner, yet remain attentive.* Be focused on the moment and take a couple of deep breaths to relax.

The five steps we take in this exercise are explained below. A shortened version of the steps will follow each *Lectio Divina* Scripture passage.

1. *FIRST READING*: Just listen.

2. *SECOND READING*: As the scripture is read a second time, listen for the word, phrase or image that catches your attention. After a silent pause the leader can ask the group, one by one, to simply share their word, phrase or image with no elaboration at this time.

3. *THIRD READING*: As you listen ask yourself, "How is this speaking into my life at this time?" Listen to discover how this passage impacts you practically in the life situations that you now face. After a pause, the leader can invite each one to share in a sentence or two, no more, how the Word is speaking to them practically in their present circumstances. For a larger group it is best if only two or three people share briefly.

4. *FOURTH READING*: Listen for what God may be inviting you to experience personally as you hear it the fourth time. What is the invitation for you at this time? After a short time of silence, let everyone share the invitation that they sensed God was giving them.

5. *RESPONSE TO INVITATION*: Pray a silent (or vocal) response to God for this invitation. Allow a few minutes for this encounter with God.

PRAYER EXERCISE 15

LECTIO DIVINA – PSALM 18 NIV   XX

Reading Psalm 18, use the five short steps below, or the longer version above to listen to what God is saying to you at this time. You may want your journal handy to record key words, messages, or your prayers.

I love you, O Lord, my strength.
The Lord is my rock, my fortress and my deliverer;
He is my shield and the horn of my salvation, my stronghold.
I call to the Lord, who is worthy of praise,
and I am saved from my enemies.

The cords of death entangled me; the torrents of destruction
overwhelmed me.
The cords of the grave coiled around me.
In my distress I called to the Lord; I cried to my God for help.

From His temple He heard my voice; my cry came before Him,
into His ears.
The earth trembled and quaked, and the foundations of the
mountains shook;
They trembled because He was angry.
Smoke rose from His nostrils; consuming fire came from His mouth...
He parted the heavens and came down...
He mounted the cherubim and flew;
He soared on the wings of the wind.
Out of the brightness of His presence clouds advanced...
The Lord thundered from heaven;
the voice of the Most High resounded.

He shot His arrows and scattered the enemies…
He reached down from on high and took hold of me;
He drew me out of deep waters.
He rescued me from my powerful enemy, from my foes, who were
too strong for me.
They confronted me in the day of my disaster, but the Lord was
my support.
He brought me out into a spacious place; He rescued me because
He delighted in me.

You, O Lord, keep my lamp burning; My God turns my darkness
into light.
With your help I can advance against a troop;
with my God I can scale a wall.
As for God, His way is perfect; the word of the Lord is flawless.
He is a shield for all who take refuge in Him.

1 Read: Listen.

2 Read again: Note a word or phrase that the Holy Spirit highlights to you.

3 Read again: How does this practically affect your life at this time?

4 Read again: What is the invitation from Jesus for you today, in this Scripture?

5 Take a few minutes to pray in response to the Lord's invitation to you.

A STORY FROM THE JOURNEY...

Eden, Jodi and I were leading a women's day retreat in Westbank, B.C., together with Anne Marie and Peter Helms who lead a fantastic teaching/equipping ministry and retreat center. Words are too limited to describe the extravagant fun, food & fellowship they serve. You can check out their ministry of teaching and leading at <www.appletreeministries.ca>.

We did this *lectio divina* exercise as usual; however, it became quite a group bonding time. I felt strongly that we should use this particular psalm that day. To our amazement the oldest woman in our group (eighty-three years old) shared that this was her "life chapter" and that the Lord had spoken to her so many times through these verses. Then as we went around the room sharing, one of the younger women with a baby in her arms shared that these were the exact scriptures that she and her husband had been praying for their child who had had a difficult birth. Hearing the testimonies of God's faithfulness through His Word in an elderly voice full of faith and a young woman's fresh encounter with God's faithfulness was such a gift to all of us.

PRAYER EXERCISE 16

LECTIO DIVINA – PSALM 36:5-9   ⏳

"Your love, O Lord, reaches to the heavens,
Your faithfulness to the skies.
Your righteousness is like the mighty mountains,
Your justice like the great deep.
O Lord, You preserve both man and beast.
How priceless is Your unfailing love!
Both high and low among men and women
find refuge in the shadow of Your wings.
They feast on the abundance of Your house;
You give them drink from Your river of delights.
For with You is the fountain of life;
In Your light we see light. "

1 Read: Listen.

2 Read again: Note a word or phrase that the Holy Spirit highlights to you.

3 Read again: How does this practically affect your life at this time?

4 Read again: What is the invitation from Jesus for you today, in this Scripture?

5 Take a few minutes to pray in response to the Lord's invitation to you.

I experienced this following exercise with Psalm 36:5-9 at a gathering led by Jeff Imbach of SoulStream Ministries. It truly is one of my very, very favorites.

PRAYER EXERCISE 17

BUBBLING UP   ⏳

1 Sit in a relaxed position and give thanks that you are in God's care.

2 Take several slow, deep breaths and then begin breathing in a relaxed, normal way.

3 Place both hands palm down over your heart. Keep them there quietly for a few minutes then repeat quietly within to yourself, very slowly, with long pauses between each phrase:

"The very life of the Trinity is bubbling up like a spring of water within my soul … filling me … calming me … restoring me …

4 Take a quiet pause while you envision a bubbling spring of life coursing through your body and then say:

"And this new life is flowing with life-giving wholeness throughout my body."

5 After a few moments when this has filled and settled within you, repeat the exercise again.

Reflection Questions:

1 Who is the "you" that Jesus loves beyond any role you have or your persona? (i.e. cherished child, precious daughter, my own son, etc.)

2 When have been the times (either in a religious context or not), that you have actually sensed that you have drunk deeply of the river of God's delights? (It could be in some relationship, some experience of nature, some cognitive awarenesses, etc.) Remember and feel the vibrancy of those moments more than the content of them.

3 What have been the blocks to the flow of life within you? (Personal failure, religious or cultural conformity, being too busy, etc.)

4 Spend some time in quietness allowing God to invite you in some way to come home to the well of water within you. Revel in the invitation and be grateful that the water continues to flow even though it sometimes gets blocked or diverted.

5 Continue to rest and receive what God is giving you.

"God of mercy and compassion,
Your Word calls us home to faith and love.
Accept all we offer you today,
and help us to continue to receive all You have given.
In the name of Jesus Christ our Lord, Amen"

"Love Never Fails"

PRAYER EXERCISE 18

LECTIO DIVINA – 1 CORINTHIANS 13:1-7, 13 NIV 𝕏

"If I speak in the tongues of men and of angels,
but have not love,
I am only a resounding gong or a clanging cymbal.
If I have the gift of prophecy and can fathom all mysteries and
all knowledge,
and if I have a faith that can move mountains, but have not love,
I am nothing.
If I give all I possess to the poor and surrender my body
to the flames,
but have not love, I gain nothing.
Love is patient, love is kind.
It does not envy, it does not boast, it is not proud.
It is not rude, it is not self-seeking, it is not easily angered, it
keeps no record of wrongs.
Love does not delight in evil but rejoices with the truth.
It always protects, always trusts, always hopes,
always perseveres.

And now these three remain:
Faith, hope and love.
But the greatest of these is love."

1 Read: Listen.

2 Read again: Note a word or phrase that the Holy Spirit highlights to you.

3 Read again: How does this practically affect your life at this time?

4 Read again: What is the invitation from Jesus for you today, in this Scripture?

5 Take a few minutes to pray in response to the Lord's invitation to you.

Prayer Exercise 19

God is Love

1 God is Love – 1 John 4:8b NIV   Look at this scripture as God being Love. What does this look like to you? Does that challenge any belief systems that you may have about God? What does God/Love want to make known to you?

2 Take time now to let Love come deeply within you.

3 How might Love help you in your present situation or relationship?

4 You carry Love within you. How may Love be inviting you to love a certain person or situation? Be mindful that Love never fails.

Wisdom is a Tree of Life

PRAYER EXERCISE 20

LECTIO DIVINA – PROVERBS 3:3, 5-7, 11-18 NIV   𝕏

(Note: the following passages have been rendered gender-neutral.)

"Let love and faithfulness never leave you;
bind them around your neck,
Write them on the tablet of your heart.

Trust in the Lord with all your heart and lean not
on your own understanding;
In all your ways acknowledge him,
and he will make your paths straight.

Do not be wise in your own eyes; fear the Lord and shun evil.
This will bring health to your body
and nourishment to your bones.

My child, do not despise the Lord's discipline and do not resent
his rebuke, because the Lord disciplines those he loves,
as a father the son he delights in.

Blessed is the person who finds Wisdom,
the one who gains understanding,
For Wisdom is more profitable than silver
and yields better returns than gold.
Wisdom is more precious than rubies;
nothing you desire can compare with Wisdom.
Long life is in Wisdom's right hand;
in Wisdom's left hand are riches and honor.

Wisdom's ways are pleasant ways,
and all Wisdom's paths are peace.
Wisdom is a tree of life to those who embrace Wisdom;
Those who lay hold of Wisdom will be blessed.

1 Read: Listen.

2 Read again: Note a word or phrase that the Holy Spirit highlights to you.

3 Read again: How does this practically affect your life at this time?

4 Read again: What is the invitation from Jesus for you today, in this Scripture?

5 Take a few minutes to pray in response to the Lord's invitation to you.

PRAYER EXERCISE **21**

WISDOM SPEAKS

1 What is Wisdom saying to you?

2 Rest with the invitation to "let love and faithfulness never leave you; bind them around your neck, write them on the tablet of your heart." What does that mean to you?

3 Ask Wisdom to show you what you are to know personally, and for your family/community.

4 Are you being invited to trust in deeper ways? Ask the Lord for a symbol or song to remind you of trust.

5 Take a few minutes to rest on the path of peace.

"His Love Endures Forever"

PRAYER EXERCISE 22

LECTIO DIVINA – PSALM 136 NIV 𝕏

Give thanks to the Lord, for He is good.

> *His love endures forever.*

Give thanks to the God of gods.

> *His love endures forever.*

Give thanks to the Lord of lords:

> *His love endures forever.*

To Him who alone does great wonders,

> *His love endures forever.*

Who by His understanding made the heavens,

> *His love endures forever.*

Who made the great lights to govern the day and the night,

> *His love endures forever.*

To Him who struck down the firstborn of Egypt

> *His love endures forever.*

And brought Israel out from among them

> *His love endures forever.*

With a mighty hand and outstretched arm;

> *His love endures forever.*

To the One who remembered us in our low estate

> *His love endures forever.*

And freed us from our enemies.

> *His love endures forever.*

Give thanks to the God of heaven.

> *His love endures forever.*

You may want to use one of these other translations:

KJV – His mercy endureth forever.

NLT – His faithful love endures forever.

NAS – His lovingkindness is everlasting.

1 Read: Listen.

2 Read again: Note a word or phrase that the Holy Spirit highlights to you.

3 Read again: How does this practically affect your life at this time?

4 Read again: What is the invitation from Jesus for you today, in this Scripture?

5 Take a few minutes to pray in response to the Lord's invitation to you.

PRAYER EXERCISE **23**

PERSONALIZE IT   ⏳

1 As you read each line in Psalm 136 pause and make that phrase personal by adding what comes to mind for you. (i.e. "to the One who remembered us in our low estate," I might add, "Like when I was so discouraged with our finances that I couldn't even imagine being well again.")

2 Take time to ponder or make a list of the following:
I give thanks for:
Great wonders and creations of God:
Ways I've been delivered:
Times I've sensed that I am remembered:

An Advent Reflection
He First Loved Us

The mystery of Christ, the gift of divine life, is a pure demonstration of God's love toward us. We were helpless and spiritually paralysed. We can never climb to Him, He must descend to us. This is most important in the mystery of Advent – God's descent to our lowliness out of pure love, not for any merit of our own. Divine mercy is most evident in tenderness with which the infinite God tempers the strength of His light to the weakness of our eyes and becomes a human being like the rest of us. "The Lord is good to all and compassionate toward all His works." Psalm 145:9

This exercise is based on the writings of Thomas Merton as shared in an Advent Devotional.

PRAYER EXERCISE 24
LECTIO DIVINA – 1 JOHN 4:7–19 NIV   **XX**

Read slowly to receive the words and thoughts

"Dear friends, let us love one another, for love comes from God. Everyone who loves has been born of God and knows God. Whoever does not love does not know God, because God is love. This is how God showed His love among us: He sent his one and only Son into the world that we might live through Him.
This is love: not that we loved God, but that he loved us and sent his Son as an atoning sacrifice for our sins. Dear friends, since God so loved us, we also ought to love one another. No one has ever seen God; but if we love one another, God lives in us and his love is made complete in us.
We know that we live in him and he in us because he has given us of his Spirit. And we have seen and testify that the Father has sent

his Son to be the Savior of the world. If anyone acknowledges that Jesus is the Son of God, God lives in him and he in God. And so we know and rely on the love God has for us.
God is love. Whoever lives in love lives in God, and God in him. In this way, love is made complete among us so that we will have confidence on the day of judgement, because in this world we are like him. There is no fear in love. But perfect love drives out fear, because fear has to do with punishment. The one who fears is not made perfect in love. We love because He first loved us. "

1 Read: Listen.

2 Read again: Note a word or phrase that the Holy Spirit highlights to you.

3 Read again: How does this practically affect your life at this time?

4 Read again: What is the invitation from Jesus for you today, in this Scripture?

5 Take a few minutes to pray in response to the Lord's invitation to you.

Ponder and Reflect:

1 Even as God created you before you knew it, can you believe this love made you before you sensed it? Be mindful that it was God who was inviting you to know and experience such love.

2 What does God loving you first look like? Feel like? Let yourself receive this powerful truth – that He first loved you. Ask the Lord if or why you may fear this love. Be open to let God's love take away this fear.

3 Do you see how you might try to "climb" to God at times? Instead, can you say "yes" this Advent as God sends Jesus to descend to you? Is there a way you can practically be mindful of Jesus loving you first each day (find a symbol of this "First" Love and put it where you will see it often, memorize a piece of Scripture, a song, or truth that you could repeat often through your day, etc.).

Entering Bible Stories
Way More Than Just a Story!

*"But these are written that you may believe that Jesus is the
Christ, the Son of God,
and that by believing you may have life in his name."*
(John 20:31 NIV)

Bible Stories may be new to you, or perhaps they were "fed" to you along with your first bites of food. No matter how familiar you are with them, however, each story brings us God's truth, insights and messages.

Usually, when any story is read to us some images come to our minds that make the story more clear and enjoyable. For instance, when we hear the story of Little Red Riding Hood we usually imagine a little girl wearing a red coat or cape with a hood on it, don't we? We can imagine her basket, her path to Grandmother's house and the big bad wolf. Less enjoyable may be the "sight" of old Granny salivating, about to chew up her granddaughter. However, you can see how easy it is for us to follow the story with our thoughts which normally include illustrations in our imagination.

God has powerfully used Bible stories that I could identify with to speak deeply into my heart and my life's circumstances. One experience happened many years ago and remarkably still impacts me; with it God illustrated how I could be different characters of the story. Another happened quite recently and surprised me. Usually these elements of surprise, or "Aha!" moments are unusual in some way, which helps confirm that they are from the Lord, as I likely couldn't have come up with them myself!

A few years ago I was feeling quite nervous while preparing for a prayer retreat that I had been asked to speak at. My insecurities were rising and I was starting to think that I had nothing of value to share with the participants. As I began to pray specifically about this and ask the Lord to help me, the story in John 6:1-15 where Jesus fed the multitude came to my mind.

Remembering the little boy who offered his lunch of two fish and five barley loaves to be shared with thousands, I sensed Jesus showing me how I could identify with this young boy who had only a little bag lunch and yet was invited to give it. As I lingered in this story I began to see how significant and perhaps even necessary this gift was – both the young boy's lunch and my contribution to the retreat. I felt like Jesus was looking right at me and bringing His peace over my shaky heart. Then came His invitation to watch what He could do with little, with the tiny bits I had to offer to Him.

When the prayer retreat was underway I had a much stronger trust that God was with us. Anticipation rose that He would be faithful to do His part in multiplying His blessings to His children in this present "story" that was now unfolding. Joy and freedom came with the reality that He was the One Who provided the miracle even as He had provided the lunch in the first place. Many in the retreat were fed the richness of a gospel or Old Testament story as they encountered God for themselves.

This has been a well practiced prayer exercise over the ages. A regular discipline of the Jesuit priests would be to read a gospel story, to learn of Christ and to experience His presence by imagining being each of the people in the story. Over the course of our lives we will likely be in the same position as the various characters in a story.

This happened in an unusual way for me while in Scotland a couple of years ago. Before we left Canada, I asked the Lord to show me what I needed to know about this trip and the ministry that we'd been invited to. The story of the wedding at Cana came to mind. Almost every day on this trip I would feel invited to meet Jesus in this story. This wedding became a meeting place for me that turned into a lifeline of His voice making things known to me as we went along. At times I felt like the Master of Ceremonies who saw they were running out of wine and I would look to Jesus for calm and trust. Other times I felt like Mary coming to Jesus with a need, like one of the servants being told what to do, or like a little girl sitting beside the water pots watching this all unfold. My favourite movement was when Jesus told me to scoop out the wine and go and serve it. What joy!

THE ROLE OF IMAGINATION IN PRAYER:

Imagination is the power of our memory and recall which enables us to enter into the experiences that come to mind. Through images we are able to touch the center of who we are and to surface and give life and expression to the innermost levels of our being. Images simultaneously reveal multiple levels of meaning and are therefore symbolic of our deeper reality. Through the sanctified & structured use of active imagination, we release the hidden energy, the truth of God, and the potential for wholeness which is already present within us by God's Spirit. When we use active imagination in the context of prayer, and with an attitude of faith, we open ourselves to the power and mystery of the truth of what God is doing in our lives and His transforming presence within us.

PRAYER EXERCISE 25

ENTERING A BIBLE STORY XX

1 Ask God to bring to mind a Bible story where you can meet today. Listen to what first comes to mind even if it doesn't seem to make sense. (If nothing comes to your mind choose one of the following invitations at the bottom of this exercise.)

2 Find the story in the Bible and read it over once.

3 Who are the characters? Who do you most identify with at this time? Why?

4 Read the story a second time as you enter into the story from this character's perspective.

5 What feelings arise as you identify with this person and what they are experiencing, as it relates to your own life? Let these feelings arise in you without fear, because God is with you.

6 Where do you see or sense God in this story? Meet God there, be aware of God's presence.

7 When God sees you, what is seen? How does God feel toward you? How do you feel?

8 What does God want to tell/show you or make known to your heart? Share whatever is on your heart with God.

9 What does God want to give to you there? Does anything change with this encounter? Rest with God and receive what is for you. Take time for giving thanks.

PRAYER EXERCISE **26**

A NO-FAIL ENCOUNTER: THE SHEPHERD OF PSALM 23　**XXX**

When I, or someone I am praying with, cannot seem to find a story or hear from the Lord very clearly or confidently I then turn to Psalm 23. This exercise seems to help us over and over. I don't fully understand the moves of the Spirit of course, but as God comes as our Good Shepherd and we recognize ourselves as a sheep something extraordinary happens.

1 Turn to Psalm 23 in a Bible and as you read the verses stop along the way.

2 Imagine yourself as a sheep. How do you feel today? What's going on for you? (I.e. happy and frolicking, tired and disoriented, beaten and bruised, lost and scared, etc.) Remember that you may see a picture, hear things, or have a sense of what God is making known to you.

3 Where does The Good Shepherd seem to be in this picture?

Close? Distant? Not present? (It may be an image of how you feel your life is at this time with God.) What is the Shepherd doing? What is the Shepherd's heart for you when you are seen? (Or what would the Shepherd's heart be for you if you were together?)

4 Allow the real presence of the Shepherd to come as close as you are able. What does the Shepherd want you to know? What does the Shepherd have for you?

5 Receive in your heart what these images are showing you, or what you are hearing or sensing.

6 Continue to move through the Psalm as you feel the Shepherd leading you. Stop when you feel this prayer time is completed, but continue to dialogue or be aware of the Shepherd with you.

7 If you were struggling to engage with the Shepherd as a sheep, you can try to be a child with a loving parent, or a character such as Lucy with Aslan in The Lion, the Witch, and the Wardrobe by C.S. Lewis.

8 Doing this exercise with someone that you trust; who is patient, kind, and experienced in meeting with God can also be a source of help and encouragement.

OTHER BIBLE STORIES YOU MAY WANT TO ENTER:

Naaman being healed – 2 Kings 5
Mary sitting at Jesus' feet – Luke 10:38-42
Peter having a vision of the food being lowered on a cloth – Acts 10
Blind Bartimaeus receives his sight – Mark 10: 46 – 52
Jesus' mercy to the woman caught in adultery – John 8:1 – 11
Four friends lower a paralytic to Jesus for help – Luke 5:17 – 26
Jesus restores Peter (a walk on the beach) – John 21:15 – 25
A woman clings to Jesus robe and is healed – Luke 8:43 – 48
Jesus' invitation to get out of the boat – Matthew 14:22 – 33
Who do you say that I am? – Mark 8:27 – 33

GROUP SHARING:

Do the exercise in a group setting and share the story and how God met each one. Listen for each other as well and share what God may show you from the story that is for someone else. Watch for a common message that God may be telling to the group.

"I'm Coming to Your House Today"

Entering a Bible Story

Jesus to Zacchaeus: "I'm coming to your house today."

Jesus entered Jericho and was passing through. A man was there by the name of Zacchaeus; he was a chief tax collector and was wealthy. He wanted to see who Jesus was, but being a short man he could not, because of the crowd. So he ran ahead and climbed a sycamore-fig tree to see Him, since Jesus was coming that way.

When Jesus reached the spot, He looked up and said to him, "Zacchaeus, come down immediately. I must stay at your house today." So he came down at once and welcomed him gladly.

All the people saw this and began to mutter, "He has gone to be the guest of a 'sinner.'"

But Zacchaeus stood up and said to the Lord, "Look, Lord! Here and now I give half of my possessions to the poor, and if I have cheated anybody out of anything, I will pay back four times the amount."

Jesus said to him, "Today salvation has come to this house, because this man, too, is a son of Abraham. For the Son of Man came to seek and to save what was lost" (Luke 19:1-9 NIV).

Wow! Imagine going from not seeing Jesus at all to having your name called by The One all are seeking for. Then imagine hearing the precious words, "I must stay at your house today." I love how the King James Version of Scripture writes Jesus' words to Zacchaeus, "For today I must abide at thy house." How would this feel? The King of kings wants to come to your house! You matter, and so does your household—even if others judge you as not being "worthy." Jesus has chosen you. Can you receive His desire to come to your house to be with you? What would that be like? What would you hope would happen?

PRAYER EXERCISE 2'7

JESUS AND ZACCHAEUS ⚸

1 Spend some time pondering this story. You may want to journal your thoughts.

2 Do you ever feel like things are really crowding out your time to be with Jesus? Perhaps there is so much happening around you. Or you can remember a time when it was like that? Is there so much noise filling the air, or your mind? Are you feeling like you want to get closer to Jesus, but it just doesn't seem to be working?

3 Jesus may have something to show you through this encounter with Zacchaeus. Can you identify with Zacchaeus. How would you feel if this happened to you?

4 What kind of fruit is or might come from Jesus abiding at your house?

5 Ask Jesus questions that might be on your mind. Get to know Him even more. How does Jesus answer you? Enjoy your time with Him and obey what He asks of you. Be at Peace.

A STORY FROM THE JOURNEY...

This came to my mind one day when I asked the Lord which Bible story He thought would be good for me. He led me to the Sycamore tree that Zacchaeus climbed up to get a better view of Jesus.

There was much "good fruit" at the house of Zacchaeus after that. Zacchaeus met Jesus and loved him. Many poor were cared for and generous restitution was made to many others.

When I did this exercise and heard the words, "Lorie, today I must abide at thy house," my heart was filled with great joy and relief as I had been feeling like He hadn't been in my home in a way

I'd wanted Him to be in quite a while. I knew He was with us, but to hear His desire to come this close, this personally, gave me a strong reminder and great hope for my family and our trying situations at that time.

I began to watch for ways that I could see He had come close to us. I watched as I was filled with joy knowing He'd make a difference. I saw myself and some of my children begin to shift towards being more mindful of God and His being present with us. I even heard comments from my children that made me mindful of God with us. I saw close up, not just from a distant tree, that indeed Jesus had come to our house!

"They saw Jesus"

"It is I; don't be afraid."
John 6:20 TNIV

Entering Gospel stories and listening to Jesus is a mighty combination of God's written and spoken Word mixing with the presence of The Living Word, Christ, to bring powerful life-giving results. Here is what came to me while I was putting life on "hold" one time to spend some concentrated time with the Lord. I sensed God inviting me to the Scriptures, to a story about Jesus and something about water and a storm. There are a few such stories so I waited for a bit more clarity. As I sat waiting, nothing more came to mind other than to open my Bible and to start looking with the thought that Jesus would guide me. As I did this it came to mind that this is what so much of life is about – simply doing what we know *so far*, only what we've been given to do, and that Jesus will guide us as we go. This is a simple, yet profound reality of life with Christ that I so often forget.

As I turned the leaves of my tattered old Bible through the gospels I came to the first mention of water and a storm in John 6. There I felt invited to enter in. I began to be deeply touched. (Watch for these heart movements within you; they are likely showing you that something important is going on within you.) When I saw the disciples in the dark wondering where Jesus was, deep within me I began to wonder if He would show up just for *them*. Would He show up for me? Would Jesus show up in my everyday problems or only in the big events of history or ministry? Would He come to my wind and waves and darkness? I had a strong reaction: *If not, I don't think this ministry thing is going to work for me.* This was my firm thought. What now?

You are invited to travel with Jesus in this passage from John 6.

PRAYER EXERCISE **28**

THEY SAW JESUS – JOHN 6   **XXX**

Read the following passage through very slowly entering into the various components of the story and the life of Christ and the disciples.

> *"When they had all had enough to eat, he said to his disciples, 'Gather the pieces that are left over. Let nothing be wasted.' So they gathered them and filled twelve baskets with the pieces of the five barley loaves left over by those who had eaten. After the people saw the miraculous sign that Jesus did, they began to say, 'Surely this is the Prophet who is to come into the world.' Jesus, knowing that they intended to come and make him king by force, withdrew again to a mountain by himself. When evening came, his disciples went down to the lake, where they got into a boat and set off across the lake for Capernaum. By now it was dark, and Jesus had not yet joined them. A strong wind was blowing and the waters grew rough. When they had rowed three or three and a half miles, they saw Jesus approaching the boat, walking on the water; and they were terrified. But he said to them, 'It is I; don't be afraid.' Then they were willing to take him into the boat, and immediately the boat reached the shore where they were heading"* (John 6:12–21 NIV).

I **God shows up in the grand scheme of things (the seen part of our journey).**

God has displayed Himself in many ways. Here are a few that come to mind for me: Creation, Virgin Birth, Resurrection, post-Resurrection Appearances, Pentecost, etc. Other times that God's presence has been evident: in documented medical and historical events, in our personal faith experiences/testimonies, the birth of a child, in the intricacies of a human body, and in the discoveries of the amazing creations on earth (such as I've been enjoying with my family as we watch the film documentaries, "Planet Earth").

Eden and I have had a full year of doing contemplative and silent retreats, prayer days, and women's conferences. Our Fresh Wind prayer teams have been a part of so many prayer ministry opportunities, personal sessions, group encounters, and a tremendous Teaching Workshop on Listening Prayer and Inner Healing. We have known and met God in our church services in worship, at the communion station, in the prayer tent, at hospital gatherings, and especially at the many funerals we have attended together.

What also comes to mind are the wonderful miracles and profound moments of God's living presence "showing up" in the Life of Christ as in the miraculous feeding of 5,000. There are also the miraculous events that we are promised, that are yet to come.

It makes total sense that the bewildered beneficiaries of Christ's miracles would come to such a conclusion as:

"Surely this is the Prophet who is to come into the world!"

2 Will He show up for me/you/us personally? (the unseen part of our journey)

Where did He go? Jesus is now unseen, and perhaps unfelt. Ever felt like this has happened to you? Jesus comes really close, and then it feels like He disappears? This brings us to look at spiritual formation (pg.129) on our spiritual journeys. It is much like a caterpillar going from summer's light to cocoon's dark. Being in the darkness of a cocoon is much like times of deep spiritual formation, being transformed but not knowing what is going on. In reality, during this change, a caterpillar's DNA is actually changed – she becomes a totally new creation.

What is going on? This is a mysterious, hidden work of God in the dark. I am presently reading, *The Dark Night of the*

Soul by Gerald May. He takes the mystical experiences of St. John of the Cross and Theresa of Avila and brilliantly brings them together with the modern findings in today's psychology and spiritual understandings. He writes simply about the deep things we experience. I will quote a few pieces of his phenomenal insights:

> "The dark night is a profoundly good thing. It is an ongoing spiritual process in which we are liberated from attachments and compulsions and empowered to live and love more freely. Sometimes this letting go of old ways is painful, occasionally even devastating. But this is not why the night is called "dark." The darkness of the night implies nothing sinister, only that the liberation takes place in hidden ways, beneath our knowledge and understanding. It happens mysteriously, in secret, and beyond our conscious control. For that reason it can be disturbing or even scary, but in the end it always works to our benefit. It is a deep transformation, a movement toward indescribable freedom and joy. And in truth it doesn't always have to be unpleasant! To be immersed in mystery can be very distressing at first, but over time I have found immense relief in it. It takes the pressure off. I no longer have to worry myself to death about what I did, or can do, because there really is no way of knowing. I realize that I'm not as much in control of life as I'd like to be."

"They saw Jesus approaching the boat, walking on the water;
and they were terrified.
But he said to them, "It is I; don't be afraid."

3 **He does show up and He always comes (the waiting part of our journey).**

Is He coming? This is the enduring question, a longing for the advent of the Christ—and now a daily longing for Him and for

His second coming, when all shall be well. We deeply sense our need of Him and our desires for Him to come. The ache of this life often seems to hurt far too much to endure. When will it end? Recently, while experiencing some extreme discomfort down deep within my being, I saw in my mind's view the words, "Primal Wound." I longed to stop the pain and found myself reaching for whatever would make it feel better, for a moment, an hour, or hopefully forever.

"Nouns" are what I call the persons, places, or things I long for or grab for when in this state of being. I was thankful that I also was sensing the Lord inviting me to be still, to not move to a "fix" to fix it. He spoke to my heart, "Be still and know I am God in this deep place, Lorie. I will meet you there. Wait for Me to come." As I used all my energy to focus, to rest, trust, to steady my heart, and to still my body, I felt the Lord come gently pouring Himself into me. It was like pure crystal water to my parched soul.

I realized that I often let Him come to me, but that I also grab a bit of whatever other "solution" is handy so that there is a mixture of God and this other thing, which is very hard thing to get out once it's in there. It can take a very long time to be removed, even years.

This time, every so often in the hours and days that followed I would feel Him come again and fill me more. How kind of Him! He was restoring my soul. What joy and freedom! I believe I was experiencing a piece of the dark night, not knowing what was happening within me, yet in the dawn I see the transformation. I see the results of greater freedom and truer love.

Often on this healing journey I have felt, "This is taking way too long," and I've joined the people in John 6, saying, "Let's make Him King by force." "Let's just get it done, and get on with it. It's all taking way too long. Let's make it happen our way, with our strength." It sounds like this may be how Judas felt: he just wanted to see Christ come into His Kingdom ALREADY!

I want to force Jesus to be King in my child's life, in my health issues, in my husband's business, in our church situations—or how about in my own weaknesses? It just doesn't work. I can see why He withdraws. It's not how He does it. He can not be forced. I must wait – an Advent wait – and let Christ be formed and born in each situation – His way, His timing, by His Spirit, where I can not control it, resist it, or manipulate it. How good it is to simply do what I've been given to do, and leave the rest up to Our Father.

In a recent scripture meditation, *Lectio Divina*, I was drawn to the verse, "Delight yourself in the Lord and he will give you the desires of your heart" (Psalm 37:4 NIV). I was enjoying the beauty of this as I sensed the Lord draw near and offer me "the desires of my heart" asking if I was ready to receive them. I stepped forward in my heart as if to say, "Of course." Suddenly I stepped back, put my hands on my hips and said, "No, actually. I wanted them then, and then, and then, and I wanted them to be like this and this and this! I don't want them now. Don't bring me flowers now." I was quite surprised at what surfaced from within my heart. I was also thankful that the Lord is full of grace and mercy and seemed to just stand there and say, "Well, what now, then? Are you sure?" Of course, one glance at Him and His perfect love, my will melted to accept His will along with His perfect timing, powerful wisdom, His love, and the fulfillment of the desires of my heart.

I like the fact that the disciples didn't recognize Jesus right away, as I wonder if that happens to us often, too. Perhaps He is in the scary, freaky, crazy, stormy things of our lives—right here—somehow? In reality, when God created us anew (2 Corinthians 5:17) He wove Himself right inside us, we carry God in us. He doesn't come and go, show up and leave. He is in us, always loving us and being God. He can withstand rejection, anger, distrust, idols, our moods, lies, confusions, etc. He can't be anything other than God, Immanuel, "God with us." Oh, how He helps us see and be aware of His presence within and about us.

Perhaps you know God's voice well by now? Or maybe it is a new experience and you will yet get to practice and learn to trust this voice that speaks to you. Let us hear Jesus say: "It is I; don't be afraid." May we then let Jesus into the boat of our life.

God can wait, and often does. I guess that's because He knows who He is and what He is capable of doing. Waiting lets the water of His Word, of His Spirit, the light of His love, take time to get to those deeper seeds inside us that otherwise may never get touched with His presence. Let us wait.

I've been reading a little old book from Andrew Murray, called, *Waiting on God*. I'd like to share a piece that is now highlighted in my personal journal:

"It is bless-ed (old English) when a waiting soul and a waiting God meet each other." It is like a kiss.

He goes on to say, "God cannot gather the fruit til it is ripe. He knows when we are spiritually ready to receive the blessing to our profit and His glory. Waiting in the sunshine of His love is what will ripen the soul for His blessing. Waiting under the cloud of trial, the breaks in showers of blessing, is as needful. Waiting makes the blessing doubly precious." He says because "then we find our life and joy in Himself." Maybe something is ripening in the sunshine of His love in you?

"...and immediately the boat reached the shore
where they were heading."

4 **He gets me/you/us to where we are to land (the truth of our journey).**

Of all the places I would like to land, the primary one is WITH HIM—either an active awareness or a deep trust that He is with me, mindful of me, caring about me and my situations. I'm sure we are all in that boat together. Often I seem to be able to get nine-tenths of the way on a path or in the race with the skills, abilities, and grace of God within me. But there is always that one-tenth when I hit the end of "myself," which wasn't "myself" at all, but His life in me, where I can't get to where I want to land. It is the place of surrender where I desperately say out loud, "I need a Savior!" Then I realize afresh, and declare with rejoicing, "And I have a Savior!"

If we could do it ourselves we certainly would have all done it by now. However, we would not actually be happy after all. We are made for the Divine and a life of interaction with the Divine, be it active or silent. Satisfaction comes with connecting with Him.

Where are we going? To Eden restored, to Canaan's freedom from bondage, to eternal life—Heaven and Earth made fully alive, new, where "every knee shall bow, every tongue confess that Jesus is LORD" (Philippians 2:10-11). That "place" where all will be healed and all shall be well! Our seed of faith that we've been given might feel really tiny sometimes, but it is mighty. God made it well. It is faith from Him. It may have a small beginning but will grow into a harvest of faith. When praying for a friend named Jacquie recently I saw her wading through a harvest field of faith and faithfulness that has grown this year. A harvest is growing in each of us, too.

Where can we land for now? Eventually we trust and hope that His kingdom will fully come and His will shall completely be done. But where is my place of rest, peace, and the fullness of God for now?

When I interacted with Jesus in the Bible story above I was delighted to see where my heart and His love had us land together. When you move to meditative moments you will see where your heart is at, where your relationship with God is at, and it is a wonderful time to meet with Him and settle things that are unsettled within us. When we "immediately" landed I was so thankful and so joyful.

At these times of His presence I don't really care where we land as long as we are together and I know He cares about me, and that He does life with me in the big cosmos and in my little row boat. Yes, I saw Jesus. I didn't land in heaven yet—with all my family, finances, health, or future issues totally resolved—but I landed in a place of peace on my journey, a place of freedom from the chaos.

He was dragging the boat up on the shore and I couldn't stop embracing Him. At first I thought He was too busy for me, but very quickly He let go of the boat and spent time with me. There we were on the beach together, Him caring for me, and me gratefully receiving His love and returning it to Him. For now, I've landed. I've come to a deeper place of peace, a deeper knowing of His love and care for me, and have a refreshed trust in His leading.

I feel it is very important to share that Gerald May describes what I have recently experienced when he goes on to say of the Dark Night:

> "The divine presence doesn't intend us to suffer, but is instead with us in all the experiences of life, in both suffering and joy. And that presence is always inviting us toward greater freedom and love. Each experience of the dark night gives its gifts, leaving us freer than we were before, more available, more responsive, and more grateful. Like not knowing and lack of control, freedom and gratitude are abiding characteris-

tics of the dark night. But they don't arrive until the darkness passes. They come with the dawn."

LISTENING QUESTIONS:

1 Take a minute to identify and feel what your wind, waves, or darkness are.

2 Sense your awareness of Jesus being with you or not. Take time to see Jesus. Listen to these words, "It is I; don't be afraid"—or other things He may be saying to you.

3 Can you let Jesus in your boat, close to you and what you are experiencing?

4 If you are able, let Jesus care, cherish, and hold you right now. If you have no sense of Jesus with you yet, can you choose to trust that he is there or that he will come? He surely comes.

5 Where does Jesus want you to land today? What is the truth in this piece of your journey? Jesus, can you give a word, a song, a scripture, or a symbol of your love today? Receive.

"They saw Jesus..."

*"Freedom and gratitude are abiding characteristics
of the dark night... they come with the dawn."*

John's Vision

"Behold I am Coming Soon"
Revelation 22:7

"I did not see a temple in the city, because the Lord God Almighty and the Lamb are its temple. The city does not need the sun or the moon to shine on it, for the glory of God gives it light, and the Lamb is its lamp. The nations will walk by its light, and the kings of the earth will bring their splendour into it. On no day will its gates ever be shut, for there will be no night there. The glory and honour of the nations will be brought into it. Nothing impure will ever enter it, nor will anyone who does what is shameful or deceitful, but only those whose names are written in the Lamb's book of life."

"Then the angel showed me the river of the water of life, as clear as crystal, flowing from the throne of God and of the Lamb down the middle of the great street of the city. On each side of the river stood the tree of life, bearing twelve crops of fruit, yielding its fruit every month. And the leaves of the tree are for the healing of the nations.

No longer will there be any curse. "The throne of God and of the Lamb will be in the city, and his servants will serve him. They will see his face, and his name will be on their foreheads. There will be no more night. They will not need a light of a lamp or the light of the sun, for the Lord God will give them light. And they will reign forever and ever.

"Behold, I am coming soon! Blessed is he who keeps the words of the prophecy in this book."

PRAYER EXERCISE **2**9

JOHN'S VISION – REVELATION **21:22-27** AND **22:1-7 NIV**   **XX**

1 Take time to imagine the fullness of the scene that John has taken time to describe. Allow yourself to be with him in your mind and take note of what he is showing and telling you. Are there particular symbols that are highlighted to you? Listen deeply, feel honestly, and be open to receive what God has for you here.

2 How does God appear to you here? What do you notice as you look at God? How does your heart respond?

3 Do any thoughts or questions come to mind? Spend time in conversation with God. Abide there and listen to any words or feelings that come to you.

4 How might this be a source of strength and light to you as you go into your day?

5 Can you receive the hope of Christ that is for you?

6 Can you offer this to others? How? Does anyone come to mind?

All Things are Possible

"Looking at them, Jesus said,
With people it is impossible,
but not with God; for all things are possible with God."
(Mark 10:27 NASB)

PRAYER EXERCISE 30

JESUS AND THE RICH YOUNG RULER – MARK 10:17-30 NIV   XX

As Jesus started on his way, a man ran up to him and fell on his knees before him. "Good teacher," he asked, "what must I do to inherit eternal life?"

"Why do you call me good?" Jesus answered. "No one is good – except God alone. You know the commandments: 'Do not murder, do not commit adultery, do not steal, do not give false testimony, do not defraud, honor your father and mother.'"

"Teacher," he declared, "all these I have kept since I was a boy."

Jesus looked at him and loved him. "One thing you lack," he said. "Go, sell everything you have and give to the poor, and you will have treasure in heaven. Then come, follow me."

At this the man's face fell. He went away sad, because he had great wealth.

Jesus looked around and said to his disciples, "How hard it is for the rich to enter the kingdom of God!"

The disciples were amazed at his words. But Jesus said again, "Children, how hard it is to enter the kingdom of God! It is easier for a camel to go through the eye of a needle than for a rich man to enter the kingdom of God."

The disciples were even more amazed, and said to each other, "Who then can be saved?"

Jesus looked at them and said, "With man this is impossible, but not with God; all things are possible with God."

REFLECTION QUESTIONS:

1 Imagine being at the scene of this event. What do you notice?

2 What thoughts come to your mind as you watch each character?

3 What might you think that you need to do to inherit eternal life?

4 Take time to sense Jesus looking at you and loving you.

5 What are you facing that is impossible with man, but possible with God?

6 Spend time receiving what the Spirit has for you in this place.

To Bethlehem

"Let us now go to Bethlehem and see this thing
that has come to pass, which the Lord has made known to us."
(Luke 2:15 NKJV)

"Do not be afraid.
I bring you good news of great joy that will be for all the people.
Today in the town of David a Savior has been born to you; he is
Christ the Lord."
(Luke 2:10 NIV)

PRAYER EXERCISE **31**

TO BETHLEHEM – LUKE 2:25 – 32 NIV   X

To Begin:

1. Be mindful of the GOOD NEWS – receiving a Saviour! Born to you – Christ the Lord.

2. Remember a time you felt lost or burdened and Jesus came to you and lifted the weight, giving you freedom. Can you remember the before and after feelings you had?

3. What is a foundational truth in this experience that can be fresh and meaningful for your heart today?

As you enter this Gospel story imagine the setting and all the people who were present. Imagine standing there; allow your thoughts and feelings to surface as you listen to what God may be telling or showing you.

> *"Now there was a man in Jerusalem called Simeon, who was*
> *righteous and devout. He was waiting for the consolation of*
> *Israel, and the Holy Spirit was upon him. It had been revealed*
> *to him by the Holy Spirit that he would not die before he had*

seen the Lord's Christ. Moved by the Spirit, he went into the temple courts. When the parents brought in the child Jesus to do for him what the custom of the Law required, Simeon took him in his arms and praised God, saying:

> *'Sovereign Lord, as you have promised,*
> *you now dismiss your servant in peace.*
> *For my eyes have seen your salvation,*
> *which you have prepared in the*
> *sight of all people,*
> *a light for revelation to the Gentiles*
> *and for glory to your people Israel.'*

The child's father and mother marvelled at what was said about him. Then Simeon blessed them and said to Mary, his mother: (The Message) *'This child marks both the failure and the recovery of many in Israel, A figure misunderstood and contradicted – the pain of a sword-thrust through you – But the rejection will force honesty, as God reveals who they really are.'"*

REFLECTION QUESTIONS:

1 What do you notice that you may not have noticed before?

2 As Simeon did, take Jesus in your arms. Is there something about Jesus that moves your heart?

3 As we are all like Mary, who represents the church and who says "yes" to the Lord, is there something that was said to her that is also for you today?

4 Christ forces honesty – how is the truth about who you are revealed?

5 Can you identify anything else that Jesus wants to reveal to you today?

6 Rest a while in the truth and comfort of Jesus being the fulfillment of God's promise to us.

That's My Story!
Using a Gospel Story to Tell Yours

"They overcame him by the blood of the Lamb
and by the word of their testimony."
(Revelation 12:11 NKJV)

"Tell your story in freedom." So says Henri Nouwen in *The Inner Voice of Love*. "The years that lie behind you, with all their struggles and pain, will in time be remembered only as the way that led to your new life." Nouwen encourages us to know our story and to move toward our new life. I have found it very healing to have those that love me listen to my story – every part of it. This has helped me to move past the parts that hindered me or that continued to cause me pain.

It is better to go in the new direction than to live feeling driven to relive painful events of the past. That can cause us to feel victimized. If we keep returning to them we may sense a need to tell it compulsively and urgently knowing that our present suffering is the result of our past experiences. "But there is another way," Nouwen says, cheering us on. "You can tell your story from the place where it no longer dominates you." We will humbly but confidently come to the place where we can speak about it with some distance and see it as part of the road to our present freedom. It no longer looms over us, it loses its weight, and, in fact, has made us more compassionate and understanding toward others.

I hadn't thought of this at first, but after many times of sharing the story of the Canaanite woman recorded in Matthew, it dawned on me that I loved this story because I could so identify with this dear woman, her journey of faith, and God's love for her. She helped me tell my story, for we walked on the same path in many ways.

The Faith of the Canaanite Woman

"Leaving that place, Jesus withdrew to the region of Tyre and
Sidon. A Canaanite woman from that vicinity came to him,
crying out, 'Lord, Son of David, have mercy on me! My daughter
is suffering terribly from demon-possession.'
Jesus did not answer a word. So his disciples came to him and
urged him, 'Send her away, for she keeps crying out after us.'
He answered, 'I was sent only to the lost sheep of Israel.'
The woman came and knelt before him. 'Lord, help me!' she said.
He replied, 'It is not right to take the children's bread
and toss it to their dogs.'
'Yes, Lord,' she said, 'but even the dogs eat the crumbs that
fall from their masters' table.'
Then Jesus answered, 'Woman, you have great faith! Your request
is granted.' And her daughter was healed from that very hour"
(Matthew 15:21-28).

This woman and I had much in common: I could identify with her powerless position, her hurdles, her desire, and her encounter with Jesus. My story is one of longing for Christ to come to that which is important or valuable to me.

She was not Jewish; likewise, I was in a sense an "outsider" in the Church who was brought to Sunday school on a bus that went around town. I was not related to one person in the church and, in a way, I was from "the other side of the tracks." The Canaanite woman persevered past laws and people. I, too, chose to keep moving toward Jesus despite the difficulties and obstacles that I faced.

A wonderful way to see a great visual of this story is to watch it dramatized on the Matthew Video/DVD series. This re-enactment showed me some things that I had never understood about Jesus and His love for this woman. Because of my mindset, as I heard it read or read it myself, I couldn't seem to get past the fact that it sounded like Jesus was speaking very unkindly to her, calling her a dog.

As I entered this story, I could see the love of Christ and the power of God rising in her as she pressed towards Jesus. It became more clear to me that our journey to Jesus is as important, or perhaps more important, than focusing on getting answered prayer. I see the wisdom of Jesus as He waits for her to come close, leading her to have an encounter with Himself rather than only getting a 'yes' to her prayer request. She was given the position of being right before Him, touching Him, kneeling at His feet, and talking to Him face to face.

I could also see that it was important for her to be challenged with the arguments that the world can use against us. Would she cave in? Would she shrink back? No, her tenacity and strong faith in Jesus – and who her heart knew Him to be – was such a delight to Christ that we can imagine Him throwing His head back with joy and laughter at her witty and trusting responses. Her posture of faithful surrender displayed in her willingness to accept even the crumbs from the table showed such beautiful trust.

Jesus commended her in the Scriptures for having great faith. She is one of only two persons in the New Testament about whose great faith Jesus comments.

Jesus is all about relationship. He seems more interested in answering prayer in ways that lead to or encourage a relationship with Himself, His Father and the Spirit.

Does a Bible story come to mind when you think of your testimony of faith? This can be a way to identify with our brothers and sisters in the Scriptures and learn more of the character of Christ who meets us.

Prayer Exercise 32

THAT'S MY STORY! XX

1 Spend some time looking at the stories in Scripture or think about the ones that seem to impact you most deeply. Is there one that you are often drawn to?

2 Ask God to highlight one to you or confirm the one that has come to your mind.

3 Putting yourself into the story, read it again. Move slowly allowing yourself to notice details or things going on, and to acknowledge your feelings.

4 What feelings arise in you? What do you feel in regards to your relationship with God? What do you learn about God? What do you notice about yourself?

5 How does the story parallel your life story? What can you strongly identify with?

6 Pause and come to some new or deeper understanding of your story and your connectedness with Jesus, and those who interacted with Him.

7 Write the key components of the Bible story.

8 Write how this story parallels yours and Jesus being with you.

PRAYER EXERCISE **33**

YOU HAVE GREAT FAITH! ⏳

The Canaanite Woman – Matthew 15:21–28 NIV.

1 *"Lord, Son of David, have mercy on me! My..."* (Put your request in here) Pause here and ask for mercy.

2 *"Jesus did not answer a word. So his disciples came to him and urged him to 'send her away, for she keeps crying out after us.'* Are you aware of any silence or rejection you may have felt or encountered? Do you have a sense of being ignored, disregarded, unwanted, or perhaps undeserving – a real bother?

3 *"I was sent only to the lost sheep of Israel."* Can you identify with a sense of not belonging?

4 *"The woman came and knelt before Him.' Lord, help me!' she said."* Offer Jesus your trust as you wait with Him.

5 *"He replied, 'It is not right to take the children's bread and toss it to their dogs.'"* Are you facing any laws or regulations in the Church or in society that might be obstructing the truth, or not in agreement with Jesus?

6 *"'Yes, Lord,' she said, 'but even the dogs eat the crumbs that fall from their masters' table.'"* Are you yielded to Jesus and prepared to receive whatever is given?

7 Ask for your faith to grow. Observe how it has already been enlarged.

8 *"Then Jesus answered, 'Woman, you have great faith! Your request is granted.' And her daughter was healed from that very hour."* Believe that your coming to Jesus with what matters most to your heart brings Him great delight! Accept that Jesus is always attentive to you, even when it doesn't seem so.

Lord, have mercy on us. Hear our prayers of faith. We trust in You. Blessed be the name of our God.

Enter Deeply into God's Word
Creative ways to enjoy Scripture

"I meditate on your precepts and consider your ways."
(Psalm 119:15 NIV)

I think that being creative with what God gives us is part of His character living and expressing itself in us—such as making an amazing salad from all the various things that grow in our gardens, or designing a building from all the raw materials that God provides. Here is a heart-felt creation designed from the traditional Lord's Prayer:

The Lord's Prayer

Ground of all being,
Mother of life, Father of the universe,
Your name is sacred, beyond speaking.
May we know your presence,
May your longings be our longings in heart and in action.
May there be food for the human family today
And for the whole earth community.
Forgive us the falseness of what we have done
As we forgive those who are untrue to us.
Do not forsake us in our time of conflict
But lead us into new beginnings.
For the light of life, the vitality of life, and the glory of life
Are yours now and forever. Amen
J Philip Newell (former rector of Iona)

I've had some life-giving experiences with God's Word being the foundational pieces to a creative prayer time. For instance, I once said the Lord's Prayer, saying one word at a time and pausing between each word. The deep and powerful truths of each word and all the meaning and significance of them filled my heart and mind with an even greater truth than I realized I could experience.

"Our," which is the first word in the Lord's Prayer, held such a fullness of being in a family with many others over the various continents and down through all the ages. After some of the deepness of that settled in my heart, I went on to the next word, "Father," which held so much strength, wisdom, and security for me. As I passed through each word, the message of this passage met me in a very profound way.

There are other ways that we can enjoy or be creative with Scripture as well. I invite you to some of these in the exercises below. Perhaps you have done this in some unique ways as well, or perhaps a new way will open up to you over the days to come.

PRAYER EXERCISE **34**

THE LORD'S PRAYER   Ⅹ

Focus: *One Word* at a Time

1 Slowly, either silently or out loud, move through this prayer.

2 In stillness or with journaling be attentive to all that you are hearing, seeing and feeling.

The Lord's Prayer – Matthew 6:9-13 NASB

"Our / Father / who / is / in / heaven,

hallowed / be / Your / name,

Your / kingdom / come,

Your / will / be / done

On / earth / as / it / is / in / heaven.

Give / us / this / day / our / daily / bread.

And / forgive / us / our / debts,

    as / we / also / have / forgiven / our / debtors.

And / do / not / lead / us / into / temptation,

    but / deliver / us / from / evil.

For / Yours / is / the / kingdom / and / the / power /

    and / the / glory / forever. / Amen."

Focus: *One phrase* each day of the week.

The Lord's Prayer
Matthew 6:9-13 NASB

Monday:	Our Father who is in heaven, hallowed be Your name,
Tuesday:	Your kingdom come, Your will be done on earth as it is in heaven.
Wednesday:	Give us this day our daily bread.
Thursday:	And forgive us our debts, as we also have forgiven our debtors.
Friday:	And do not lead us into temptation,
Saturday:	but deliver us from evil.
Sunday:	For Yours is the kingdom and the power and the glory forever. Amen.

PRAYER EXERCISE 35

INSERT YOUR NAME   X

1 Open the Bible to Psalm 91.

2 Proceed through the passage as I have illustrated below:

Based on Psalm 91 NIV

I, (your name) , who dwell in your shelter, O Most High, rest in your shadow, Almighty.
I will say of you, Lord, "You are my refuge and my fortress, my God, in whom I trust."
Surely you will save me from the fowler's snare and from the deadly pestilence.

Continue on in Psalm 91...

a.) Do you notice anything different about this passage as you read it this way?

b.) Does it seem more personal or fresh to your ears?

c.) Can you relate it more practically to your present life situations?

d.) Try this with other passages such as Psalm 23.

PRAYER EXERCISE **36**

LET GOD SPEAK IT TO YOU   ⏳

1 Open the Bible to Psalm 40:1-11

2 Proceed through the passage as I have illustrated below:

Based on Psalm 40:1-11 NASB

You, (your name), waited patiently for Me;
and I inclined to you and heard your cry.
I brought you up out of the pit of destruction, out of the miry clay,
And I set your feet upon a rock making your footsteps firm.
I put a new song in your mouth, a song of praise to Me, your God.
Many will see and fear and will trust in Me.
How blessed are you, (your name), who has made Me your trust....

Continue on in Psalm 40...

a.) Can you imagine God sitting with you sharing His heart for you, speaking love and truth over you? Try to receive the unseen real presence and Word of God to you.

b.) Respond with a personal prayer of gratitude to God.

PRAYER EXERCISE 37
IT'S ABOUT US! – PSALM 5   X

Focus: Reading as given to the community rather than to an individual.

1 I invite you to feel the strength of belonging to the family of God.

2 What feelings or thoughts emerge in your heart as you hear this?

Based on Psalm 5:1–4, 7–8, 11–12 NIV

Give ear to our words, O Lord, consider our sighing.
Listen to our cry for help, our King and our God,
for to you we pray.
In the morning, O Lord, you hear our voice;
In the morning we lay our requests before you
and wait in expectation.
You are not a God who takes pleasure in evil;
with you the wicked cannot dwell.
But we, by your great mercy, will come into your house;
In reverence will we bow down toward your holy temple.
Lead us, O Lord, in your righteousness
because of our enemies—
Make straight your way before us.
But let all of us who take refuge in you be glad;
let us ever sing for joy.
Spread your protection over us that we who love your name
may rejoice in you.
For surely, O Lord, you bless the righteous;
you surround us with your favor as with a shield.
Amen

Invited to Rest

"We need silence to be alone with God,
To speak to Him, to listen to Him,
To ponder His words deep in our hearts.
We need to be alone with God in silence
To be renewed and to be transformed.
Silence gives us a new outlook on life.
In it we are filled with the grace of God Himself,
Which makes us do all things with joy."

Mother Teresa

Entering His Rest

"I have stilled and quieted my soul."
(Psalm 131:2 NIV)

I lead a contemplative prayer hour at the MARK Centre each week called "Sacred Space" – a drop-in invitation to those feeling led to a quiet hour that includes Scripture reading, reflection questions, and a time of listening to God. It was June and the final hour of being together before heading into the summer months. I wondered, "What will we hear to carry us through the many days of summer that lay ahead?"

One of the questions that day was, "God, what are You inviting me to this summer?" I was quite surprised when what I heard was "Enter the Sabbath Rest." As I sat still hoping for a bit more clarity, I sensed that God was asking me to experience the weekly Sabbath Rest of 24 hours of not working, but resting, slowing down life, and enjoying quiet and stillness. And not just doing it once, but weekly. It intrigued me. What was this? You see, I was living free from a legalistic trap of my past where the "Sundays are holy," mentality plagued me, so what did this mean?

I went to my Bible to read and hopefully understand this invitation better. As I read, a powerful desire to move toward this rose up from within me. I looked at my schedule and the summer days were much more accommodating to add this huge request. So I picked the day that it would be each week, thought through how I could unplug from work, have an easy meal ready, still care for the needs of my family, and enter into this Sabbath Rest.

I woke up on the appointed day, stayed in my pyjamas, took my Bible and journal and headed to a restful spot in my house. "Hmm," I thought, "I've never really entered into this restful location in my house like this." I love decorating my house with whatever is beautiful to me. I like to make spaces be inviting and lovely, so I had a few such spots throughout my house and yard. The sad reality was that I had never really sat in them long – they just *looked* really nice!

What happened next astounded me. As I sat becoming aware of stillness, quiet, and a sense of "nothing-ness," a whole new world appeared to me. I saw, heard, and sensed as never before. My eyes beheld things I never had time to notice before, my ears heard things that made me smile, and I sensed the beautiful and surrounding presence of God in such an intentional, yet peaceful way.

My eyes were drawn to my Bible which I had used for over a decade. I felt led to pick it up tenderly and to gaze upon it. I lingered over the worn-out cover that made people think I must be very godly – or scholarly at least. I saw, as if for the first time, how tattered the pages had become, and, how the ribbon that hung out from the pages had become a very faded pink on the end, but the rest of it that was tucked inside was a more vivid rose color. I cannot adequately express the profound fondness, the deep love and appreciation that came upon me for this Book, and all that it held for me, and all it had given me.

I noticed an ever-deepening peace coming upon me, and yet my body seemed to still hold tension and anxiety. I saw in my mind's eye a child's wind-up toy. I sensed the Lord showing me that I was like this, all wound up tight inside and physically as well. As I sat still at the beginning of this Sabbath I felt invited to let go, just to let it all go and unwind until all the unwinding was done. How scary! What would happen? Would I fall apart?

And what about everything in my life that I held together? What would happen? Would I ever wind up or get going again?

I took the leap of faith and settled back into the chair trusting that Jesus would catch me at the end, or the bottom, or wherever we were going. I would rest until I felt unwound then do it again, and again, like stages, or layers, going deeper and deeper into stillness. I was surprised and glad at how wonderful it was feeling. What a release of all that I did not need to be holding, or worrying about, or mindlessly clinging to for some unknown reason. I liked this and felt it was to be part of the beginning of each of the Sabbath days to come. And so it is to this very day.

The day unfolded with much-needed sleep, reading great books I had been longing to get into, making tea and leaving any mess for later, interacting with God, and actually experiencing the many beautiful restful spots around our property that I had usually only enjoyed from a distance.

The day, the Sabbath, God's presence, it all got even better; I was in our back yard lying in the beautiful hammock that my daughter, Tiffany, brought me from one of her trips. I read, rested my eyes, and enjoyed the natural beauty that surrounded me. Suddenly, a baby fawn came dashing across the rocks above me into my view. The little one was baaing and bleating with such earnest cries. My heart leapt to come close and comfort her, yet I dared not move as I didn't want to startle her even more. She was looking feverishly around the hill making this noise that I had never heard before.

I heard some rustling in the trees and out sprang a large deer, very abruptly. It was obviously the fawn's mother. She, too, was making a loud calling sound as if to reassure her baby that she was near. The mother came swiftly and directly across the rocky edge with her neck outstretched to reach her little one long before she could actually get there. When she got near the fawn she affectionately put her nose upon the little one. The crying instantly stopped, they were reunited, and went on grazing as if nothing had happened. All was well.

I sat enthralled by this live and moving performance that seemed to be coming out of a nature show on television, but was right before my eyes. I likely would have totally missed it in an average busy day. I was captivated by this event.

Then it struck me that this is exactly how I had been feeling toward one of my children who seemed to be a bit lost in their life, a bit too far from home. Tears fell as this situation spoke deeply to my heart and life, and encouraged me to continue to love and watch over those entrusted to me.

Usually what happens is that the longer you linger the more you notice or comprehend. As I continued to embrace and ponder these moments and what God was showing me I sensed His intense love and devotion toward me as His child – that He would never let me go too far, was always attentive to my whereabouts, and comes quickly when I call (See Jeremiah 33:3).

Not much in my life is as contended-for as my weekly Sabbath rest hours. Outside requests, obligations, responsibilities, and my own inner struggles compete in the on-going challenge of entering this rest and then staying in it as led by God. Not much in my life gives me as much as I receive in these hours. The bounty of His loving presence that God offers and bestows upon me, body, soul, and mind, is abundant in so many ways. Of course, some Sabbath days are full of what appears more rich or extravagant, and others seem sparse and God is less apparent. When days seem more ordinary, or even empty, I must choose to continue being obedient, and to be with God whatever that may or may not look like.

I am finding that if I listen to what my body, mind and heart are telling me or what I am strongly feeling, He uses this to guide me into what I am to do, or not to do. For example, when I open my email I feel very uncomfortable if I start to check any work-related email rather than just notes from my kids. One time while taking a rest, before I knew it, I had a dust-buster vacuum in my hand and was scooping up some debris in a corner of my house. When I realized what I was doing, I was so surprised that I laughed out loud. As I turned my focus upon the Lord, I sensed His smile too. Rather than beat me up, He was there to gently remind me and invite me back to the break I needed from all the busy-ness.

There are some things that I've had to adjust in my life and ways that work for me to have a Sabbath day when the rest of the world isn't having one; not so easy!

1. The first thing I do is to pencil off the full day each week in my Daytimer so I remember that this is not to be touched for anything that is work-related, ministry- related, or electrical. I say "electrical" because if I am working it usually includes various house or yard appliances or tools. I invite everything in my life to rest as much as possible—even equipment! I will not answer email (unless it's a limited chat with one of my children or a friend). I take phone messages to call back, or let the answering machine take them for me. If I have a ministry weekend, trip, or important family event that prohibits a proper Sabbath, then I choose a different rest day that week. But most typically it works for me to start my Sabbath on Friday afternoon and go until Saturday afternoon.

2. Friday afternoon I unplug from the usual work world and enter my unwinding. I will try to do something restful for self-care such as enjoy a massage that I've booked ahead, have a long relaxing bath, or meet a friend or one of my children for a peaceful cup of tea. I slow everything down, even my walking and actions. I invite my family to participate as they are able. I have a prepared dinner ready just to warm up, or plan a simple all-make-together meal and enjoy my family or community. Often we will visit and enjoy the evening.

3. Saturday I sleep in. (My youngest children are now teenagers so this works. When our five children were little and we wanted rest, my husband and I would take turns so we couldn't both rest on the same morning together, but each of us would get a full rest every other day of the weekend, or vacation day.) I enter the morning simply and peacefully by relaxing with nothing booked and enjoy a time of quiet non-activity, by myself or with my family. We will only book things that need to get done in the yard, around the house, or preparing for Sunday ministry for later in the afternoon.

4. I plan my rest days from: noon – noon, or 3:00 pm – 3:00 pm (it depends on the rest of the world and what is going

on), and at some point in the 24 hours I will always journal. The top of my journal page starts: Sabbath, and the date. I share my unwinding with God, either how lovely it is, or how difficult. I love having time to write, think, or sketch without time constraints. I listen to God, read, but mostly try to sit in silence with non-activity to become aware of all the sounds, sights, and beauty around me—letting my body relax and my mind feel the stillness. Often I will be filled with gratitude and a sense of God with me that is both natural and enjoyable. From my times in stillness I may realize that I need some sleep so I go for a rest. I may realize that I want some fresh air and will go outside to sit or walk. Or I may remember a book I've been waiting to read.

5. If my children need me to help them with something that cannot wait, I help them, but I do it from a place of rest and slowness. If they need a ride and it cannot wait, I will drive them, again from a place of peace and enjoyment. If a meeting is booked that I sense God wants me to attend, I will, but again, I do it in a relaxed manner. If I prepare tea or some food, I do it slowly, smelling, tasting, enjoying each movement I make. One of the goals I have is to take this pace, this restfulness into the rest of my days; I trust God is growing that in me.

6. I endeavour to remember that God is at work even when I am at rest. He is able to do all that I can not. I am growing in trust that everything will still get done, and probably better, as I obey this time of rejuvenation and space for God.

My favourite things about practicing the Sabbath are; the joy and anticipation I have of connecting with God more intentionally, the space that is made for Him to fill, and, of course leaving dirty dishes all over the kitchen and not making the bed. The physical rejuvenation and energy I receive is so exciting to me. Doing the tasks and activities that I am given to do on the other days are so life-giving now. I go into these days filled with rest and peace, and can work vigorously with enjoyment, rather than feeling guilty or being exhausted. There is also the sheer delight that comes from obeying Christ when it isn't always easy.

What I hope for, and do see growing in my life, is the ability to take God's Sabbath Rest into the other days, nights, situations, relationships, activities, etc. that I am given.

I invite you to look at this area of your life and to hear God for yourself and what He may be inviting you into in the area of Sabbath Rest.

PRAYER EXERCISE 38

SABBATH-REST FOR THE PEOPLE OF GOD XX

1 Meditate on these scriptures:

"Therefore, since the promise of entering his rest still stands, let us be careful that none of you be found to have fallen short of it. There remains, then, a Sabbath-rest for the people of God; for anyone who enters God's rest also rests from his own work, just as God did from his. Let us, therefore, make every effort to enter that rest, so that no one will fall by following their example of disobedience" (Hebrews 4:1, 9-11 NIV).

"But I have stilled and quieted my soul;

like a weaned child with its mother,

like a weaned child is my soul within me.

O Israel, put your hope in the LORD,

both now and forevermore" (Psalm 131:2-3 NIV)

2 What message do you hear from the Lord for yourself? What is His invitation to you?

3 Recall a time of rest that was particularly meaningful for you. What did that feel like? Why was it meaningful? Rest a couple of minutes in this memory and receive what the Lord wants to give you.

4 See if you are falling short of a Sabbath-rest in your life, a time of stopping for quietness, listening, restoring, and reviving. If you are invited to more Sabbath Rest in your life, wait on God with a listening posture and an attitude to receive what God has for you – encouragement, strengthening, a strategy, peace, etc. I highly encourage you to read the guiding principles of spiritual disciplines (pg.123-127). How can this be applied practically to your life? What do you need to pre-plan or adjust in your schedule and/or family life? What way can you have a peaceful Sabbath-rest in your life?

PRAYER EXERCISE **39**

A WIND-UP TOY **XX**

1 Could you be wound up tight like a child's toy? Perhaps you've been wound tighter and tighter as days and hours have passed. Something seems out of place, or not quite right. What is it?

2 Find a comfortable location and chair. Sit upright with feet re-laxed but on the floor in front of you. Lay your head back if you are able but do not take a sleeping position.

The invitation comes to you to relax, slow down, chill out, let go, unwind.

3 Then perhaps the fear of unravelling arrives – "What if I let go? What will happen if I totally relax and let all the tension out of my body? Will I fall apart? Will things in my life get done?" What are your questions or concerns? Can you relinquish them and trust God at this time? If so, continue on. If not, be at peace to receive as much rest right now as you are able.

4 As you sit and do this "unwinding" allow yourself to go deeper and deeper into a place of peace, and become more and more still and restful. You may actually fall asleep. If so, that's possibly what you needed. If you doze, when you come back to the present moment, continue to be mindful of your unwinding state.

5 When you feel you have unwound, rest there and be aware of God's presence. Let Him surround you and fill you. What are you aware of? What do you see, feel, smell that you didn't notice before? Enjoy this awareness and what the Lord may be giving you at this time. Be at peace in this place of God's rest. "Be still, and know that I am God" (Psalm 46:10 KJV). Continue the layers of unwinding as you feel led.

6 When this non-activity feels completed you can do this if you feel led: Imagine instead of the wind-up toy, that you are a spool of thread that is wrapped neatly and tightly, but not tense. Feel that God is winding Himself and His love around you binding you to Him.

7 In the hours/days to come, notice if or when you are becoming tense or winding up. Give yourself the gift of rest and calm right at that moment if you are able. Take the Sabbath Rest that you receive into the other days, events, or times of your work and life.

Resting In God's Grace

"...the riches of God's grace"
(Ephesians 1:7).

Oh, how God loves us! The extent that He goes to save and rescue us astounds me. Have you ever struggled with the many thoughts that go racing through your mind? How about the ones that get stuck on repeat and seem to come fleeting by every so often simply to drive you crazy, or so it seems? "God, please stop these thoughts from coming to me! I know You can, and in an instant!" I prayed, I begged, I repented, I did everything I knew to do to remove some nasty thoughts from repeating in my mind. It seemed that the harder I prayed, the worse it got.

In my desperation I finally sat down, feeling very defeated, to inquire of God as to why I could not seem to have "deliverance" from this frustration. When I finally was quiet long enough to hear God's wise and loving voice I heard, "I don't plan on helping you with this until you accept the fact that I love you just the way you are, even with this weakness." *Great*, I thought. *What do I do in the mean time?* "Come meet me in The Grace Room," I heard. Not sure of what the Grace Room was I sat still longer. Slowly I began to feel that my heart indeed had a Grace Room complete with a hammock where I would certainly need to rest from all my striving. It was a most simple, but exquisite place. The room was lit, but gently, as if by candlelight. The air was warm and tender, relaxing and receiving, and full of God's healing love.

Since that day, whenever I have felt overcome with chaotic thoughts or by my inability to think straight or cope in some situations I would turn to God in my heart's Grace Room. As I accepted the truth that God's grace is enough for me and that I am loved completely regardless of my negative propensities, my whole self began to settle. My serenity was restored, my negative inclinations lessened, my overambitious efforts diminished, and life was far more undisturbed. I still visit this place when God brings it to my mind.

God's understanding and grace are so complete and restorative.

One day I was going about ordinary chores when I sensed the Spirit inviting me to spend some time together. I was so excited. I grabbed my Bible and journal, a pillow to sit on the patio, and headed out into the sunshine. I got all set up ready to listen. *I wonder what we will do today?* I thought. *Would I be taught something spectacular? Would the Spirit move in healing, restoration, or surprising visions?*

As I stilled my soul, I heard a tender voice say, "I just wanted to be with you." I don't think any other seven words could mean so much to me as these. I was taken aback, yet deeply moved. Simply being together without something having to happen was a new reality for me in my relationship with God. I had been enjoying a more interactive relationship over the past while and this felt a bit strange, but mysteriously wonderful.

More and more I am realizing that God gives me everything I need, and that it is the Spirit that moves upon my body, soul, and spirit to lead me into what is best for me, which could be rest, energy, grace, freedom, service, etc. The invitation to rest in so many more areas of my life is becoming more and more noticeable and appealing to me.

Recently, a state of worry was stirring in me and I was tempted to give in to it, when once again, while standing right in my kitchen, the tender voice of God said, "Lorie, why are you worrying? You belong to Me. You gave yourself to Me, remember? You died, that I would live in you." It hit me right between the eyes, and I melted into this peaceful love and this wonderful place of belonging. I sensed God looking at me saying, "Just go with Me, honey. It will be okay." That made me smile. This verse now means so much more to me: "I have been crucified with Christ and I no longer live, but Christ lives in me. The life I live in the body, I live by faith in the Son of God, who loved me and gave himself for me" (Galatians 2:20 NIV).

PRAYER EXERCISE 40

RESTING IN GOD'S GRACE ⏳

1 Is there a specific area in your life that you feel invited to rest or receive God's grace? It could be an outward activity or one in your interior life.

2 Let these scriptures flow over you as you read them slowly, one word at a time, pausing in between each word or thought. Receive God's love and message to you. Accept His grace and let His rest remain in you.

> *"The Lord your God gives you rest and will give you this land ... cross over before your brothers ... and help them until the Lord gives your brothers rest, as He gives you, and they also possess the land which the Lord your God is giving them" (Joshua 1:13 NASB).*

> *"Heaven is my throne, and the earth is my footstool. Where is the house you will build for me? Where will my resting place be?" (Isaiah 66:1 NIV)*

> *"Moses answered the people, 'Do not be afraid. Stand firm and you will see the deliverance the Lord will bring you today.... The Lord will fight for you; you need only to be still" (Exodus 14:14, 15 NIV).*

> *"He who dwells in the shelter of the Most High will rest in the shadow of the Almighty" (Psalm 91:1 NIV).*

> *"His place of rest will be glorious ... There will be a highway for the remnant of His people" (Isaiah 11:10 NIV).*

Swimmers, Floaters, or Drifters

"I have been crucified with Christ and I no longer live,
but Christ lives in me.
The life I live in the body, I live by faith in the Son of God,
who loved me, and gave himself for me."
(Galatians 2:20 NIV)

Do you ever get tired and feel like you've been swimming upstream for such a long time? Perhaps you don't realize how hard you've been paddling to move your life along. As you know, you can do this for only so long. "I quit," or "I hate this," or "I'm drowning," might be sentiments that come out of your mouth or resound loudly in your heart and mind.

Recently I encountered a season of being very tired. After a full year of ministry and focus on my family, I was facing extreme challenges in numerous areas of my life all at the same time. To top it off, in the midst of this time, I was also experiencing a sense of God not seeming to be very present to me in ways that were familiar, easily recognizable, and reassuring. This sense, known as a dark night of our senses or dark night of our soul, was quite discomforting, even distressing, especially in the middle of the night. (See pages 12-14, 70, 71, and 76 for more on *Dark Night*.)

While unable to move about with a normal amount of energy and zest for life, I saw a book that I had picked up at a second hand store. It had been on one of the reading lists given to me years before. You may recognize it: *When the Well Runs Dry, Prayer Beyond the Beginnings* by Thomas H. Green, S.J. I skimmed through the contents, flipped through the pages and thought, "This book looks really good." However, my get-up-and-go had gotten up and left, so I was extremely thankful that what caught my attention was the Epilogue. The heading read, "How blest are the poor in Spirit; the

111

reign of God is theirs." Matthew 5:3. In my lethargic state I was convinced that the book had much more to offer me at another time. But for now I would be satisfied with the short but powerful message that Father Green shared with me in the Epilogue.

I can remember reading three key words—swimmers, floaters, and drifters. Father Green explained a part of our spiritual journey and what we are invited to as we go. We are guided by God's grace and find ourselves at the water and are led to swim towards God, by our own will and God's will—but this is only part of the journey. God, at some point in our transformation, will change us from swimmers into floaters, moving us from our own will to being one with His will. This can seem very awkward after getting fairly good at swimming or being exhausted and not knowing how to float.

"It is not natural for man to be a floater," Father Green states. "Even when he does learn a bit about floating and acquires some skill at it, there still lurks in him a suspicion that he should be doing something, controlling events, working for the kingdom according to his own lights and his own God-given natural gifts." However, even God-given gifts and reason will never make us into floaters he tells us.

"Floaters are not drifters," he states. They may appear the same as they are moved by the water, but floating is far more dynamic and responsive than it appears. Drifting leads us to lazily sink to the bottom or lose all balance and become lost. However, one who floats has let the movement and will of the water, which is God, become their own as they let go of the swimming, the striving, or controlling their own journey. The will of God "has become the dynamic force of his life and all his energies are spent in responding fully to the ebb and flow of the tide. He is intensely active." "It is only the floater, who has allowed the will of the Lord to become his own will, who will be intensely active and yet tension-free."

What we discover as we become one with God's will is order and peace, since the tension of pulling in different directions has ceased. We also discover that surrendering to God does not make us lifeless, pathetic or feeble. Rather, when tapping more fully into God's will and moving with His work and energies, our lives and talents become limitless.

Father Green ends this beautiful message telling us that as floaters, we will discover that the river we are floating on comes from the heart of God and that the tide is now reversed and draws us back to its Source. He asks, "But who can describe, or even imagine, what the floater will discover There?"

PRAYER EXERCISE 41

ARE YOU SWIMMING, FLOATING OR DRIFTING?

1 Rest as you become aware of God's presence with you.

2 Give thanks for God's grace leading you to life-giving water and for giving you strength to follow.

3 Continue to surrender your will to be one with God's. Is there an area of your life that comes to your mind that God wants you to let go of?

4 Ask God to help you move from being a swimmer to a floater.

"God, if there are areas in my life where I still want to control or strive to get where I think I need to be, I humbly ask You to help me trust You as You transform me as You see is best. Amen."

5 Receive the love of God as you are invited to move from swimming to floating. Close your eyes and become open to God's will and love. Imagine lying back into God's love like you would lay back into water. Feel the movements of God's heart of love for you and where you are being led. Look to God to hold you, guide you, and take you where you are being drawn by the Spirit of God.

6 Meditate on Revelation 22:1, 2 which is printed below.

7 Receive God's life flowing to you as God takes you. Be open to receive rest, trust and surrender and whatever else you are given. Give thanks to God.

> *"Then the Angel showed me Water-of-Life River, crystal bright.*
> *It flowed from the Throne of God and the Lamb,*
> *right down the middle of the street.*
> *The Tree of Life was planted on each side of the River,*
> *producing twelve kinds of fruit, a ripe fruit each month.*
> *The leaves of the Tree are for healing the nations."*
> (Rev. 22:1, 2 MSG)

When the Well Runs Dry, Prayer Beyond the Beginnings by Thomas H. Green, S.J. – Ava Maria Press 1979

Rest and Intercession
They Go Together?

By Fiona Calder

"Be still and know that I am God;
I will be exalted among the nations,
I will be exalted in the earth!"
(Psalm 46:10 NKJV)

Please meet a dear friend of mine, Fiona Calder, known as "Fi," (pronounced, Fee.) Fi is one of the people who always sticks out in my mind because she is just that special and she is always "about her Father's business." She has a passion for Jesus and being with Him in the various ways that He lays on her heart. Usually these ways involve people and prayer. She oversees the intercessor team at Fresh Wind Church and is also likely to be baking cookies for someone, or cleaning their toilets. Along with her regular family and home duties, she spends her days with Jesus listening, praying, and encouraging us with what He shows her.

I love watching, hearing about, or joining the little intercessory group she leads; it is small in size, but mighty in God's kingdom of prayer and intimacy. One of Fi's messages on Rest is so vital and yet so simple. It is my hope that we will enter into prayer and intercession with faith and trust as she shares with us now.

Fiona: Our little intercessory prayer group started in the spring of 2005. We were an unusual team; four women with ages spanning four generations. All were seasoned intercessors with an array of church backgrounds and experiences, and a combined total of 120 years of intercession behind us.

Right from the start we practiced listening to how the Holy Spirit might ask us to pray about any given situation. We listened for scriptures, images and hymns and used these to fuel our prayers. Things seemed to be going pretty well.

Then in the summer of 2006 came something which changed our whole emphasis. The church leadership team sent out a message to the entire church that God was asking us to use that two month summer season as a Sabbath Rest. And so it was that our little intercessors group was also asked to continue to meet together for fun and fellowship, but NOT to pray. O dear! We balked! This just could not be right! To ask intercessors to stop interceding is like asking us to stop breathing! It's the one thing that brings us life. We emailed back and forth with the leadership, pleading our cause, but the message always came back 'God has asked us, as a church, to REST.' Finally, with heavy hearts and a few tears, we agreed.

Towards the end of that summer our dear Anne, the oldest member of our group, had an encounter with God. She was reading in Leviticus when she stumbled upon the "fallow field" (a programme of rest, required every seven years for the farmland), and it was into this field that God asked her to lay her intercessions. She explained to us that just as the land was required to rest (to improve its longevity and fruitfulness), this was a picture too of how the intercessors were to rest. Not to pray for people or situations in this season, but simply to place them in God's fallow field and to trust Him to take care of them. (See Leviticus 25:3–4.)

Another piece of the puzzle came in the words of Hebrews 4:1 (NIV), "Therefore, since the promise of entering into his rest still stands, let us be careful that none of you be found to fall short of it." There was a serious warning in this verse: we needed to be vigilant not to fall short of God's rest, even in prayer. At the same time, we were hearing the Holy Spirit say, "Cease striving," and again and again we mulled over Jesus' invitation of rest for all those who are weary and heavy laden (Matthew 11:28).

Learning how to enter into God's rest was to become the bedrock of all our intercession. Choosing to "cease striving" (or "cease labouring") in prayer uncovered some of the driven-ness of our Christian practices and challenged our sense of worth and efficacy as intercessors. Our very identity felt threatened. If we weren't labouring in prayer, were our prayers going to work? Could we still call ourselves intercessors?

We chose to follow through with REST because we truly believed God was asking this of us. At first we thought this didn't require enough from us to be valid. But we quickly came to see that rest is not an easy option, and that it is often contrary to our natural instinct. Rest is, in fact, a discipline.

We discovered that the practice of rest in prayer greatly increased our trust and confidence in God. When we rest we stop "doing" and it means we have to trust that God will do the "doing" instead. Trust is a sweet and powerful component of intercession. It has child-like qualities of simple, holy faith, and it relies on the character of God. Sometimes when we meet to pray our group does little more than allow our hearts to rest in His promises (in scripture and song). We are united in trusting that God is good, He is near and that He loves to take care of us. There is little need to "ask" anything of our heavenly Papa when we are resting in such a sacred spot.

We keep a prayer basket. Into this basket we place all the names of those we've been asked to pray for. This basket is like the fallow field … it requires hardly any work from us. But it's because we believe that this basket is God's basket, and in placing the prayer needs into it, we are in fact placing the requests right into God's hands. He knows the needs, and we rest in that knowledge. We keep the basket on the coffee table that we sit around as we pray. In this way it is surrounded by our love and unity. Most weeks we lay hands on it, or simply lift it up before Him.

From the flow of rest our intercessions often focus around worship, gazing into the face of Him who has won our hearts. No matter what the disease, misfortune, injustice or difficulty that we are praying about, when we focus on Him our assurance of His power and love increases and the problem shrinks. Again, we trust in Him, and this trust spills over as a covering of blessing over all those concerned. Our faith in Him and His character opens the door for Him to "enter in" and take action as He chooses.

Surprisingly, rest has proved to be a form of warfare in our intercessions. There are moments when we shout and do our war-dance with passion, but by and large, warfare has become less about taking up arms and more about standing still and watching God fight the battles for us (Exodus 14:13; 2 Chronicles 20:17). Our valiant and powerful Warrior God rises up and melts our hearts (with love), and the heart of the enemy (with fear)!

Rest in prayer takes many forms for us: silence, worship, praise, humming, singing in tongues together, playing the drums (or the furniture when there is no drum!), meditating on the Scriptures, laying or sitting very still, dancing, taking communion, listening and writing. Rest is such a great equalizer. Those of few words are no longer disadvantaged, since the labour of verbal petition and declaration is no longer the main focus. Yes, we do still ask God some very specific requests as He lays these on our hearts, but usually this is a relatively short part of our prayer time.

Personally, I often use the imagery of rest in my prayers. If God has laid someone on my heart, He may also give me a mental picture of the distress they are encountering. For instance, with a person in crippling financial debt, I might have the sensation that they are being held in a vice, like the one on my husband's work-bench. When God asks me to intercede for them, He might ask me to allow myself to be in that vice, to identify with what they are going through and to stand with them. As I am feeling the pressure and tightness in my spirit, He then asks me to pray by simply entering into His rest on behalf of that person.

This is different from asking for God to change their situation, for the vice to be loosened etc. It is easy to enter into rest on lazy days at the beach, but can I really enter into His rest and allow trust to flow when I'm in a tight vice? This is why I say rest is a discipline! By my choice and by God's grace and strength I do it. And in that place of pressure which is squeezing the life out of the person in its grip, I create a "sacred space" of peace and rest and trust. I believe God uses this.

Learning to pray from the resting place has been the best thing that's happened to our little intercessors group. We go home most weeks with hearts so light and free, and with such a sense of having completed what God gave us to do. He carries the weight of the multitude of prayer requests for us.

PRAYER EXERCISE 42

REST AND INTERCESSION – THEY GO TOGETHER?

1 Jesus, how can rest become a more significant part of my prayer life?

2 Why is rest difficult for me?

3 What is it about being yoked to Jesus that is restful? (Matthew 11:28)

Invited to Solitude

He Desired Me So I Came Close

He desired me so I came close.
No one can come near God unless He has
Prepared a bed for you.

A thousand souls hear His call every second,
But most everyone then looks into their life's mirror and says,
"I am not worthy to leave this sadness."

When I first heard His courting song, I too
Looked at all I had done in my life
and said,
"How can I gaze into His omnipresent eyes?"
I spoke those words with all
My heart,

But then He sang again, a song even sweeter,
And when I tried to shame myself once more from His presence
God showed me His compassion and spoke a divine truth.

"I made you, dear, and all I make is perfect.
Please come close,
for I desire you."

St. Teresa of Avila
Love Poems from God – Twelve Sacred Voices from the East and West
Translated by Daniel Ladinsky

A Contemplative Life
Whatever?

"For with you is the fountain of life; in your light we see light."
(Psalm 36:9 NIV)

Contemplative Living is the fountain and source out of which all our ministry will flow. Without a contemplative life pattern, it is impossible for us to help others discern the reality of Christ in the whole of their life.

What do we mean by a contemplative way of life? What is its essence? It is not something to do, but a life – a way of life centered on God. It is a life that flows out of a response to God's love for us. It is God's life *in* us. Another way of saying it could be: living the new life we have already been given.

Contemplative Living affects how we view and act in relationship to:

- our body

- our family, friends, co-workers, fellow students, strangers

- our vocation and/or our main occupation

- our role as a citizen

- our role as a consumer

- the created world

I'm not sure it's a way of life for the faint of heart! It is a life of continuously offering ourselves to be purified of all that is not of God in us.

"The disciplines are activities of the mind and body purposeful-

123

ly undertaken, to bring our personality and total being into effective cooperation with the divine order." – Dallas Willard

Some of the practices (disciplines) that support the contemplative life:

> *Prayer silence fasting simplicity consciousness Examen worship music volunteering doing art celebration confession solitude submission study journaling walking advocacy etc...*

Spiritual disciplines are part of a contemplative life. Spiritual disciplines demonstrate our availability and openness to the work of the Holy Spirit in shaping our lives, restoring the beauty of the image of God in us. They are the choices we make to nurture and support the Life of God emerging within us and which help us to resist distorting the power of this life and becoming captive to our fallen nature. They are activities that we consistently choose that shape our experience into character—habits or regular patterns in our life that repeatedly bring us back to God and open us up to what God is saying to us.

The Latin word for discipline (rule) is "*regula*" which originally meant "*trellis.*" If you picture a trellis in a garden, likely you will think of a vine growing over and around it. The spiritual disciplines are the structure that helps us to grow in a direction that is good and stable, rather than on the ground to be trampled upon. The trellis (discipline) is not the Life-giving Source, rather it is simply the means to shape or form us as God leads us.

No discipline, prayer bead, cloth, icon, symbol, or other object, nor any devotional practice, body position, sequence of words, etc. makes God respond any better to any prayer, nor will they make heaven, earth, or hell bend to our bidding. God does not work that way; the world God created does not work that way. Devotional aids are to help us be directed toward God. They are our response to His invitations to be with Him. The moment we believe they have any powers or merit of their own we are being idolatrous or worshipping a form of godliness, rather than God. If you find yourself having that attitude, it is best to stop doing the practice or using the devotional aid. Become aware of any such tendencies you may have and try something else that might cause less of a problem for you. Listen and watch what the Spirit may be inviting you to that brings you life and joy and is easy and light, not another burden.

Some features of a contemplative practice:

- It is my response to the deepening experience of God's love for me, a way of being that springs from my heart.

- It is created as the Holy Spirit invites and inspires me.

- It will be unique to me, suited to me as a unique creation of God.

- It doesn't depend on my feelings or mood or what else is happening; it is a discipline not done out of a sense of obligation or rigid legalism, but as a response to God's drawing – yet at the same time, trusting that there is treasure to be found when I stay at it.

- It includes a daily practice – i.e. there is something I will do every day as well as perhaps things I do regularly but not daily, such as participating weekly with others in worship or keeping Sabbath.

- It is do-able in my life; realistic.

- It is a small practice – it's best to undertake something modest.

- Quiet time/prayer each day.

- It is balanced in 2 ways: - Natural to me in keeping with my personality, and at the same time challenges my weaker side.

- It nourishes my mind, body, spirit, relationships and community.

One of the powerful outcomes of a contemplative life is an active and practical response to the world and its needs that are around or in ones life such as justice issues or environmental concerns, serving the poor, or other areas God may lead us into. The results are good fruit that grows out of a healthy, vibrant, and connected tree or vine to its Source. Therefore, we have two components that fit together: Contemplation and Action. We will live out who we are and live out God in, with, and through us.

PRAYER EXERCISE **43**

A CONTEMPLATIVE LIFE – WHAT-EVER?   **XX**

Set aside some time to listen to God and your own heart. Receive what is for you.

1 **A Contemplative Life:**

Why is a contemplative life important to you?

What life patterns do you have that show you that you live or value a contemplative life?

Ask Jesus for a picture, scripture, song, or symbol of what contemplative living looks like or means to you.

2 **Spiritual Disciplines:**

What spiritual disciplines are you presently maintaining? Do you sense a shift or change in this?

Ask:

- What will nurture the presence of God's life in my soul?
- What will allow it to come forth into my daily & bodily experience?
- What will keep me from being discouraged?
- What do you believe God is inviting you to now?

Working on our own Rule: (Rule – Discipline, habit)

- Go slow and take small steps.
- Realize that it can be adapted.
- Concentrate on the things that have become central in your life.
- Focus first on values.
- Then choose actions and orientations that give substance to the values.

Handling a Rule over time:

- Suspend long-term choices only after clear reflection.
- Suspend (for at least some time) any practice that leads you to shame or that seems (with the advice of trusted people) to contradict the moving of the Spirit in your experience.
- Ask God to heal you and to find a way to make this practice a liberating and soul-nourishing practice for you.

3 Contemplation and Action:

Do you sense a healthy balance of contemplation and action in your life?

What actions or fruit are in your life as a result or in response to a contemplative life?

What actions do you feel invited to experience or practice?

What might God be inviting you to let go of? To hold on to? To be open to receive or embrace next?

Some of the above teaching on Contemplative Living was received from SoulStream Ministries: The following chart, Movement from Compulsion to Contemplation, is also from them. Used with Permission <www.soulstream.org>.

MOVEMENT FROM COMPULSION TO CONTEMPLATION	
COMPULSIVE LIVING	**CONTEMPLATIVE LIVING**
Driven approach to life	Open ended and free-flowing approach
Narrow vision of reality	Expansive vision of reality
Control; rigidity	Surrender; spontaneity
Obsessed and anxious	Accepting and serene
Holding on; possessiveness	Letting go; freedom
Past and future oriented	Living in the present moment
Self absorbed	Self aware
Strong defences	Necessary boundaries, vulnerability
Self-disgust and self hatred	Self-acceptance and self-love
Emotional Distance; dissonance with self	Intimacy with self, God and others;
Dealing with people	Relating with people
Inordinate (misdirected) desires	True longing for God
False self	True self/authentic self
Emphasis on pleasure	Emphasis on true joy
Living at the surface	Living from the heart

Spiritual Formation
Out of the Cocoon!

Spiritual formation is the means by which we are transformed into the image of Christ (for the sake of others and ourselves.) Let's take a look at inner landscapes that nourish spiritual formation, the desire and activity of God in our formation, and how we personally affect the process. Let's also look at what constitutes spiritual formation—the involvement of God and ourselves in the process and the resistance we experience in our formation.

Spiritual Formation is the work of the Holy Spirit in us. It's about our receptivity. Spiritual Formation takes time; it is a transforming process; it is ongoing, lifelong, beautiful, organic, intelligent and orderly; it is not straight-line but spiral, gathering up and deepening all that has gone before.

In the expansive area of Spiritual Formation, key components are prayer and our experience of life. These are infused with the redemptive grace of God to create beauty out of chaotic mess, taking into account both the developmental process and how personality type influences receptivity and resistance to the shaping process.

Scripture and spiritual reading, the wonder of the Living Word, which speaks us into existence and then transforms the distorted broken image of God that we have become, are an integral part of our spiritual formation. Meditating on God's Word through exercises such as *Lectio Divina* (pg.39,43) and contemplative prayer exercises such as Centering Prayer (pg.134), are valuable for our deepening and broadening journey with God.

We look to spiritual disciplines and our openness to the work of the Spirit of God in shaping our lives into the restored beauty of the image of God. Spiritual Disciplines are the choices we make to nurture and support the life of God emerging within us and to resist becoming captive to the ways we distort the power of this life. They are oft-chosen activities that shape our experience into character.

A Spiritual Discipline is a habit or regular pattern in our lives that repeatedly bring us back to God and open us up to what God is saying to us. More about the disciplines further on.

An important component in our spiritual formation is our connectedness with community. Community plays a significant part in our being formed. Spiritual Direction is an aide in our spiritual formation. A spiritual director is recommended for those who value their spiritual journey and formation (pg.219).

A Prayer of Desire for Transformation

Gracious and loving God,
You know the deep inner patterns of my life
that hold me in bondage and keep me from being completely and
freely Yours.
In Your faithful goodness You are crumbling my defenses,
and molding me into the wholeness of Christ.
Melt my innate resistance to Your love.
Awaken me to the glory of Your presence within.
Deliver me, I pray, from the easy habit of thinking
that my spiritual transformation is my own, in private, apart
from my life with others.
And live out Your purposes through me within the possibilities
and impossibilities of my daily life.
Lord, have mercy. Christ, have mercy.
(Author unknown)

PRAYER EXERCISE 44

SPIRITUAL FORMATION – OUT OF THE COCOON XXX

1 What do you consider one of the most pivotal moments in your life or spiritual experience? What happened at this moment? How did your life change from that moment on? How did you identify yourself as a child, teen, young adult, and now as an adult? What changed it? Recall one or two times you sensed that God's redemptive grace obviously created beauty out of chaos in your life.

2 In your relationship with God do you sense that you initiate the relationship more or less than He does? How much is up to you? Do you see him as the initiator?

3 How would you describe your Christian Community? Is there anything you sense God might be inviting you to develop or be a part of to better your community of faith?

4 Is it easy for you to allow process in your and others' lives or is this difficult or a weakness? Why? What might God want to grow in your life?

Prayer is All of Life

"Prayer is to descend with the mind into your heart
and there stand before God."
Theophan the Recluse

"If you sincerely want to learn to pray: Keep silence."
"Listen in silence, because if your heart is full of other things
you cannot hear the voice of God. But when you have listened to
the voice of God in the stillness of your heart,
then your heart is filled with God."
Mother Teresa

Prayer is the centerpiece of our relationship with God. Let's ask ourselves: What is prayer? How do we pray? Is it simply words, or thoughts that are spoken or quietly offered to the Lord? Or is prayer more than that? It is suggested that we see all of our life as prayer – living our life in conscious gratitude, continuous awareness, continuous openness to God, continuous listening, praising and thanking, *a way of being*, rather than a method or type of praying; prayer is the experience of life in the presence of God. I have discovered that for me, my every day thoughts, my deep silent laments, my simple sighs, my abandoned laughter are all prayer, they are all my interacting with God apart from words.

Common movements of prayer: process, change, transformation, intimacy, darkness, and revelation.

In his book, *Prayer, Finding the Heart's True Home*, Richard Foster describes prayer as having three parts. He calls them Trinitarian Movements. They are a.) Inward prayer to the Son – seeking the transformation we need. B.) Upward prayer to the Father – seeking the intimacy we need. C.) Outward prayer to the Holy Spirit – seeking the ministry we need. He goes on to say that, "To be spiritually fit to scale the Himalayas of the Spirit, we need regular exercise in the hills and the valleys of ordinary life."

PRAYER EXERCISE 45
PRAYER IS ALL OF LIFE   XX

Journaling Exercise:

1 How would you describe *PRAYER*? How do you move with prayer in your life? How can you identify with the common movements of prayer: process, change, transformation, intimacy, darkness, and revelation?

2 How do you describe yourself as it relates to prayer?

3 Do you struggle with spending intentional time with God in prayer? If so, explore these possible reasons for this happening and bring whatever comes to mind to God: Fear of change, the unknown, failure, loss of control, desire to keep God at a safe distance, your image of God, time, lifestyle change, busy schedule, cluttered life, solitude and silence seems too harsh, hard to stop your mind from racing, discipline, hard work, seems unproductive, sense of being unworthy, need empowerment of Living God through Scripture, some methods might seem questionable or New Age-ish or crazy, you think they won't help, you're just not in the habit of it or used to it, etc.

4 Ask God to show you a picture of yourself and God as it relates to prayer. What do you see or hear? Invite God to be with you in this. Receive clarity, truth, and peace.

Suggestion: Do a 24-hour silent retreat, alone with God (maybe even without your journal or Bible). Experience yourself with God in silence.

Centering Prayer
The Best Gift to Give God

"But when you pray, go to your inner room, close the door,
and pray to your Father in secret.
And your Father who sees in secret will repay you."
(Matt. 6:6 NAB)

Practicing Centering Prayer has become one of my favourite times with God. It is an ancient Christian prayer exercise that, when I first heard of it, I thought would be really easy. At first it seemed so uneventful that I thought there must be something wrong. Was I doing it right? Was anything happening with me and God?

As I have continued practicing this method of contemplative prayer I have come to see some of the value of it and the good fruit in my life, and I now love meeting God in this way. It is the exercise I miss the most if I miss doing it. I often feel the Lord leading me to do it and it is one of the Spiritual Disciplines that I endeavour to practice daily.

Contemplative Prayer is opening our whole being, heart and mind, to God. There are times to use words in prayer and to interact with God; however, this contemplative prayer exercise takes us beyond thoughts, words, feelings, and actions. It is an invitation to open our awareness to God, who we know by faith, is within us (1 John 3:24). Centering Prayer helps us develop our faculties to receive communion with God rather than conversation with God.

I've heard it said that Centering Prayer familiarizes us with God's first language, which is silence. I've also heard it said that God loves meeting us in this manner the most since we are so clearly invited, "Be still and know that I am God" and the Psalmist speaks of quieting himself at times instead of crying to God (Psalm 46:10; 131:2 KJV). I do like the fact that during this time in prayer I am not asking anything of God, nor am I am engaging to listen for anything for myself; this allows us simply to be together and that is beautiful and it is enough.

The principle fruits of the prayer are experienced in daily life and not during the prayer period. Centering Prayer is not limited to the "felt" presence of God but is rather a deepening of faith in God's abiding presence. It is not reflective or spontaneous prayer, but simply resting in God.

PRAYER EXERCISE 46

CENTERING PRAYER

To Begin – We choose a *sacred word* as a symbol that expresses our intention to consent to God's presence and action within.

1 The sacred word is chosen during a brief period of prayer asking the Holy Spirit to inspire us with one that is suitable for this time with Him. E.g., God, Jesus, Peace, Trust, Abba, Yes, etc.

2 The sacred word is said when we wander off in our thoughts, and helps us come back to an awareness of God's presence with us. It is not to be used repetitively. It is to be spoken quietly within to gently turn us towards God.

3 Instead of a sacred word, a simple glance toward the Divine Presence or focusing on one's breathing may be more suitable for some people.

4 Sit comfortably with backs straight so as not to encourage sleep during this time. We close our eyes as a symbol of letting go of what is going on around and within us. Legs and arms need to be set comfortably as straight as possible to rest for the full 20 minutes.

5 We introduce the sacred word inwardly as gently as laying a feather on a piece of absorbent cotton.

a.) Should we fall asleep, we continue with the prayer when we awake. When engaged with our thoughts, we return ever so gently to the sacred word. Thoughts are inevitable, an integral and a normal part of Centering Prayer. Thoughts include body sensations, feelings, images, and reflections. They may be ordinary wanderings of the imagination or memories. Thoughts and feelings that come may bring feelings of attraction or aversion. Insights and psychological breakthroughs may come, as well as self reflections such as, "How am I doing?" or, "This peace is just great!" They all arise from the unloading of the unconscious mind. When you realize you may have become engaged with any of these thoughts return gently to your sacred word, leading you back to an awareness of God's presence.

b.) We avoid analyzing our experience, holding expectations, or aiming at any goal such as: having no thoughts, making the mind a blank, feeling peaceful, repeating the sacred word continuously, or achieving a spiritual experience.

c.) We may notice slight pains, itches, or twitches in parts of our body, or a generalized restlessness. These are usually due to the untying of emotional knots in the body. We may notice heaviness or lightness in our extremities. This is usually due to a deep level of spiritual attentiveness. In all cases we pay no attention and gently return to the sacred word and to focus on God.

6 This prayer normally lasts for 20 minutes.

a.) It is recommended that we practice this exercise twice daily, first thing in the morning and in the afternoon or early evening. With practice the time may be extended to 30 minutes or longer. (Once a day works well, too.)

b.) Using a quiet timer will help to tell us when the time is done. In a group setting it is nice to be brought back from the prayer time with someone leading in the Lord's Prayer or another gentle form of re-entry.

7 Remain silent at the end of the prayer period for a couple of minutes. The additional 2 minutes enables us to bring the atmosphere of silence into everyday life.

I heard one of my favourite comments after leading a Centering Prayer time which my friend, Eric, was attending. I thought that fifteen minutes would be long enough for our first time doing this together. I wondered if some of the people attending the retreat might not be able to focus like this for very long or find it very uncomfortable. Being silent, especially in a room full of people, can feel like a long time, even though doing this together in a group is a very wonderful experience. I was concerned that this lively group would be grumbling when we finally moved from the prayer time. However, instead of any negative complaining, I heard Eric sigh and say, "No, I don't want to stop this." Thankfully it isn't expensive, doesn't need a lot of equipment, and can be taken with you into every day.

One day I saw some lovely fruit coming from my Centering Prayer times. A lot of busy activity was happening around me on this particular day, yet I was able to lightly let each thing go and stay in a deep peacefulness. It wasn't until later that I realized that my heart had taken Centering Prayer with me into the day.

Andrea Kastner, a well-learned teacher and encouraging facilitator of SoulStream, had some brilliant insights into Centering Prayer that she graciously shared with me. She writes:

"Centering Prayer is very hard at first. Everyone who has practiced contemplative prayer/centering prayer over the ages says this same thing. It takes a LOT of practice. It gets easier, then it gets harder, then it gets easier.... In a large sense it is the practicing itself that holds the transformative power of the prayer. For one thing, staying with it, no matter what the immediate experience/'effect' shows us just how deeply addicted we are to our belief that we can improve ourselves spiritually by trying hard. Most of us expect there will be some reward, including the reward of feeling like we are 'getting it' or feeling peaceful. It is helpful to remember that all we are doing is making ourselves available, to the best of our human ability that day, to receive the love of God pouring around and through us. God is doing the transforming in us whether we feel it or not. Everything that happens is a gift from God: our ability to 'show up' in the first place when there are so many other demands from the world – even our desire to show up on the days when we avoid it or forget to show up, our noticing our frustration at not being able to pay attention for very long, and the more rare moments when we glimpse the face of God gazing at us with love. It's all a gift. And God is so touched, so delighted when we make even the smallest of steps.

"The alertness or paying attention, the 'being present with God,' is important and not quite the same thing as the kind of cosy nestling up one might do in another kind of prayer such as the kind of rest we might experience in imaginative prayer where we might picture ourselves as a small child snuggled in God's arms.

"I find it helps to think of this kind of rest as the kind that comes from stopping. Where I stop trying. Stop planning. Stop trying to figure things out. It is a giving up of all effort for 20 minutes. In time, stopping brings rest; rest is the result of stopping.

"It is a big challenge for us to enter into this prayer as a response to God, out of the place of our desire to be with God and enjoy God, rather than out of our more usual place: the habit of doing, or trying to achieve yet one more thing. Again and again we meet this mistaken impulse, this weakness in ourselves. Perhaps with a little light humour and the reminder that Jesus understands our human weakness, and without beating ourselves up when we notice we are back in our habit again, we can just gently return to our word, the sign of our desire, our intention."

I'd like to invite you to ponder two phrases that Andrea gave:

"Being present to God." And *"Rest is the result of stopping."*

Prayer of Examen
What a Day!

"By day the LORD directs his love, at night his song is with me
a prayer to the God of my life."
(Psalm 42:8 NIV)

As you practice the "Prayer of Examen," joy, love and gratitude will fill you at the end of your day. This prayer will also reveal some deep truths about you and the things going on in your life.

Spending a few minutes to reflect upon the day that you just lived can bring much love and healing to your heart as you go to rest for the night. This prayer exercise is an outstanding gift from St. Ignatius. "Examen" is the Latin word for "a consideration, an examining," and as practiced daily by the Jesuits, means "an examination of conscience."

My journal, with many Examens written in its pages, has become a source of astonishing memories that I otherwise might not have recorded. Some of the little, seemingly insignificant moments of my life come to flood me with much more joy and peace as I read them again and receive what was given to me. As well, some of the very painful or difficult struggles that once nearly overwhelmed me become a place of refuge as God meets me there with peace and solutions. I am discovering the truth that God is indeed, in all things.

Some nights, however, I simply collapse into bed and they never get recorded; I merely try to look to my Loving God while I drop off to sleep. I used to feel terribly guilty if I fell asleep while praying. When I asked God about this, I was reassured that I wasn't doing something bad or neglectful; instead I learned that falling asleep while sensing such nearness with God is a beautiful resting place. (Psalm 4:8).

When I do a Prayer of Examen, I may light a candle, take a moment to breathe in and out deeply a few times as I focus on breathing in God's Presence and emptying myself of hindrances, fears, or stress that may have accumulated through the day. As my body, mind, and heart begin to settle I focus on the day that has just finished.

PRAYER EXERCISE **47**

PRAYER OF EXAMEN   ⏳

Pause now and enter the Prayer of Examen. Prepare by sitting in a quiet place, breathing deeply as you settle and quiet yourself.

1 **Most grateful:** As the events of the day come to your mind, ask God to bring to your awareness the moment for which you are most grateful.

(Which moment would you re-live? When were you most able to give and receive love today? Ask yourself what was said or done in that moment that made it so good.) Breathe in the gratitude you felt for this and receive a life-giving moment. Rest in this place and receive all that this moment gave you.

2 **Least grateful:** Ask God to bring to your awareness the moment for which you are least grateful today. (When were you were least able to give and receive love? Ask yourself what was said and done in that moment that made it so difficult.) Re-visit the feelings you had without trying to change or fix it in any way. Take deep breaths and let God's love fill you just as you are. Be loved with things just as they are.

3 **Give thanks** for whatever you have experienced. If possible, share as much as you can of these two moments with a friend.

My friend, Irene, has a wonderful addition when she does Prayer of Examen. In the second step, "When remembering ungrateful moments, those that involve my wrong responses, I ask forgiveness.

Then I ask the Lord to help me imagine a different response, and I imagine myself doing that."

Being and feeling loved in moments that we are grateful for, the beautiful moments, is one thing. Sometimes they fly by so quickly that we really don't fully receive what we were given in that one precious moment or event. How rewarding to return to it and receive all that God had intended for us to receive. It is like eating some fruit from the Tree of Life.

Experiencing love in times that are filled with anguish or sorrow is quite another thing, especially if we have been a contributor to those emotions. We do not always relish such re-visits, especially at bed time! However, powerful Love Encounters can happen when we cease from fixing, changing, interceding, etc. and simply let ourselves be loved there. This is a vital life skill as so many things in our life cannot be fixed quickly, or changed at all, yet we can experience the deep love of God regardless. This prayer exercise has brought me clarity about my days and is allowing me to live in greater acceptance and peace, both while awake and asleep.

When journaling Examens I've noticed some of my entries are lengthy, full of great detail, and others are simple, only a few words that remind me of the event and lead me into prayer and intimacy with God.

Here are a couple of Examens from my journal:

Examen: Monday, Nov. 19, 2007

1. **Most grateful** for the wonderful aroma of the roast cooking with all the spices, as it filled the house this afternoon. The delicious fragrance led me to feel that all was well. I had prepared a meal and others would be blessed by it. I also felt joy and wellness at the simple act of cooking a roast, caring for my family and them knowing that they are loved and cared for. I am very grateful for the simple smell – the simple act – bringing amazing truths of love, security, acceptance and belonging.

2. **Least grateful** today for the time when people were visiting at my doorway as they prepared to leave our time together. Anxiety grew as they lingered and I realized that I had to get on with my day. The negative feelings were quite intense as a battle popped up within me. Perhaps I was selfish to not care enough about what was mattering to them? Perhaps they were taking from my time? I do not know; it's just the way it was. "Be loved there, Lorie."

3. **Thank you**, for these gifts today and you being in them. Jesus, I love how you fill my home and I'm so thankful for being loved by you even when I'm not at my best. "Perfect love casts out all fear" (1John 4:18).

Examen: Friday, Nov. 23, 2007

1. Most – So thankful that my child is feeling better today.

2. Least – Being taped during a prayer session without being asked.

3. Thankfulness

As a Group Exercise: For retreats, with colleagues, and family prayer times.

This exercise is very effective at a retreat setting. We often do this each night of a retreat as we come together for the close of the day. We share with the one sitting next to us, or our room mate, whatever came to our mind and how God met us there. Sharing these testimonies of God's love and faithfulness to us is so encouraging. When we've been travelling we will often do this prayer exercise in our hotel room to help us focus on the God and as a way of "washing off" things that happened or that we were around in the day.

My brother and sister-in-law, Gary and Ronda, used their family devotion time with their three children for a while to do this prayer exercise with them. Roger, Amy, and Nicole enjoyed the simple time of listening to God and sensing God's love and friendship.

EXPANDED PRAYER EXERCISE WITH PRAYER OF EXAMEN:

1 Record your most grateful, and least grateful, moments of the day while doing the Prayer of Examen over many days, even weeks.

2 Look at the series of things that brought you life, and those that did not. See what moments or situations are strongest over a length of time. What do they have in common? What are you noticing when you look at these?

3 Ask God for wisdom and to show you ways that you can incorporate more of those things that bring you life into your daily living. Does anything need to happen regarding the least grateful moments in your life? Do you need to make some changes in your life to bring greater health and wholeness?

4 Take concrete steps to help bring about any changes God is showing you to make.

This simple three-part exercise reminds me of one of my favourite sisters of the past, St. Therese of Lisieux. She often shared of her "littleness." She believed she was a little soul and could offer only little to God. "Is this enough?" she wondered.

One afternoon at a weekend prayer retreat, one of my friends, Lora, sensed that the love she had to give Jesus was a very small portion in a cup. She shed tears as she told the story of offering her "littleness" to the Lord as she poured it into the river of God's love that she imagined before her. As she did, however, she saw the river swell. Her love may have seemed little, but it was enough to make a difference to God and to His Kingdom.

The very next morning, the person speaking at our church, encouraged us to "take the cup we are given and pour it out." This could have meant many things to many people—such as our talents being given to bless others or to share whatever might be in our hearts—but for Lora, it was her "little" love.

If our love can make God's heart swell, then truly God's love will make our hearts expand and enlarge. God fills us with more Light and we are transformed. May you receive the peace of God as you practice the Prayer of Examen.

TO PONDER:

> St. Therese of Lisieux taught me that
> the closer to God we come,
> the more simple we will become.

Practicing His Presence

"Your beauty and grace chase after me all the days of my life."
(Psalm 23 MSG)

I used to think I could only connect meaningfully with God when I set aside a lengthy chunk of time for extreme quiet and focus. Although I truly do love these encounters, God surprised me by integrating my daily activities and my "holy" times so that they are both times of loving and knowing God. This did not come easily to my busy, passionate, focused personality.

It actually came about during a time when I was angry at God for not doing something that I wanted the way I wanted it. For quite a few days I felt a very strong resistance to being with God and when I would walk by the room where the chair was that I usually sat in for our prayer times it felt like the chair was calling me to come. Part of my heart wanted to be there, yet something inside me had a strong aversion to being close to God. This was very unusual for me, a new experience, or at least new to my awareness. Resistance that I had before must have been quite subtle, not as noticeable or agonizing as this time.

I told myself that if God wasn't going to look after my children the way I wanted, or the way I thought that should look, then I better keep busy for them and do it myself and not "waste" my time sitting in "that" chair. As you can see, I had quite the attitude! I had felt quite enough pain around this recently and somehow staying away from God helped me think I was staying away from the pain. This was a scary time for me as I realized some very ugly feelings and recognized how painful it is to feel separated from God like this. I saw quite clearly how my anger and disappointment can build walls in our relationship. Of course, God had never abandoned me, or my children, but somewhere in my unhealthy understanding I thought I knew best on how that should look. Blaming God for the situations and the pain that followed wasn't working very good for me and my

145

heart eventually realized that it was actually God who would rescue me, and it was God who would comfort and strengthen me, and it was God who would lead my family in The Way.

The surprise encounter came when I was busy doing the ordinary things of life. I was standing at the kitchen sink washing dishes and it felt like God tapped me on the shoulder to get my attention and let me know I wasn't alone or far from God. He was right there with me. He was impressing on me that I didn't need to go somewhere special to meet. Then I heard these words to my heart, "I'll just come and meet you here at the sink, I understand."

I know this is a very basic truth, but it had eluded my deeper understanding of God. This also brought to my deeper understanding the truth that God comes to me, God invites me, God is the initiator in our relationship, I respond.

What is "practicing the Presence of God?" There are probably many answers from many viewpoints. Here is one: it is paying attention to the fact that God is present and active everywhere and responding out of that awareness in every moment. We are invited to live this way with a greater sense of quiet and a peaceful pace of life, with awe and wonder. It leaves us refreshed and nurtured, having a sense of joy and freedom, and it also requires nothing less than everything! It is a death to much; sometimes painful. It also requires perseverance.

When we practice God's Presence we will be noticing more and more our attitudes and failures in our everyday life with our family, co-workers, etc. Its gift is to allow us to see these things and our helplessness to change. This brings us again to an awareness of our utter dependence on God to free us and to heal us. How? Just practice being mindful of God as often as you can in an hour. Persevere, and it becomes automatic. Offer all things to God. Thank God for all. More and more in every moment, we find we are whispering to God, praising, seeking God's advice for how we are to be in this specific moment, asking to be filled with strength, or asking for patience, courage, and thanking God. Here are two good questions:

- How is God making Himself known to me in this moment?

- In what way is this situation I am in right now a sacrament?

Thomas Merton (1915–1968), wrote many books that made a significant impact on Western spirituality. He is known for his journal writing, meditations, and social critique, and held tightly to his belief in the importance of a relationship with God through Jesus Christ. His life and writings continue to inspire countless men and women who long to go deeper in the spiritual life. He held a delicate balance between the inner and the outer life – contemplation and action. I love his perspective on effort and exertion in the spiritual life. He believed that these were helpful only if we are being led by God; if we are in fact resisting God's leading, "no amount of effort can produce a good result."

Merton believes that we need to cultivate an "attitude" in our life before God. He lists eight attitudes that unite us to God: faith, openness, attention, reverence, expectation, supplication, trust, and joy.

PRAYER EXERCISE 48

MY EFFORTS – FOR OR AGAINST ME?   XX

Good questions for us to ask ourselves are:

1 Do my present practices of prayer describe me as one who is led, or one who is still trying to lead? Why?

2 How might God lead me?

3 Are my efforts led by God? Are they leading me to God?

4 Set aside fifteen minutes a day for solitude and meditation. Relax from strain and stress and simply rest in God's presence.

5 During your times of reflection, choose one of these attitudes and nurture it by concentrating on offering short, simple prayers:

Faith, openness, attention, reverence, expectation, supplication, trust, and joy.

(Inspired by: "Devotional Classics" by Richard Foster and James Bryan Smith)

I'd like to share a wonderful way we can stay aware of God being with us throughout our day. I learned this from Andrea of SoulStream Ministries.

PRAYER EXERCISE 49
TRANSITION TIMES

1 Notice as you move from one activity in your day to another; such as moving from reading the paper to going outside to cut the lawn, or from reading a story to your child, to doing a load of laundry, or going out to do an errand, etc.

2 In this transition between activities, become aware of God being with you. Interact as you would a friend (perhaps how the disciples did life with Jesus).

3 Continue to do this as much as possible and it becomes a good habit.

4 Notice how you feel in these times, and what this tells you about God.

PRAYER EXERCISE 50
5 MINUTE WATCH ALARM

My friend, Mike Stewart, Rector of St. Matthews Anglican Church in Abbotsford was spending the evening with a group of us. Every few minutes his watch alarm would 'beep.' Eventually one of us asked him what was happening with all the beeping.

He humbly replied that he was practicing God's presence. He wanted to be continually mindful of God with him and this was improving his attentiveness to God's presence and His love. Try it, you might like it!

A STORY FROM THE JOURNEY...

One of my very favourite stories of God's presence happened with my precious mother-in-law, Vi Martin. She is one of the most wonderful people in our family's lives. Mom highly values the first part of the day, before everything else gets going, to sit with God, read Scripture and pray. The peaceful atmosphere in her home, and her caring qualities, reveal that she spends committed time with God. If you met her, or sampled her amazing baking that I'm always sharing, you'd love her too! Her and Dad (Richard or Dick) were married for 54 years, but had known and loved each other for even longer.

Dad passed into heaven in 2008, and Mom was not looking forward to being alone in her home. She was looking to God to help her in this "new normal," as she called it. Val and Jude, her daughters, were with her for quite a few weeks after the funeral, and then the day came when she was alone.

She seemed to be coping extremely well when we would check in on her the following days. About a week later she told us what was going on. The first morning alone she woke up early morning sensing that Dick or one of the girls were still in the apartment. Then she would remember that they were gone. Even through the day she had a strong sense that someone was there with her. After a couple of days she realized, "It's the Lord! It's the Lord! He is here." I can still hear her voice telling me of this amazing experience. She had such a tangible sense of God's real presence, and still eighteen months later she often feels that Someone is with her, that she is not alone. To God be the glory, great things He has done.

I'd like to share this poem that my friend, Anne Lawless, wrote. Anne is in her eighties and is the eldest woman in our church family; she is one of our key intercessors and even preached a powerful sermon this past year. Her walk with Jesus has been long and adventurous. She is a radiant light and source of wisdom and strength to us. Anne has spent much time in God's presence. Her life is very full of the Spirit of God as she continues to love and serve God faithfully.

You Listen.

In Your presence is fullness of joy.
In Your presence I find perfect peace.
In Your presence there is a quiet, healing balm to my spirit.
So quiet,
So peaceful.
I listen, and wait. I listen and wait.

Then I tell You all I have on my heart,
And I know that You are listening, and waiting.

I know that You listen with great love and compassion.
You are never too busy.
You are always waiting for me to come and talk to You.

You are King and Lord of all, You are the Creator of the universe.
Yet You wait for me
To come and talk with You.

My heart cries out,
'Who am I, Lord, that You should listen to me?'
Surely I am the very smallest part of Your great plan.

But, You listen to me.
You love me and You forgive all my sins.
You renew me, day by day, hour by hour, and moment by moment.

I love You so Lord, and I say thank You.
Thank You for waiting.
And loving,
and healing.
Thank You Lord.

Anne Lawless

Living Life in God's Awesome Presence

"Teacher, which is the greatest commandment in the Law?"
Jesus replied: "'Love the Lord your God with all your heart and
with all your soul and with all your mind.' This is the first and
greatest commandment. And the second is like it:
'Love your neighbor as yourself.'
All the Law and the Prophets hang on these two commandments."
(Matthew 22:36-40 TNIV)

By Ward Draper

Meet my friend, Ward Draper. Ward is married, has three children, and has been a "Kingdom Citizen" for about twelve years. There is much about him that is fascinating, but here he shares a bit about what he's been up to in Abbotsford lately with a fantastic ministry called *The 5 and 2*.

Ward: The 5 and 2 exists to encourage an individual's knowledge, love and service of Jesus; particularly as He is found in the lost, the broken, and the poor. The 5 and 2 is a ministry devoted to the Greatest Commandments. Careful study of Scripture reveals that a personal compassion and systemic justice for society's most vulnerable members are integral aspects of the gospel Jesus preached and lived.

Poverty on all levels, material, spiritual, and psychological, robs a person of hope, a sense of self-worth and the ability to engage in positive relationships that foster community, creativity and achievement.

The Church has a mandate to end poverty rather than to manage it. The point is not simply to bring marginalized individuals into the centre but to allow their experience and talents to improve it. It is by exercising these truths that both mutual transformation and mutual education occurs.

152

Currently there are three primary areas of focus in the arena of poverty and homelessness. These being housing options, support services, and adequate income. The 5 and 2 works in all three areas with our emphasis on support services. Providing practical needs while going even further by developing lifelong relationships.

Genuine relationships are the key to victory when fighting the war on poverty and homelessness. Relationships are the glue that makes recovery possible, relationships are the frame from which lives are rebuilt, and relationships are what give life purpose.

This is where The 5 and 2 stands. We are all about relationships above all else. We know nothing in life is worth having if you do not have someone to share it with.

Lorie: When I was chatting with Ward over coffee, I was intrigued to learn from him how He viewed His relationship with God. He shares some of it here. Enjoy!

Ward: Experiencing God. It is an interesting phrase and presents me with many questions of how our faith is realized. It is my belief that the use of this type of phrasing *can* build narrow walls of thought within our inner world. The words *Experiencing God* seem so limiting *to me*; it carries a singularity and not the actual reality of life with Him. To experience God seems to convey an occasional event that if we work hard at it we will be lucky to have an amazing direct contact and will be blessed by a divine chance meeting. I think this is nothing more than our little minds placing safe parameters on being in relationship with God. Do we articulate our earthly relationships in these terms? Do we say "experiencing Mom," or "experiencing Jesse"? No that is not something commonly articulated; we simply say I am visiting mom or having coffee with Jesse.

I wonder if we ground down our language to earthier, more practical words that our "experiences "of God will simply become old hat. I don't mean that in a derogatory way or to minimize the value of these "experiences" but rather it would simply be just a part of daily life.

This is my approach, I make a concentrated effort to *remove the vocabulary that might only been known in Christian circles, and to merely be in life with God and view it as simply another relationship.* A relationship of great value with a Great Being, but a simple relationship none the less. I spend time with God as I do most people. We have coffee *together*, we watch movies, we go for drives, we shoot the "chat," and we do what most good friends do.

It is from this, some would say sacrilegious, way of living that I "experience" God. I know of no other path that produces as many experiences as this simple act of friendship and intentional relationship. Flip through history books and you will find countless stories of those who simply spent quality time with Him and they never had a shortage of God in their lives. Live in the realization that God is with you always, not just on Sundays between the hours of 9 am and 12 pm, during specific times of crisis, or scheduled prayer. Rather God is with you when you are shopping for groceries, when you grab a beer with your co workers, and when you gaze out a window at the setting sun. Living in the absolute truth of God's constant presence *means* experiencing Him will be just like breathing, there is *not always* thought involved, no need for *constant* solo reflection; no, He is beside you at all times. It is this frame of mind that we of faith must stand; it produces a life so abundant you will grow tired of even speaking of it because the fruit and encounters will be more numerous than the stars in the heavens.

When I say tired of *talking about it* this is not because I see no value in it but rather you will be so busy living with God and doing stuff with Him that a new adventure is only minutes away. So I run off in His direction, God and me on our next grand adventure like Pooh bear and Christopher looking for Heffalumps and Woozles. I do not want to waste the time we have together; it is so very magical. I am always inviting friends and acquaintances along to come and see what our next trip will be. This is the primary way I share the Gospel; by bringing along a hunting party as we search for the dangerous Heffalumps. Along the way we laugh and play as co-adventurers living life in God's awesome presence.

This is experiencing God to me. Living in the moment with Him; knowing Him as my dearest and most trusted friend. We work together, we live together, we scream together, we drink together, and we do everything together. There is nowhere that God and I don't go together. We are inseparable and it is here that "experiencing" God becomes common place. The grass is green, the sky is blue, and God is with you always. It is a given that when one recognizes that God is at their side always that seeing and hearing Him is like hearing the giggles of children, the tears of the homeless, the professor's voice echoing through the auditorium. His voice becomes something you just know. It is here that God is experienced. He is experienced in simply spending time with Him, actively setting your mind and heart on the reality that He is always with you. Never lose sight of Him and your life will become a wondrous adventure.

PRAYER EXERCISE 51

LIVING LIFE IN GOD'S PRESENCE

1 Think of your relationship with God. Are there words that you use to express your relationship with Him that are limiting?

2 What are these words?

3 What words will you replace them with to open new doors to encountering God?

Lorie: It is with great joy that I received this message. When reading it I discovered in a fresh way the timeless message of God's heart to us. It spans all of history and geography. The message that we hear from Ward resounds the voices of those who deeply love God, those who simply like being with God, and those who follow The Way of Jesus personally, and join Him on the streets to help many. May we link with those like Ward in 2010; Brother Lawrence whose message has been heard for nearly 300 years in *The Practice of the Presence of God*, and King David who said in the Psalms, "Yet I am always with you; you hold me by my right hand" (Psalm 73:23 NIV).

The Meeting Place
Friend to Friend

A Song of Ascents.
"I will lift up my eyes to the mountains;
From where shall my help come?
My help comes from the Lord,
Who made heaven and earth.
He will not allow your foot to slip;
He who keeps you will not slumber."
Psalm 121:1-3 NIV

When things get confusing, crazy, and chaotic where do you go, what do you do? Let me share what has been so helpful for me when my emotions rise and my mind can't think straight, often unable to connect with the Lord, when I seem to need Him most.

A bit of background…One of the key ministries at Fresh Wind Christian Fellowship in Abbotsford, my church family, is the Listening Prayer Ministry (pg.301). One of our core values is hearing God's voice for ourselves and one another. We listen and pray at Sunday ministry times, during the week with healing prayer sessions, and in church or leadership team meetings. We teach it, we share it, and we live it with each other and in our families. Listening to God and meeting with Him is a main ingredient in how we pray.

Brad Jersak, one of the pastors who planted Fresh Wind, who is now an itinerant conference speaker/teacher and author of many books, taught us this great way to connect with Jesus in prayer. He calls it "The Meeting Place." I highly recommend one of his books, *Can You Hear Me?* That clearly teaches "The Meeting Place." One of Brad's gifts is that he teaches difficult concepts or theology in very easy to understand ways. In *Can You Hear Me?* Brad shares how his prayer life evolved from a one-way verbal communication pattern into "a visual, internal meeting with the indwelling Spirit

156

of Christ," prayer as an intimate meeting place with Jesus. He encourages us that we can and probably have experienced it already ourselves.

"By way of definition, we will describe a "place" as "somewhere – whether physical, historical, or spiritual – where we meet with Jesus to behold and be held." Meeting Places can be Biblical images or locations such as: the Cross, Psalm 23, the Tent of Meeting, The Strong Tower, etc. We can connect or join Him when we step into Bible stories (pg.59) such as Daniel in the Lion's Den or one of the many Gospel Stories of Jesus with his disciples.

Meeting Places can be actual places in nature or in our homes where we sense the presence of God easily, or a place in our memory of where we sensed being close to God; at church, or perhaps at camp when we were a child. We can meet God in dreams and visions, and in so many more ways. The point is – we purpose to meet Him in our hearts and these are simply venues that help us connect intimately with Him and hear His voice to us as C. Austin Miles clearly shares with us in the words of his song, *I Come to the Garden Alone:* "And He walks with me, and He talks with me, and He tells me I am His own, and the joy we share, as we tarry there, none other has ever known."

The basis is that the Lord lives in our hearts and wants to meet with us. Sometimes the reality of that truth is hard to grasp, so we see our heart as a house, a cottage, a cave or castle. There are many ways He may show us how He lives with us in our hearts.

My main meeting place with the Lord is a lighthouse. Some times He brings this place to my mind, especially if I am having trouble focusing on Him. It is an established place of safety and God's presence that I can tune into within where God abides.

There is no end to meeting places. Many people I've met with have met Jesus on the beach, in the woods, in the Throne Room, by the quiet steams of Psalm 23, or the valley of the shadow of death. My lighthouse has expanded over the years as I now enter the grounds around it, the veranda, the basement, the castle that it is attached to and the woods and bridges beyond it. These experiences with Jesus help to give me an inward picture of the unseen reality of what He is saying and doing in my life.

Some of the ways you may often be hearing or seeing Him with you might be in songs, in Scripture verses or stories, through a preacher, friend or parent (pg.5).

> *"He who forms the mountains, creates the wind,*
> *and reveals His thoughts to man,*
> *He who turns dawn to darkness,*
> *and treads the high places of the earth –*
> *the Lord God Almighty is His name."*
> (Amos 4:13 NIV)

Once this interactive safe place is established to meet with the Lord, He may invite us to a time of inner healing as memories or thoughts may come up when we meet with Him (pg.261).

If I am going into a potentially difficult situation I ask the Lord to show me where I am with Him in my Meeting Place before I go. I listen there for anything He may want to show or tell me. Often He reminds me of His love, fills me with His truths and peace, and gives me wisdom, strategies, and guidance. This has proven to be so successful in helping me be at peace when I otherwise might be thrown off course.

For example, one time I was going to meet one of my children's teachers. I was nervous and didn't know what was coming. Before I went the Lord showed me that my child and I were safe with Him in a tucked in part of my Lighthouse. A couple of times in the meeting I remembered this truth and Him being our Strong Tower and that He was with us, protecting us and covering us. I prayed silently for my child and the situation from this place with Jesus even as we sat together around that table. I received strength, courage and comfort. I know these truths in my mind, but sometimes a picture helps me to identify with it stronger and know God is with me more clearly.

Here is one of my very favourite songs; it reminds me of this special safe place that the Lord is and the Meeting Place He has given to me. It is written by Kevin Boese. Kevin has been a worship leader in Abbotsford for the past 10 years, and helped put together the "Love Abbotsford Live" recording with other Abbotsford worship leaders; he is also part of a number of other city worship events. Kevin has written a number of passionate, prayerful songs that connect deeply with our journey of faith. His lyrics are honest, authentic and come from his personal story. I suggest you hear him and this song: <www.kevinboese.com>.

Safe Place
Kevin Boese

I cannot live beyond your reach
You hold me in your arms of peace
I cannot live beyond your reach
You hold me in your arms of peace
My world may suffer war
But you have proven your control
I've never been alone
You're my safe place
You cannot be moved, You cannot be shaken
You're my safe place
You stand in the storm
You are my defence
You surround me with songs of deliverance

© 2002 ION Publishing

I don't always feel led to my Meeting Place. Sometimes God shows me some other place to meet Him. Sometimes He just wants to sit with me where I am and this becomes a Meeting Place. We are often quiet, simply just being together.

I could, however, write an entire book with many pages and

chapters full of Meeting Place experiences and encounters with Jesus. I can believe that He wants to meet with us countless times and in a multitude of ways and share His heart and thoughts with us.

I'd like to invite you to ask the Lord to give you a Meeting Place. If you already have a few, I wonder what He might have for you now?

PRAYER EXERCISE 52

THE MEETING PLACE – FRIEND TO FRIEND   XXX

1 Come to a place of quiet and stillness while you wait on the Lord.

2 Ask the Lord if there is a place He would like to meet you.

3 See what comes to your mind, what it looks like, ask Him to show you as many details as He wants.

4 Ask Him to make Himself known to you there. Where is Jesus?

5 Ask if there is anything He has to tell or show you? This is to be a time of blessing, promise, and intimacy.

6 Perhaps He'd like to tell you why He is telling or showing you this, or how He sees you. Feel free to interact with Him with thoughts or questions.

7 Spend some time with Him there as He makes Himself known to you.

8 Thank Him and ask if you can meet Him there again.

9 Be mindful of this place and open to go there with Him again.

It is always good to be aware that it is God who initiates our times of connecting and to keep our posture as one responding to God's invitations. I would like to suggest that He is always inviting us to Himself. You may sense Him inviting you to prayer in different ways.

There may be times when it is hard to tune into this kind of praying. Don't worry. There may be some very good reasons for that. It could be about timing, or being with others, or there may be blocks to hearing that you may want to explore. Brad goes into these in detail in His book. It could be anything from the simple fact of being tired to the revelation of a lie that you might believe about God not wanting to meet with you. It is important to pay attention to any blocks that come up so our relationship with God can continue to flourish.

GROUP EXERCISE

Invite people to share the *Meeting Places* God is or has given them and their experiences with Jesus. People will be blessed and filled with encouragement – this exercise builds faith and fellowship in community.

My friend, Sue Vander Woude, who generously helped me with some tweaking of this book, added a great point to this section; "Doing it together is a nurturing and sensitive way of helping others to enter into this type of prayer."

"I Can't Hear or See God"

What about me? I'm not hearing, seeing or anything! This is part of the journey and not to be stressed about. You can ask Him to show you why this is happening. If nothing comes to mind it is okay for you to pick a place that is safe to you, a place you have met Him before, or Psalm 23. This is really okay. He is delighted that we want to spend time with Him and come close.

When people share with me that they struggle to find a Meeting Place, I invite them to come to the green pastures and quiet waters of Psalm 23. He comes to show that He is their shepherd and they are His sheep. This is very successful in helping us get past that we can't seem to see. Often it helps so ask:

- "If God is my Shepherd, how would He want to meet me today?"

- "How might He see me as His sheep at this moment?"

- "What do I think He wants to give me?"

Let God give this to your heart as you receive it.

A STORY FROM THE JOURNEY...

At a retreat in Alberta we were a bit short on time to help a few people who wanted to have meeting places, but it wasn't coming easily to them. So I met with a few people together at one time and invited them all into Psalm 23. We had a most amazing time together.

One woman was meeting Jesus for the very first time. I was astonished later to learn that she wasn't a Christian when we began the encounter. She saw Jesus was far away from her. She was a sheep on a hillside. She longed to be near the Good Shepherd and when her niece asked if she wanted to give her life to Christ she cried out, "Yes," and she was rescued. She prayed and was repenting of things, and then great joy came upon her and all of us.

While this was happening, another woman was having an encounter with Jesus. She had been quite sad because she had heard of so many people having wonderful meetings with Jesus and she had not yet experienced this. When I asked where she was in the Psalm, she said she was one of many sheep in the pen. When I asked where Jesus was she spotted Him watching His sheep. She was okay with this, but when I asked Jesus if He would come close to her, she exclaimed quite loudly, "It's Him, He's coming to me, oh my!!! I've always wanted this." Jesus to come to her and specified her as His own daughter and precious lamb. He noticed her and she was overjoyed at the reality of His love that was for her specifically.

Time after time, God meets with us. Usually, if there is something in the way of these encounters we are shown what it is and Jesus meets us there to take care of it. I encourage people who struggle with this to meet with someone they trust and do it together as Jesus teaches us in Matthew 18:20, "For where two or three come together in my name, there am I with them."

The Unseen Real Presence

"[Jesus:] No one can snatch them out of my Father's hand."
(John 10:29 NIV)

One of the greatest revelations we can gain on earth is to know as deeply as humanly possible, and to experience the unshakable and steadfast love of our Heavenly Father. Jesus modelled this perfectly as He consistently went away to a solitary place to meet with His Father (Mark 1:35). In return, He was loved and given everything He needed from His Father. I want to experience this kind of relationship with the God of the Universe—close, comforting, and caring.

St. Therese of Lisieux has taught me much about "confident love," which is what she calls being loved freely and fully by God. I learned much of her understanding of Christ's marvellous love in a book by Father Jean C.J. d'Elbee entitled, *I Believe in Love, A personal Retreat based on the teaching of St. Therese of Lisieux.* It is a delightful book of God's love and I so cherish it that I have underlined nearly every sentence in it.

There was a group of people in the days of St. Therese of Lisieux (1873-1896) who had a view of God that she disliked. She tells us that they believed that God has one arm of love and in the other God carries a rod to punish us. A picture can easily come to mind of God's arms stretched out wide to receive us, BUT, one hand has a weapon in it. It's hard to trust or come too close to a God who looks like this.

She was very upset by this view of God for her message of God's love was that God is all love. Both hands and all of God are always open to embrace us. This is how we see God in the parable that Jesus gave us of the son who left and returned to an extravagant Father (Luke 15:11–24). This perfect love reminds us that we are always accepted. "Oh, this desire, this need of the Father of Mer-

164

cies to retrieve His lost child and give him life! That is the Heart of God!" she says.

Can you sense the freedom that you have when you are in a place of safety? Safe enough to dance with utter, joyous abandon? Safe enough to give yourself fully to love without fear of rejection or judgement? When we are in a place where we are fully known and deeply loved, it seems to be rich soil for the life of the Spirit to grow, flourish and produce a harvest of good fruit.

At a time when I was struggling to understand the Father's true love for me, my Spiritual Director of eight years, Karin, suggested that I might want to enhance my experience with God by trying something new. She suggested that I find a place in my home where I could be with God in a more tangible kind of way.

For instance, she suggested that I could choose the dining room table as a place to sit and be mindful that God is truly with me. "Not a god who is looking at me from a distance, but the "with-me-God," I would tell myself.

So I set up two plates and cups on my dining room table as a re-minder that I abide with God, and He lives with me. "Jesus replied, 'Anyone who loves me will obey my teaching. My Father will love them, and we will come to them and make our home with them'" (John 14:23 TNIV). Setting this up and intentionally meeting with him at this location had a great impact on me. My mind started to grasp the reality of the security and strength of God's loving pres-ence. It was as if my faith in God that I had in my heart was connect-ing with a stronger knowing it in my mind.

I would move toward the table often and enjoy the truth that God loves to be with me. As we spent this time together God would listen to me as long as I needed to talk, we would sit in silence. It was a great delight knowing that God was gazing upon me as I sat or moved about my house.

During the weeks that I was doing this, I woke up one night with a nightmare. It reminded me that, like all children, I had had the occasional nightmare when I was a child. I also remembered not knowing what to do as the fear and anxiety would grip me. Upstairs, in the middle of the night, I was drawn to my dining room table, to this special holy place. I sensed God, my Heavenly Father, saying to come close and be cared for. I can still remember walking past my chair over to God's chair and sitting down thinking that I needed a sturdy and solid lap with warm embracing arms. I wept there as the truth that God is always with me, and always has been calmed me— this love sinking in even deeper and stronger. I slipped back into bed for a very restful remainder of the night. It was a victory night.

Other memories or circumstances came up during these weeks. Once, a memory left me feeling very cold and abandoned. I found myself quickly grabbing a big warm towel and wrapping myself up to receive the tangible, yet unseen, touch of my Heavenly Father, holding and loving me, satisfying my fear and insecurities.

These physical actions led me to accept a more concrete understanding of the truth of God's very present self in my life.

I wonder how you might be invited in a tangible way? Be open and receptive to your own encounters.

PRAYER EXERCISE **53**

THE UNSEEN REAL PRESENCE

1 Find a quiet place for you and God to meet.

2 Meet regularly. Plan what will work for you; meet as often as you feel led.

3 Use tangible items in your meeting times. (i.e. two cups of tea, an extra chair, a blanket to snuggle in, etc.).

4 Journal your visits. Receive deeply what you are being given as God's child.

"That He would grant you, according to the riches of His glory,
to be strengthened with power through His Spirit in the inner man,
so that Christ may dwell in your hearts through faith;
and that you, being rooted and grounded in love,
may be able to comprehend with all the saints
what is the breadth and length and height and depth,
and to know the love of Christ which surpasses knowledge,
that you may be filled up to all the fullness of God."
(Ephesians 3:16–19 NASB)

Praying the Creation Story

By Steve Imbach

"The Lord God called to Adam, 'Where are you?'"
(Genesis 3:9 NLT)

Lorie: When I first experienced this prayer encounter it exposed an incorrect view I had of God. My view certainly missed the mark of who God really is. The prayer exercise brought a great truth to my mind and corrected my mistaken understanding of God true love and grace for each of us. I received two years of teaching and training on spiritual direction with SoulStream Ministries. This was absolutely one of the most valuable courses I've taken; the two years were filled with rich teaching and thorough understanding on the contemplative life and experiences with Chirst. Steve Imbach, Director of SoulStream Ministries led this prayer encounter for our class. You are invited to join in this wonderful meeting with God; I only wish that you could hear him lead it in his own voice. This encounter was most moving for me.

Steve began with comments and descriptions that set the stage of Eden. He did this to help us enter the Creation Story and learn from it in a very profound way.

I think most of us have a picture in our mind of what the Garden of Eden looks like. Sunday School teachers may have described it to us over the years and if we've read it, certain images come to our mind. Some of us have also seen illustrations that stick in our minds to this day.

Unfortunately, for most of us, by 11 years of age a large majority of our imagination is no longer used. Our imagination is such a great thinking and feeling skill and is beautifully active as children. I believe the Spirit of God wants to awaken, restore and heal our imaginations to become one of God's most vivid ways to meet with

168

us. This part of our mind can make things come alive, and helps our heart to feel, understand, and believe (pg.5,61).

Perhaps you can imagine God being with you when you are on a nature walk. This might be a similar experience to what may have happened for Adam and Eve in the story of Creation. You may be able to imagine the trees, paths, birds, smells, and sounds of the garden. Imagining this as close to how it really is told can be very encouraging and helpful as we spend time with God.

To sit comfortably for the time it will take to do this exercise, put your feet on the floor, sit up straight, breath in deeply and exhale fully. If the story is being read to you, you may benefit from closing your eyes to let pictures of what you are hearing come to mind, and a more full awareness of God's presence being so close to you.

PRAYER EXERCISE **54**

PRAYING THE CREATION STORY **XXX**

Steve begins…

Our Holy Scripture opens with a pivotal expression of God's heart of pleasure and love toward us as His creation. Imagine that we were all present at Creation. We are caught in a time warp. Now, God sat back after six days of marvellous, energizing, extravagant creativity. God sat back and took a long look around. (Pause and imagine what He saw.) From a deep sense of pleasure and satisfaction the Scripture tells us He said that all He had made was "very good!"

YOU AND I ARE PART OF THAT PROCLAMATION!
THAT MARVELLOUS, ALL ENCOMPASSING
BLESSING OF GOD!!!

The context of our life, that sense of pleasure and delight of God in what He had made, was affirmed in His response to the deliberate, rank disobedience of Adam and Eve. They were getting along well. Delightful encounters of intimacy in the cool of the evening.

Adam and Eve followed their self-centeredness and self-interest, and disobeyed. God came to spend time with them, as usual, and they weren't there. God could have exercised several options. He could have left because He was busy. He could have devised an appropriate punishment. (Sounds like the choices I would make.)

But what did God actually do? True to His character/essence, He called out to them, "Where are you?" God wanted to be with them. They were missed. (Wouldn't every good parent go looking for their children and every caring artist go looking for their precious creation?)

This is the moment when God's heart of love poured forth in redemptive restoration. He put salvation's plan into action. He made them clothes! Wow!

Steve now invites us deeper into the story.
I invite you to pray this story – Imaginative Prayer
In your imagination…

1 Using all your senses (smell, sight, taste, hearing, feeling) visualize yourself in a beautiful, extensive, profuse, lush garden. There are meadows, streams, trees, flowers, ponds, meandering paths, with snow-covered peaks in the distance.

2 You begin to notice that the sun is getting closer to the western horizon. Feel the cooling air, a soft breeze against your skin. You revel in the delight of this golden time of day. You relax into the pristine beauty.

3 Your delight and serenity begins to crumble. Within yourself you find you are wrestling deeply with a heavy, restless sense of guilt. You become uneasy and agitated. The conflicted moment is punctuated with a familiar sound… God approaching. Immediately you feel a rising sense of shame, dread, and fear.

4 You scurry around to find a safe place to hide as you respond to the pressing need to avoid meeting God.

5 As you settle into your hiding place you feel your heart pounding and your breath coming rapidly. You hear the deep, strong voice of God calling out…

"Where are you?" "Where are you?"

6 Your mind races in deep inner conflict.

a.) I want to be with God.

b.) He'll be angry.

c.) Our times in the garden were so intimate, so beautiful.

d.) I'm embarrassed, ashamed.

e.) God says He loves me.

f.) I'm afraid.

PRAYER REFLECTION QUESTIONS:

Take a few moments to be in the story… hear the voice of God calling you.

1 What tone of voice was God using to call you? How did you hear it?

2 How did it make you feel?

3 What is your response?

4 What would it be like for you to come out of hiding and walk into the embracing presence of God's redemptive, restorative love?

Behind the bush—what a fearful, lonely, and desolate place. I always imagined God in this moment, while "hunting down" Adam and Eve, as being very angry at them and just waiting to punish them severely. I remember thinking, as well, that there is no way they could endure such wrath. They were trapped. How horrible this was.

What I experienced behind the bush while hiding was a great revelation for me. I heard the voice of God being full of longing, full of love, and full of caring concern. He likely was angry at what the serpent had done and what Adam and Eve had agreed to, but the new realization was that when I disobey my Father comes looking for me to help me. As I sat in this hiding place I discovered Jesus was with me—that because of God's redemptive love and salvation I was safe and restoration surrounded me despite what I had done.

The picture of God making them clothes (Genesis 3:21), covering their shame and caring for them in their time of disobedience was most comforting to me! How does this unselfish love feel for you? We no longer have to live in the fear of God's wrath, or our own guilt, rather, as much as we are able, let God come close to find us and receive tender love and full forgiveness.

I have noticed that God gives comfort and understanding to me when I am surrendering something that is difficult for me to give up. Even greater to me is the realization and my experience that even when I am relinquishing something that I have held so tightly instead of God and divine love, still bestowed on me is healing compassion and gentle comfort. How great is the love of God. This is what it could sound like in my words: "So you've chosen something or someone instead of Me. Oh, you're having a hard time letting it go. I understand it's hard. Here, let Me help you, let Me love and hold you, let Me set you free." Is this not extravagant love!

Stations of the Cross
Encountering God at Easter

The glory of Easter is the heart of the Christian gospel. It is the center of the Church's faith and worship. In the earliest days of the Church it was the only Christian festival, an annual celebration of Christ's life, death, resurrection, ascension, and His sending of the Holy Spirit. The celebration lasted fifty days in one continuous festival of adoration, joy and thanksgiving, ending on the Feast of Pentecost.

I invite you to do this exercise, The Stations of the Cross and contemplate the sufferings of Jesus and unite with Jesus in your life. You may do it over a few days, or take a retreat day and go somewhere to meet with Jesus as you walk or journey quietly through these stations of prayer and listening. There is an opening prayer at each station that you are invited to do together if you are going through this in a group.

Each of us frequently finds our self fleeing from the cross of everyday life (challenges, struggles...) Jesus makes us return into our town, into our village, into our house, to our families, to our working places, and into our life, so that in faith we do what we have to do and so that all that is temporary and fleeting within us may die and all that is eternal may remain.

PRAYER EXERCISE 55

STATIONS OF THE CROSS   XXX

Preparatory Prayer

> Jesus,
> I would like to meet You. Guide me on my way. Teach me to hold on to Your Word when I have to walk up the Calvary of my life.

Help me so that – like You – I am ready to obey and say,
"May Your will be done."
Help me to do what You ask me to do.
Father, here I am.
I would like to embrace the secret of your Son so that You may
acknowledge me as Your child who is returning to You. Amen.

Opening prayer at each station: Please read out loud together.

**We adore You, O Christ, and praise You, because by Your
holy Cross You have redeemed the world.**

FIRST STATION

Jesus is Condemned to Death
Opening prayer together:
**We adore You, O Christ, and praise You, because by Your
holy Cross You have redeemed the world.**

> *"Now the chief priests and the whole Council kept trying to
> obtain false testimony against Jesus so that they might put
> Him to death"* (Matthew 26:59 NASB).

> *"Finally Pilate handed him over to them to be crucified"*
> (John 19:16 TNIV).

Be still and know God.

Walk over to where Jesus is standing and allow Him to place
His arms around you. Also picture a person out of your past
who has condemned you, labelled you, misjudged you, or deeply hurt you. As that person now stands before you, Jesus takes
your hand, placing it into the hand of the person who has hurt
you. Jesus says, "Do not judge, and you will not be judged; do
not condemn, and you will not be condemned; *pardon, and you
will be pardoned*" (Luke 6:37 NASB).

SECOND STATION

Jesus Receives the Cross
Opening prayer together:
We adore You, O Christ, and praise You, because by Your holy Cross You have redeemed the world.

> *"Surely he took up our infirmities and carried our sorrows"* (Isaiah 53:4 NIV).

Be still and know God.

Allow Jesus to carry the cross for you, bearing upon His shoulders the primary responsibility for your burdens and those of mankind. Give Him the associated pain and let go of what He is asking you to release. Experience now the peace of Jesus as He provides the strength and consolation you need at this moment.

> *"Come unto me, all ye that labour and are heavy laden, and I will give you rest"* (Matthew 11:28 KJV)

THIRD STATION

Jesus Falls the First Time beneath the Cross
Opening prayer together:
We adore You, O Christ, and praise You, because by Your holy Cross You have redeemed the world.

> *"Christ loved us and gave himself up for us as a fragrant offering and sacrifice to God"* (Ephesians 5:2 NIV).

Be still and know God.

Ask Jesus to help you to accept your weaknesses, as difficult as that may be.

As you accept your weakness, offer it to the Lord, asking that every time you fall He will help you begin anew just as He did on the way to Calvary. The important factor is not falling, but "rising" as we follow the Lord in this way.

> *"And He has said to me, 'My grace is sufficient for you, for power is perfected in weakness.' Most gladly, therefore, I will rather boast about my weaknesses, so that the power of Christ may dwell in me"* (2 Cor. 12:9–10 NASB).

FOURTH STATION

Jesus Meets His Mother
Opening prayer together:
We adore You, O Christ, and praise You, because by Your holy Cross You have redeemed the world.

> *"This child is destined ... to be a sign that will be spoken against, so that the thoughts of many hearts will be revealed. And a sword will pierce your own soul too"* (Luke 2:34-35 NIV).

Be still and know God.

Ask Jesus to comfort you in any memories or present situations where you have disappointed or distressed your mother, a friend or family member. Feel the peace of God flowing to you and those you have brought pain to. Experience the love flowing through Jesus to you, your mother, and others that come to mind.

> *"Bear with each other and forgive whatever grievances you may have against one another. Forgive as the Lord forgave you"* (Colossians 3:13 NIV).

FIFTH STATION

Simon of Cyrene Helps Jesus Carry His Cross
Opening prayer together:
We adore You, O Christ, and praise You, because by Your holy Cross You have redeemed the world.

> *"But rejoice that you participate in the sufferings of Christ, so that you may be overjoyed when His glory is revealed"* (1 Peter 4:13 NIV).

Be still and know God.

As you see Jesus humiliated in this station, extend forgiveness to your own earthly father or someone else who may have humiliated or hurt you. Also receive forgiveness from Jesus for any disappointment or hurt that you gave to your father or another.

Have courage to receive help from your parents or others. Let others surpass you, let them take care of you, and admit that you need them.

> *"Forgive us our sins, for we also forgive everyone who sins against us"* (Luke 11:4 TNIV).

SIXTH STATION

Veronica Wipes the Face of Jesus with Her Veil
Opening prayer together:
We adore You, O Christ, and praise You, because by Your holy Cross You have redeemed the world.

> *"Whatever you did for one of the least of these brothers and sisters of mine, you did for me"* (Matthew 25:40 TNIV).

Be still and know God.

Think of a time someone gave to you and you were unable to return the favour. Have courage to be indebted to others. Learn to receive without thinking of giving in return. You will meet Jesus in this and recognize that you cannot reward your heavenly Father for what He gives you. Be your Father's child. Accept that you cannot repay God for all His love. Give Him thanks.

SEVENTH STATION

Jesus Falls the Second Time
Opening prayer together:
We adore You, O Christ, and praise You, because by Your holy Cross You have redeemed the world.

"All who see me mock me; they hurl insults, shaking their heads. 'He trusts in the Lord,' they say, 'let the Lord rescue Him. Let him deliver him, since he delights in him" (Psalm 22:7-8 TNIV).

Be still and know God.

Remember a time of falling or showing weakness. Can you see how you wanted to show your own strength in this? Let go of defending or justifying yourself or wanting to put things right. Look for how God showed you that you were stronger than the offence or weakness and that it is/was His strength that raised you.

"Whoever wants to save their life will lose it, but whoever loses their life for me and for the gospel will save it" (Mark 8:34-35 TNIV).

EIGHTH STATION

Jesus Meets the Women of Jerusalem
Opening prayer together:
We adore You, O Christ, and praise You, because by Your holy Cross You have redeemed the world.

"Daughters of Jerusalem, do not weep for me; weep for your-selves and for your children. For if people do these things when the tree is green, what will happen when it is dry?" (Luke 23:28, 31 TNIV)

Be still and know God.

Be mindful of any grief you may be experiencing. Ask Jesus to come and comfort you. Jesus, help us to recognize resurrection beyond each death, recovery beyond illness, reunion beyond fare-well. Who has grief to whom you can bring the compassion you have been given? Receive human comfort when it is given. Have courage to do without human comfort and ask God for strength.

"Finally, all of you, be like-minded, be sympathetic, love one

another, be compassionate and humble. Do not repay evil with evil or insult with insult. On the contrary, repay evil with blessing, because to this you were called so that you may inherit a blessing" (1 Peter 3:8-9 TNIV).

NINTH STATION

Jesus Falls the Third Time
Opening prayer together:
We adore You, O Christ, and praise You, because by Your holy Cross You have redeemed the world.

"My strength fails because of my affliction, and my bones grow weak. Because of all my enemies, I am the utter contempt of my neighbours" (Psalm 31:10-11 NIV).

Be still and know God.

Can you see Jesus standing at the door of "I can't go on," to meet you? Receive His presence and His strength. Receive His grace to go on in the face of discouragement and despair.

Jesus says: "Do not let your hearts be troubled. Trust in God; trust also in me" (John 14:1 NIV).

TENTH STATION

Jesus is Stripped of His Clothes
Opening prayer together:
We adore You, O Christ, and praise You, because by Your holy Cross You have redeemed the world.

"People stare and gloat over me. They divide my garments among them and cast lots for my clothing" (Psalm 22:17-18 NIV).

Be still and know God.

See yourself standing at the cross with Jesus as He is stripped of His garments. Tell Jesus at this moment that you do wish to let go and give up to Him all that you hold dear, particularly that one item or that one person that you cherish the most, for this is where you are held in bondage and live in fear. Ask Jesus for the strength to do this. Sense Jesus' love as He returns the gift to you in a new way. It will then not possess you, but rather you will possess it. Let Jesus come to your fear that it may dissolve in His love.

"Perfect love drives out fear" (1 John 4:18 TNIV).

ELEVENTH STATION

Jesus is nailed to the Cross
Opening prayer together:
We adore You, O Christ, and praise You, because by Your holy Cross You have redeemed the world.

"When they came to the place called the Skull, there they crucified him, along with the criminals" (Luke 23:33 NIV).

"By his wounds we are healed" (Isaiah 53:5 TNIV).

Be still and know God.

Can you identify with the sense of being nailed to the Cross, where there is no escape; only death? Do you have a sense that you might be fighting some thing in your life that must die? Ask the Lord to help you accept this place and to not be afraid. Remember, you will rise again. Give thanks for the pain and ultimate vulnerability that Jesus underwent to bring us life and freedom.

"Greater love has no one than this: to lay down one's life for one's friends" (John 15:13 TNIV).

TWELFTH STATION

Jesus Dies on the Cross
Opening prayer together:
We adore You, O Christ, and praise You, because by Your holy Cross You have redeemed the world.

"Jesus called out with a loud voice, 'Father, into your hands I commit my spirit.' When he had said this, he breathed his last" (Luke 23:46 NIV).

Be still and know God.

Reflect now on these last three hours of Jesus' life. Ask for the grace of an abundant life, given to you through Jesus' death on the cross. What is the area of greatest need in your life at this time? As you are there at Calvary with Jesus crucified, expect Jesus to bless you and set you free, imparting to you the life, the abundant life that He died to give to you. This is the beginning of real life.

"I have come that they may have life, and that they may have it more abundantly" (John 10:10 NKJV).

THIRTEENTH STATION

Jesus is Taken from the Cross and Laid in Mary's Bosom
Opening prayer together:
We adore You, O Christ, and praise You, because by Your holy Cross You have redeemed the world.

"All you who pass by ... look around and see. Is any suffering like my suffering that was inflicted on me?" (Lamentations 1:12 NIV)

Be still and know God.

Join Jesus at the Cross where He rests in Mary's arms. Receive such tremendous love. Let this love nurture you in the deep places of your being. Go there often. It is a safe place where Jesus went often and He invites you to be loved. God has both the love of a Father and a Mother for you to receive.

FOURTEENTH STATION

The Body of Jesus is laid in the Tomb

Opening prayer together:
We adore You, O Christ, and praise You, because by Your holy Cross You have redeemed the world.

"Unless a kernel of wheat falls to the ground and dies, it remains only a single seed. But if it dies, it produces many seeds" (John 12:24 TNIV).

Be still and know God.

What does Jesus want you to bury? Wish-dreams that you have designed? Egoism where you try to save yourself and others? Ask Him to show you the resurrection He has for you beyond this tomb. Do you fear death for yourself or a loved one? Ask Jesus for the grace to accept death knowing that it is the door to life. Receive healing from fear of death and walk in freedom and peace as He gives you this important grace.

In the end, He says it is He who knows you.

Receive joy and union with Christ as you bridge from death to risen life with Him. Let this be the fulfilment of all your wishes and longings. He has gone this way and is waiting for you.

"Jesus said to her, 'I am the resurrection and the life. Anyone who believes in me will live, even though they die; and whoever lives by believing in me will never die'" (John 11:25-26 TNIV).

May you enter into the dawn of Easter and may it be a light for you.

"If the Son sets you free, you will be free indeed" (John 8:36 NIV).

"Then the disciples went out and preached everywhere, and the Lord worked with them and confirmed his word by the signs that accompanied it" (Mark 16:20 NIV).

Based on a meditation I read from Tomislav Ivancic, The Stations of the Cross, on Mountain of the Cross – Medjugorje, Feb. 20, 1986

Holy Week

An invitation to journey
through the week leading up to Easter Sunday

The glory of Easter is the heart of the Christian gospel. It is the centre of the Church's faith and worship. In the earliest days of the Church it was the only Christian festival: an annual celebration of Christ's life, death, resurrection, ascension, and His sending of the Holy Spirit. The celebration lasted fifty days in one continuous festival of adoration, joy and thanksgiving, ending on the Feast of Pentecost.

Contemplate the sufferings of Jesus and unite with Jesus in your life.

Each of us may frequently find our self fleeing from the cross of everyday life. Jesus invites us to return to our own town, to our own village, to our own house, to our families, to our working places, into our life, so that in faith we do what we have to do and so that all that is transitory within us may die and all that is eternal may remain.

PRAYER EXERCISE 56

HOLY WEEK – EASTER (DAILY)

Preparatory Prayer

> Jesus,
> I would like to meet You. Guide me on my way. Teach me to hold on to Your Word when I have to walk up the Calvary of my life.
> Help me so that I – like You – am ready to obey and say, "May Your will be done."
> Help me to do what You ask me to do.
> Father, here I am.
> I would like to embrace the secret of Your Son so that You may

acknowledge me as Your child who is returning to You. Amen.

The Sunday of the Passion – Palm Sunday

Triumphal Entry

> *"Blessed is he who comes in the name of the Lord! Hosanna in the highest!"* (Matthew 21:9 NIV)

On this day our Lord Jesus Christ entered the holy city of Jerusalem in triumph. The people welcomed Him with palm fronds and shouts of praise, but the path before Him led to self-giving, suffering, and death.

Today we greet Him as our King, although we know His crown is thorns and His throne a cross.

We follow Him this week from the glory of the palm fronds to the glory of the resurrection by way of the dark road of suffering and death.

United with Him in His suffering on the cross, may we share His resurrection and new life.

Monday in Holy Week

Almighty God,
whose Son was crucified yet entered into glory,
may we, walking in the way of the cross,
find it is for us the way of life,
through Jesus Christ our Lord,
who is alive and reigns with You and the Holy Spirit,
One God, now and for ever.

In Your light, O God, we see light.

Tuesday in Holy Week

O God,
by the passion of your blessed Son,
You made an instrument of shameful death to be for us the

means of life.
May our lives be so transformed by His passion that we may
witness to His grace,
Who lives and reigns with You and the Holy Spirit, One God,
now and for ever

From my mother's womb You have been my strength

Wednesday in Holy Week

Lord God,
Your Son our Saviour gave His body to be whipped
and turned His face for men to spit upon.
Give your servants grace to accept suffering for His sake,
Confident of the glory that will be revealed,
through Jesus Christ our Lord
Who is alive and reigns with You and the Holy Spirit,
One God, now and for ever

O Lord, make haste to help me

Maundy Thursday

This is the day that Christ the Lamb of God
gave Himself into the hands of those who would slay Him.

This is the day that Christ gathered with His disciples in the
upper room.
This is the day that Christ took a towel
and washed the disciples' feet, giving us an example that we
should do to others
as He has done to us.

This is the day that Christ our God gave us this holy feast,
That we who eat this bread and drink this cup, may here proclaim His Holy Sacrifice and be partakers of His resurrection
and at the last day may reign with Him in heaven.

I will lift up the cup of salvation

Good Friday

Enter this day in silence.
Christ the Lord became obedient unto death, even death on a
Cross.

Almighty God,
Our heavenly Father, we have sinned in thought and word and
deed; we have not loved You with our whole heart; we have not
loved our neighbours as ourselves.
We pray You of Your mercy; forgive us all that is past,
and grant that we may serve You in newness of life to the glory
of Your name.
Almighty God, look graciously, we pray, on this Your family,
for whom our Lord Jesus Christ was willing to be betrayed
and given into the hands of sinners, and to suffer death upon
the cross;
Who now lives and reigns with You and the Holy Spirit, one
God, for ever and ever.

Almighty God,
Kindle, we pray, in every heart the true love of peace, and guide
with Your wisdom those who take counsel for the nations of
the earth, that justice and peace may increase, until the earth
is filled with the knowledge of Your love; through Jesus Christ
our Lord. Amen.

Holy Saturday

Christ became obedient unto death, even death on a cross.
Therefore God has highly exalted Him and bestowed on Him
the name which is above every name.

O God,

Creator of heaven and earth, as the crucified body of Your dear Son was laid in the tomb and rested on this holy Sabbath, so may we await with Him the coming of the third day, and rise with Him to newness of life;

Who now lives and reigns with You and the Holy Spirit, one God, now and for ever.

"Father, into your hands, I commit my spirit" (Luke 23:45 NIV).

Easter Sunday

Father,

We share in the light of Your glory through Your Son, the light of the world.

Sanctify this new fire, and inflame us with new hope. Purify our minds by this Easter celebration and bring us one day to the feast of eternal light. We ask this through Christ our Lord. Amen.

For the light of Christ we give thanks to God.

May the Morning Star which never sets find this flame still burning: Christ, that Morning Star, Who came back from the dead, and shed His peaceful light on all creation, Your Son Who lives and reigns for ever and ever. Amen.

Almighty and eternal God,

You created all things in wonderful beauty and order.

Help us now to perceive how still more wonderful is the new creation, by which in the fullness of time You redeemed your people through the sacrifice of our Passover, Jesus Christ, Who lives and reigns for ever and ever.

Protect me, O God, for I take refuge in You.

I will sing to the Lord for His glorious triumph.

You have brought me up, O Lord, from the dead.

You shall draw water with rejoicing.

O God,
by the power of Your Word You have created all things, and by Your Spirit You renew the earth. Give now the water of life to those who thirst for You, that they may bring forth abundant fruit in Your glorious kingdom. We ask this through Jesus Christ our Lord.

Alleluia!

(A Compilation of Meditations)

Invited to Community

Serenity Prayer

God, give us grace to accept with serenity
the things that cannot be changed,
Courage to change the things
which should be changed,
and the Wisdom to distinguish
the one from the other.

Living one day at a time,
Enjoying one moment at a time,
Accepting hardship as a pathway to peace,
Taking, as Jesus did,
This sinful world as it is,
Not as I would have it,
Trusting that You will make all things right,
If I surrender to Your will,
So that I may be reasonably happy in this life,
And supremely happy with You forever in the next.

Amen.

- Reinhold Niebuhr (1892-1971)
Complete, Unabridged, Original Version

The Trinitarian Dance
Community and Self-Sacrificing Love

"Dear children, let us not love with words or tongue but with
actions and in truth."
(1 John 3:18 TNIV)

When we encounter Jesus, we also encounter God, and God reveals that His essence is self-sacrificing love. This is witnessed and experienced in history, in reality, and in community. The powerful image of The Trinity – our Creator, Redeemer, and the Spirit – being a family and moving in full love and unity, invites us to the holy Trinitarian family. What do you notice when you look at how they live as "family?" What do they model for us?

Can you see how they are always honouring each other; lifting up, or elevating the other?

Jesus: "My Father, who has given them to me, is greater than all" (John 10:29 NIV).

Father: "This is my Son, whom I love; with him I am well pleased. Listen to him!"(Matthew 17:5 NIV)
"The Father loveth the Son, and hath given all things into his hand" (John 3:35).

Spirit: "This is ... Jesus Christ.... And it is the Spirit who testifies, because the Spirit is the truth." (1 John 5:6 NIV)

"All that belongs to the Father is mine. That is why I said the Spirit will take from what is mine and make it known to you."(John 16:15 NIV)

I learned from Wm. Barry's book, *Spiritual Direction & The Encounter with God*, that the Greek Fathers used to describe the mutual indwelling of the three persons of the Trinity *Perichoersesis*, which literally means, "dancing around." To describe this mutuality of relationships the best metaphor the Greek theologians could come up with was *THE DANCE*. The One God is *dance*, the perfect relationships which we call Father, Son, and Spirit. The pain we feel when we love someone deeply, yet cannot be perfectly one with him or her, is another indication that we are made in the image and likeness of God, with Whom such union is the reality.

Barry describes a Christian community in a very simple, yet refreshing way: "The primary motivation for our togetherness is our friendship in the Lord and our desire to celebrate that friendship. The primary purpose is not to feed the hungry, to educate our children, to take care of the sick, but to enjoy one another's company in celebration of the Lord." Of course, because we love one another and that love is outgoing, we may decide together to do these things. "Works" demonstrate our love and flow out from our love.

We are a community because we love one another; let's call this, "Trinitarian love." We are invited to be Christians in direct relationship with one another, like the words in this song tell us, "They will know we are Christians by our love." (See John 13:35.)

Barry tells us: "The glue that makes us community is our mutual intentional friendship and care for one another in the Lord." That glue is produced by the indwelling Spirit of God.

We, as Christians must intend to be communities first of all, because that is what the Lord wants of any grouping of His followers. Secondly, we must do that because that alone will satisfy our members' deepest desires; and thirdly, only in such communities do we "preach" by our very being and living and interactions that God is the perfect community of love. The real effectiveness of a group's ministry varies directly with the group's approximation to being friends in the Lord. Religious groups will attract followers in direct proportion to their approximation to being friends in the Lord.

Barry believes that there is only one thing that hinders this; it is the voice saying, "It can't be, it's not realistic." The ideal of religion is an inclusive community in which everyone cares for everyone else. "This ideal is endangered by our un-integrated fears which can evolve into hatred," Barry explains.

A person's perception of another person can largely be a projection of his/her own fears and past relationships; i.e. distant, cold, demanding, frightening, etc. The first step toward a closer relationship comes with the realization that the other person really cares for me. I am filled with gratitude to him/her and trust in that person. When this attitude is relatively firmly established in me, I have an affective foundation for the positive development of the relationship.

Barry shares with us from *Glittering Images* (a spiritual novel on grace and mystery by Susan Howatch) a strong message in a dialogue between a priest and a person who has deeply sinned:

Sinner: "He's (God is) not here, I've sinned. I'm cut off."
Priest: "Take this (a cross in his hand). No demons can cross this path."
Sinner: "He's not here."
Priest: "He's here. Whenever His followers are gathered together in His name, He's here."

In childhood we learn both love and fear. We experience an inner drawing towards and a resistance to God's love. This is the rhythm of withdrawal and return. As we mature, we face our un-integrated fears. When we withdraw from God or other people for whatever reason, the return is the overcoming of the withdrawal. It goes like this: we fear – we withdraw – we reconcile – we return. This happens by the grace of God.

When we continually act out of love we see fear breaking down. Fear loses its hold and there is eventually little room for it left. Withdrawal shows itself in our resistance to God's offers of intimacy. We have a honeymoon experience with God and each other, then a falling out (hurt); then we wonder about one another's continued love. (This is where un-integrated fears can take over: we can be dominated by fear for self rather than by love for others.) This is part of spiritual formation described in more detail on page 129.

We move from the radical love of God where we feel close to Him, to a resistance where we feel unworthy and distant due to sin; so we withdraw, and there is an illusion of absence of God, believing that God does not love sinners. By God's grace we eventually sense His closeness again when we realize God loves us as we are, sin and all.

I love the limited role we have, as humans, in the unfolding love of God. Barry invites us to just accept the call to communion with the Trinity and with one another without attempting to earn our way. It may be hard for our egos to accept that we can't earn our way, yet it is really the only way to find peace.

Friendship means that love predominates over fear, and it must be freely given, not coerced. Friendship means a sharing of all that one is and has with one's friends; friendship is love. St. Ignatius tells us that love ought to manifest in deeds rather than in words, and it is to consist in a mutual sharing of goods. Whatever is possessed is shared, whether it be knowledge, honour, riches, etc. One always gives to the other and is always giving. Since "perfect love casts out fear" (1 John 4:18 NKJV), fear is cast out or at least put permanently in subordination to love. Again we see in the Trinity that they share all that they have and all that they are with one another; they are one. God has emptied self, without any fear at all, in order to become what we are. (See Philippians 2:6–8; Hebrews 2:14–17) God models community life, He shares at His deepest level His dreams, values, hopes, desires, and intentions.

Conversion is a lifelong process of letting God remove the scales from our eyes so that we can more and more embrace the reality of God's overwhelming love for us. In this lifelong process of withdrawal and return we need one another to help us overcome our resistance to the Light. We all thirst and resist. In community fear is subordinated to love. Augustine confesses to God, "You have made us for Yourself, and our hearts are restless until they rest in You." When we experience that restlessness for "we know not what," we experience that the motive of God is superabundant, freely-given love, the reason or intention that all persons join the community of the Trinity.

The aim of all ministry must be to make it more possible for us to pay attention to and to carry out the deepest desires of our hearts – namely, to live in community with the Trinity and with one another.

This message has encouraged me many times to continue in relationships with the true love of God as I move about in community.

PRAYER EXERCISE 5·7
THE TRINITARIAN DANCE

1 Ask God for a picture of what the Trinity might look like.

2 Notice the Trinity lifting up each other, always honouring the other.

3 Think of your church community and imagine it operating as the Trinity does.

4 What would be different? What might God like to give you and your community?

5 What un-integrated fears might you be projecting onto your friends or community?

6 Remember times when you have felt loved and cherished in community.

7 Accept this loving care and let it dissolve the fears that want to keep you from experiencing a loving community as God desires you to have.

8 Can you relate to withdrawal and return in your relationships?

9 Ask God to help these times lead you to greater love and trust in God and others.

10 Ponder St. Augustine's words here and come to a deeper rest in God:

> "You have made us for Yourself,
> and our hearts are restless until they rest in You."

We are often wounded in community, and therefore, we will be healed in community. It is my hope that you will find a safe community in which you can be authentic with your fears and your journey and come to greater freedom and healing. If you have a safe community (even if it is 2 or 3 others) share the above exercise with them and move in caring ways to each other. When your love and trust is established what might God be inviting you to do together from this place of love and Good News?

One of my closest life companions, Herta Klassen, has generously contributed to my life in community. She was my first new friend when we moved from Edmonton to Abbotsford, eighteen years ago; and thankfully Herta is still a part of many areas of my life today. She brings healing to my life with loving actions, attentive care, and we share memories and laughter. From our loving friendship we serve in community as God leads us.

Herta lives a life of excellence in all areas of her life; family, teaching, ministry, kitchen and garden, and now a new passion has risen ~ she is an artist. I have one of her prints; the most gorgeous large canvas painting of bright Echinacea waving in the light; called The Healing Dance <www.hertaklassen.myartchannel.com>.

When I spend time gazing at this beautiful work of art it reminds me of The Dance of Life that we are all in with the Trinity and each other. This art piece represents the lives of those that fill these pages. All are part of the greatest Healing Dance; a divine dance between heaven and earth; and all that is in them. Come, dance, be healed, and set free as the loving light of God warms, holds, and gazes upon you, whispering your name.

"Lord, bless our friendships. Amen"

Burden Bearing

"Praise be to the Lord, to God our Savior,
who daily bears our burdens. Selah."
(Psalm 68:19 NIV)

We are invited to look at two types of burden bearing. One is where we are carrying our own burdens, and the other is where we are carrying someone else's burdens. Both are significant in our lives and in the kingdom of God.

Let's look at the gift of burden bearing and how it is intended to be just that – a gift. "Bear one another's burdens, and thereby fulfill the law of Christ" (Galatians 6:2 NASB). "The Father of mercies and God of all comfort, who comforts us in all our affliction so that we may be able to comfort those who are in any affliction with the comfort with which we ourselves are comforted by God" (2 Corinthians 1:3-4 NASB).

Have you ever felt the deep pain or grief that someone you know is experiencing? This gift can be very strong in some people, to the point of being extremely overwhelmed and feeling very chaotic, and often not knowing "who's who in the zoo."

I've had the privilege of being taught about burden bearing by Brian and Della Headley, Listening Prayer Community. For a more extensive understanding of this subject, I would highly recommend that you contact them <office@listeningprayer.ca>.

Burden bearing is a type of intercession, a form of prayer where we receive the Lord's heart about something and we invite God in prayer to act upon what we've been shown. It is His invitation to participate in His work. When God is hurting about something and He shares that burden with you as His friend, you have an opportunity to bless God.

In such Christian service we are assisting people to appropriate what is already available to them by bringing them to the cross of Christ. We see, hear about or sense someone's trauma/wound and the Lord uses us to help them through it. We join the Lord in lifting emotional pain to Jesus and He will bring restoration to the person. Joy and freedom can be lost and life becomes sad and heavy if we do not lift burdens to the Lord. "Cast your burden on the Lord, and He shall sustain you" (Psalm 55:22 NKJV). Sometimes it only takes a minute. Sometimes it takes many years. The Lord will lead. The Lord will carry burdens, hold pain, etc. as we ask, but we are joining Him, not taking over.

Our daughter, Adri, is a burden bearer. This gift runs in the family! One day when she was in grade two she came home from school noticeably upset. When I asked what had happened she poured out the story. Two girls were celebrating their birthdays on the same day, so both brought cupcakes to share with the class as was the custom. One of the girl's cupcakes looked so beautiful with lots of icing and sprinkles on top but they didn't taste very good and the garbage can was full of half-eaten or bitten-into cupcakes. When Adri saw this she was so sad for the little girl. She picked up the burden (if there even was one) and came home heavy-laden with sorrow.

When we went to the Lord and He showed her that He would take care of the little girl, Adri was quickly able to release her to the Lord. It happened so fast I wondered if it could be that easy. Well, when I checked on her heart she was happy and ready to move on. The light came and the heaviness left. It was great to pray for this little girl and trust Jesus with Adri and teach her how to move with this gift.

Burden bearing is not about what we do; it is about what the Holy Spirit does through us. We are not to take people's pain or circumstances into ourselves. This is called "substitution" and it is not healthy or advised. Rather, our purpose is to connect people to God for restoration and to each other to be reconciled.

Ask God questions as you proceed, because the answers will guide you. Do not assume you know all of what is going on by the one piece of information you have been given. Della says it well:

"Some strengths of a burden bearer are: to identify good and evil very quickly and accurately; to easily perceive character in individuals and groups; to be very compassionate and caring; to sense others' feelings and be understanding; to intuitively feel God's heart and be prophetic' and to be called to intercession. Burden bearers can function very well in caring and helping others, in mediating and restoring relationships, and connecting people to people.

"Some weaknesses are: they can be judgmental (see the flaws in people, which they are to pray about, but not to hurt the person with); they can be pushy with their discernment, wanting others to see or move toward spiritual maturity, intolerant of opinions and views that differ; sometimes they read into things without the facts and communication; they can fail to see true spirituality in other giftings such as serving or administration; and they can tend to be overly introspective.

"Burden bearing can become heavy and harmful to us if we do it in the flesh or out of our own woundedness or unmet needs. Burden bearers will need teaching or healing themselves if they were a sensitive, perceiving child who grew up without guidance and protection. They may have developed their own defences to keep their vulnerable self from being hurt, crushed or overwhelmed. They may appear overly strong, weak, rebellious, isolating, or they may take on the role of scapegoat, or become people pleasers or enablers in order to cope with all that they have to deal with. They may develop physical problems such as depression or frequent illnesses because they cannot vent their emotions. They may distrust God, judging that He does not care about the world because so many suffer and He allows it, or they may minimize their own needs.

"Burden bearers will need to hold onto who they are, or find their own identity if they have lost their own.

"It's important that burden bearers understand what is going on with themselves and this gift, how to operate with it in healthy ways, and to regularly meet with Jesus to dialogue about what they are feeling or experiencing and to learn to listen to His voice to have the burdens lifted."

We were teaching this to a group and one young man stared intently at me the entire time. This was unusual because for all the other sessions we were teaching he would not engage in eye contact at all but preferred to look down. When the session was over he came right up to me and said, "That was me!" He couldn't believe his ears. I was describing his life and all that he struggled with. He felt so good to finally identify what was happening to him all the time and to have some clear helpful answers in how to improve his life.

At the end of these sessions we pray, asking the Lord to restore the gift of burden bearing that has become so dreadful for some people. Below is a prayer for you if you sense the need to receive healing and restoration to this splendid gift from God.

My friend, Eden, has constructed this extremely effective prayer exercise to help with the burdens we have picked up or the ones that feel just got dumped onto our laps. It is one of our very favourite tools to use when praying for others. It is easy and always has lasting results. Should a burden return after doing the exercise, we simply meet Jesus with it again to receive comfort, wisdom, or to simply have Him lift it again as we are strengthened in the Lord.

PRAYER EXERCISE 5*7

BURDEN BEARING X

Matthew 11:30
"For my yoke is easy and my burden is light" (NIV).
"I won't lay anything heavy or ill-fitting on you. Keep company with me and you'll learn to live freely and lightly" (MSG).
"For My yoke is wholesome (useful, good) – not harsh, hard, sharp, or pressing, but comfortable, gracious, and pleasant; and My burden is light and easy to be borne" (AMP).

1 Go to a meeting place where you feel safe and where Jesus is close to you, either in your heart, or a physical safe place.

2 Identify the burden. What does it look like? If it were an object, what would it be?

3 Where do you carry that burden (or object) in or on your body?

4 What has it or does it cost you to keep carrying that burden?

5 What is the payoff of keeping and carrying the burden? (What do you get out of it?)

6 What does Jesus want to do with that burden?

7 Can you let Him take that from you now? Does anything prevent you from giving that burden to Jesus, such as responsibility, familiarity, etc.? Tell Jesus.

8 What is Jesus doing with that burden?

9 What does Jesus want to give you to replace that burden?

You will usually sense that some weight has been lifted from your heart. Now you can really use this as an opportunity to intercede. When you feel the familiar weight of this burden come on you, be quick to bring it to Jesus – that's intercession! Ask Him what He wants to do with it, and then let Him direct you. That's what makes the yoke easy (bringing it to Jesus) and the burden light (letting Him take it).

PRAYER TO RECEIVE BURDEN BEARING AS A GIFT:

Almighty God,

Thank You for the gift of burden bearing. I can see that it is so close to Your heart as you share Your love and concern for me and others. I want to use this gift for Your glory and for it to be for my joy in connecting with You and serving You as You lead me.

This gift has not always seemed like a gift to me, and has often been hard to bear. Please come to the places in my heart, mind and body that have been wounded or affected by wrong use of this gift. I lay down these unhealthy thoughts or behaviors.

Please forgive me for any ways that I have been moving in ungodly ways with this gift. (Name them if things come to your attention.) I receive Your forgiveness to the depths of my being.

I give You my burdens of pain or sorrow (or whatever else may come to mind). I trust that You are able to carry all of this for me and for other people that I may have thought I was to carry. I receive the compassion of Christ and the comfort of the Holy Spirit. (Pause to receive deeply all that God has for you.)

Please restore this gift to me, give me Your wisdom, and guide me in the ways everlasting. In Jesus' name, Amen.

"Surely our griefs He Himself bore, and our sorrows He carried."
(Isaiah 53:4 NASB)

I'd like to take this opportunity to celebrate a special place; Life Recovery Home, Abbotsford, B.C. The women who serve there, and those who come for the recovery of addictions are some of the most beautiful and courageous people I've met. My friend, Karen Robertson (and each precious team member) give strength and hope from their own hearts and lives to many.

Karen has a wonderful story of recovery and for many years has been faithfully caring for the many women who come to "Life." She is convinced that there are two main ingredients to a healthy recovery. The first vital component is a safe and well run home, such as Life Recovery. The second is encountering God in listening prayer. Learning and having access to prayer ministry for inner healing, intimacy, and an ongoing personal relationship with God brings the deep inner restoration needed to overcome the roots of addiction, and leads to the personal connecting with God needed to heal and sustain a healthy, growing life.

Our regular visits to teach that everyone hears God and to offer listening to God encounters, like this Burden Bearing prayer exercise in this chapter, to those who are in the midst of recovery are truly some of my most life-giving experiences. The open and receptive hearts of the women to receive the love and healing of Christ are truly the most beautiful displays of God's mercy and redemption. Thank you to each lady that I've met – you have touched my life and encouraged me on my journey of healing and freedom. I am grateful to each of you.

RECOMMENDED READING:

The Highly Sensitive Person by Elaine Aron
The Highly Sensitive Child by Elaine Aron
The Highly Sensitive Persons Survival Guide by Ted Zeff
The Mystery of Spiritual Sensitivity by Carol Brown

Praying with the Household of God
Morning Prayer and Compline

By Irene Gifford-Cole

You are no longer strangers and sojourners
but fellow-citizens with the saints
and members of the Household of God (Ephesians 2:19)

Therefore, since we are surrounded
by such a great cloud of witnesses,
let us throw off everything that hinders
and the sin that so easily entangles,
and let us run with perseverance the race that is marked out for us,
keeping our eyes on Jesus.... (Hebrews 12:1-2a)

I'd like you to meet my friend, Irene. For nearly 30 years Irene has served as Anglican priest, clinical psychologist, retreat leader, and spiritual director to many. Irene, and her husband, David, (also an Anglican priest) serve as honorary associates at St. Peter's Anglican Church in Comox. David and Irene also offer retreat locations and spiritual care. Dwight, my husband for 32 years, and I thoroughly enjoy spending time retreating at either The Well in Qualicum Beach, Vancouver Island, or The Hermitage, which is further up in the mountains. Both of these locations welcome spiritual directees and retreatants <the_well@island.net>. We not only enjoy the quiet rest, and the beautiful facilities, but our hearts and lives are enriched by spending time with David and Irene. They live a monastic type of lifestyle focusing on daily prayer and working in their gardens, properties, and offering spiritual direction (info on spiritual direction on page 219). One of the activities that Dwight and I value doing when with David and Irene is doing *Daily Morning Prayer* and in the evening, *Compline*. Neither Dwight nor I come from a traditional background so these have been delightful additions to our devotional experiences with God.

Irene: When I was a young woman sitting in the pews of a large church with my husband and children, it seemed to me a dead thing to be praying prayers out of a book. Why not pray spontaneous prayers all the time? Surely when we pray we are talking to God, and why would we need canned prayers to do that? Aren't we in a real relationship with God through Jesus Christ? So for goodness' sake put away that Prayer Book, and let's get on with it! And surely, even if you *have* to bow to convention and use a Prayer Book at church for communion and baptism, you wouldn't *dream* of using "canned prayers" when you are praying at home....

Well, things have changed. I still pray spontaneously, probably more than I used to. I also spend more time in silence with the Lord, and more time listening. But the really radical change is that now I am deeply nourished by praying Morning Prayer every morning with my husband. Usually I don't even rely on the Prayer Book because I have memorized the prayers. And when David is not with me, I pray Morning Prayer by myself. Not only that, but when we have guests in the evening we pray Compline with them before they leave. Compline is the last prayer of the day, also found in the Prayer Book, and has been prayed by Christians for many centuries.

So why would I, of all people, now regularly use the Prayer Book, even at home? There are two reasons. First of all, I have come to appreciate the fact that, as Paul puts it, we are actually members of the household of God; members of God's family and fellow-citizens with the saints. That is an awesome thing. And it is an even more awesome thing to be actually surrounded by those who have loved God in every age, though they are in a dimension of reality that we cannot now perceive (Hebrews 12:1). The author of Hebrews seems to be saying that they are actually cheering us on as we run the race that is marked out for us, keeping our eyes on Jesus. And when I pray the prayers that my sisters and brothers in the faith have prayed for centuries, I am in a very real sense joining in prayer *with them*. No matter how alone I may feel in this alienated and fractured twenty-first century, I am not alone. David and I are not alone. We are surrounded by this great cloud of witnesses, and we pray Morning Prayer *with them*.

And when we and our guests pray Compline together in the evening, we know in a fresh way that we are not just a little knot of Christians huddled together in a hostile landscape under a threatening sky, trying to keep warm together. We are here with Jesus, who promised never to leave or forsake us (Hebrews 13:5), and we are also present to the People of God in every generation and from every corner of this earth. Nor are they ghosts, these faithful witnesses, because as Jesus once told the Sadducees very clearly, God is not the God of the dead, but of the living (Matthew 22:32). Praying the prayers which have expressed the worship and love and longings of our brothers and sisters for generations past is both acknowledgement and reassurance of their presence *with* us in the communion of saints, as we pray together now.

But there is another reason why praying Morning Prayer from the Prayer Book nourishes me as it does; it has a profound impact upon my emotions. Praying these prayers makes a difference to the way I enter the new day. The prayers of that ancient service are inspired by the Holy Spirit. Many of them are actually Psalms written by David and others many hundred years before the Incarnation of Jesus the Messiah. For instance, the first two prayers, the Invitatory Psalms in Morning Prayer, (the *Venite* and the *Jubilate*) are found in Psalm 95 and Psalm 100 respectively. The *Venite* begins:

"Come, let us sing to the Lord; let us shout for joy to the Rock of our salvation!" And the *Jubilate* begins: "Be joyful in the Lord, all you lands! Serve the Lord with gladness and come before his presence with a song!" Even though the night may have been uneasy and the morning dark, those Psalms, quickened by the Holy Spirit, offer me a template of joy into which I can choose to step that day. And because they and other prayers have moved from the printed page into my memory, and from my memory into my heart, they are able to nourish me *during* the day, as I remember and ponder them.

I would like to offer you, the reader, abbreviated versions of both Morning Prayer and Compline here. Before I do though, I need to say a couple of things. First of all, these prayers are not magic. I suppose you could call them potential vehicles of grace. They are means of communicating with God, in the company of all the heavenly host, as we choose to be really present to the Lord in the praying of them. They also offer us a means of shaping our thoughts and our emotions to conform more closely to the patterns of wholeness laid out for us in the Scriptures.

And then in regard to *how* to pray these prayers, I would suggest praying them slowly, savouring them and actually picturing the reality they describe. In the *Venite* (Psalm 95) for instance, where the Psalmist praises God in whose hands are the caverns of the earth, the heights of the hills, the seas and the crafted contours of the land, I imagine all of those and allow the imagining of them to mould my own praise of God.

Secondly, I would strongly suggest praying out loud. There are a couple of reasons for this. First of all, praying out loud seems to be assumed in the Scriptures. That was why Jesus told his followers to go back into an inner room and shut the door when they prayed (probably the inner room was the storehouse, since that would be the only room in the house other than the room everybody used for everything else). A more significant reason, though, is that when we pray the prayers out loud rather than just in our minds, we have a feedback loop. The words are going out from us, and we ourselves hear them. That gives the words of our praying another avenue to affect who we are as we pray them. This is not to denigrate silent, inward prayer. It is only to say that when we are praying with all the company of Heaven, it is a good thing to pray with mind and heart *and* voice.

Finally, Morning Prayer and Compline, which I offer here, are just two of the daily services of the historical Church. Some of my friends also use the service of Evening Prayer regularly with their families. These and other services can be found in *The Book of Common Prayer* (According to the Use of the Episcopal Church), *The Book of Alternative Services of The Anglican Church of Canada* and *The Book of Common Prayer, 1962* (Canada).

Prayer Exercise **59**

Morning Prayer and Compline **XX**

An asterisk (*) is used for antiphonal reading (the leader reads aloud up to the * and the congregation or the person you are praying with takes over for the rest of the verse). This works well with even two people.

DAILY MORNING PRAYER:

Rite Two

Easter Season, including Ascension Day and the Day of Pentecost (Opening sentence varies, according to the season of the Church Year.)

Officiant: Thanks be to God, who gives us the victory through our Lord Jesus Christ.

Officiant: Lord, open our lips.
People: **And our mouth shall proclaim your praise.**

Officiant and People: **Glory to the Father, and to the Son, and to the Holy Spirit: as it was in the beginning, is now, and will be for ever. Amen.**

From Easter Day until the Ascension

Alleluia. The Lord has risen indeed. Come let us adore him. Alleluia.

Venite *Psalm 95:1-7*
(the following 3 Canticles in unison or antiphonally)

Come, let us sing to the Lord;*
    Let us shout for joy to the Rock of our salvation.
Let us come before his presence with thanksgiving*

And raise a loud shout to him with psalms.

For the Lord is a great God,*
    And a great King above all gods.
In his hands are the caverns of the earth,*
    And the heights of the hills are his also.
The sea is his, for he made it,*
    And his hands have moulded the dry land.

Come, let us bow down and bend the knee,*
    And kneel before the Lord our Maker.
For he is our God,
And we are the people of his pasture and the sheep of his hand.*
    Oh, that today you would hearken to his voice.

Jubilate *Psalm 100*

Be joyful in the Lord, all you lands;*
    Serve the Lord with gladness,
    and come before his presence with a song.

Know this: The Lord himself is God;*
    He himself has made us, and we are his.
    We are his people and the sheep of his pasture.

Enter his gates with thanksgiving;
    go into his courts with praise;*
    Give thanks to him and call upon his Name.

For the Lord is good;
His mercy is everlasting;*
    and his faithfulness endures from age to age.

The Song of Mary *Magnificat (Luke 1:46-55)*
Another psalm can be used instead of the Song of Mary for Morning
or Evening Prayer.

My soul proclaims the greatness of the Lord,
My spirit rejoices in God my Saviour;*
    for he has looked with favour on his lowly servant.
From this day forth, all generations will call me blessed:*
    for the Almighty has done great things for me,
    and holy is his Name.
He has mercy on those who fear him*
    in every generation.
He has shown the strength of his arm,*
    He has scattered the proud in their conceit.
He has cast down the mighty from their thrones,*
    and has lifted up the lowly.
He has filled the hungry with good things,*
    and the rich he has sent away empty.
He has come to the help of his servant Israel,*
    for he has remembered his promise of mercy,
The promise he made to our forebears,*
To Abraham and his children for ever.

Glory to the Father, and to the Son, and to the Holy Spirit:
As it was in the beginning, is now and will be forever. **Amen**.

*Lessons from the Old and New Testaments are read here, each fol-
lowed by silence. (Available at http://www.crivoice.org/daily.html
Daily Bible Readings)*

Officiant: The Lord be with you.
People: **And also with you.**
Officiant: Let us pray.

Officiant and People:

Our Father in Heaven,
  hallowed be your Name.
Your Kingdom come, your will be done,
  on earth as in Heaven.
Give us today our daily bread,
  and forgive us our sins
  as we forgive those who sin against us.
Save us from the time of trial,
  and deliver us from evil,
For the Kingdom, the power and the glory are yours,
  now and forever. Amen

Officiant: Show us your mercy, O Lord;
People: **And grant us your salvation.**
O: Clothe your ministers with righteousness;
P: **Let your people sing with joy.**
O: Give peace, O Lord, in all the world;
P: **For only in you can we live in safety.**
O: Lord, keep this nation under your care;
P: **And guide us in the way of justice and truth.**
O: Let your way be known upon earth;
P: **Your saving health among all nations.**
O: Let not the needy, O Lord, be forgotten;
P: **Nor the hope of the poor be taken away.**
O: Create in us clean hearts, O God;
P: **And sustain us with your Holy Spirit.**

A Collect for Peace (Officiant)

O God, the author of peace and lover of concord, to know you is eternal life, and to serve you is perfect freedom: Defend us, your humble servants, in all assaults of our enemies; that we, surely trusting in your defence, may not fear the power of any adversaries; through the might of Jesus Christ our Lord. **Amen.**

A Collect for Grace (Officiant)

Lord God, almighty and everlasting Father, you have brought us in safety to this new day. Preserve us with your mighty power, that we may not fall into sin, nor be overcome by adversity. In all we do, direct us to the fulfilling of your purpose; through Jesus Christ our Lord. **Amen**.

A Collect for Guidance (Officiant)

Heavenly Father, in you we live and move and have our being. We humbly pray you so to guide and govern us by your Holy Spirit, that in all the cares and occupations of our life, we may not forget you, but may remember that we are ever walking in your sight; through Jesus Christ our Lord. **Amen**.

Prayer for Mission (Officiant)

Lord Jesus Christ, you stretched out your arms of love on the hard wood of the cross, that everyone might come within the reach of your saving embrace: So clothe us with your Spirit that we, reaching forth our hands in love, may bring those who do not know you to the knowledge and love of you; for the honour of your Name. **Amen**.

Other prayers and intercessions may follow here. This is also a possible time for listening prayer.

The General Thanksgiving (Together)

Almighty God, Father of all mercies,
We your unworthy servants give you humble thanks
For all your goodness and loving-kindness
to us and to all that you have made.
We bless you for our creation, preservation
and all the blessings of this life;
but above all, for your immeasurable love

in the redemption of the world by our Lord Jesus Christ;
For the means of grace, and for the hope of glory.
And we pray, give us such an awareness of your mercies
that with truly thankful hearts we may show forth your praise,
not only with our lips but in our lives,
by giving up ourselves to your service,
and by walking before you
in holiness and righteousness all our days;
Through Jesus Christ our Lord,
to whom with you and the Holy Spirit
be honour and glory throughout all ages. Amen.

A Prayer of St. Chrysostom (Together)

Almighty God, you have given us grace at this time with one accord to make our common supplication to you; and you have promised through your well-beloved Son that where two or three are gathered together in his Name, you will be in the midst of them. Fulfill now, O Lord, our desires and petitions as may be best for us; granting us in this world knowledge of your truth, and in the age to come life everlasting. Amen.

Officiant: Let us bless the Lord.
People: **Thanks be to God.**

All: **The grace of our Lord Jesus Christ, and the love of God, and the fellowship of the Holy Spirit be with us all, now and forever. Amen.**

An Order for Compline
(Abbreviated)

The Officiant begins:
The Lord Almighty grant us a peaceful night and a perfect end.
Amen.

Officiant: Our help is in the name of the Lord;
People: **The maker of heaven and earth.**

Officiant: Let us confess our sins to God.

Officiant and People:
Almighty God, our heavenly Father: We have sinned against you in thought, word and deed, and in what we have left undone. For the sake of your Son our Lord Jesus Christ, forgive us all our offences; and grant that we may serve you in newness of life, to the glory of your Name. Amen.

Officiant:
May the Almighty God grant us forgiveness of all our sins, and the grace and comfort of the Holy Spirit. **Amen**.

Officiant: O God make speed to save us.
People: **O Lord make haste to help us.**

All: **Glory to the Father, and to the Son, and to the Holy Spirit:**
    as it was in the beginning, is now and will be forever. Amen.

Psalm 134
Behold now, bless the Lord, all you servants of the Lord,*
    You that stand by night in the house of the Lord.
Lift up your hands in the holy place and bless the Lord;*
    The Lord who made Heaven and earth bless you out of Zion.
Glory to the Father, and to the Son, and to the Holy Spirit;*
    As it was in the creation, is now and will be forever. Amen.

The following Scripture is read:
Jesus said, Come to me, all who labour and are heavy laden, and I will give you rest. Take my yoke upon you and learn from me for I am gentle and lowly in heart, and you will find rest for your souls. For my yoke is easy, and my burden is light.
(Matthew 11:29-30)

People: **Thanks be to God.**

Officiant: Into your hands, O Lord, I commend my spirit;
People: **For you have redeemed me, O Lord, O God of truth.**
Officiant: Keep us, O Lord, as the apple of your eye,
People: **Hide us under the shadow of your wings.**

Lord have mercy. **Christ have mercy.** Lord have mercy

All:
Our Father in heaven, hallowed be your Name, your Kingdom come, your will be done, on earth as it is in heaven. Give us today our daily bread. Forgive us our sins as we forgive those who sin against us. Save us from the time of trial, and deliver us from evil.

Officiant: Lord, hear our prayer,
People: **And let our cry come to you.**

Officiant:
Be our light in the darkness, O Lord, and in your great mercy defend us from all perils and dangers of this night, for the love of your only Son, our Saviour Jesus Christ. **Amen.**

Keep watch, dear Lord, with those who work, or watch, or weep this night, and give your angels charge over those who sleep. Tend the sick, Lord Christ, give rest to the weary, bless the dying, soothe the suffering, pity the afflicted, shield the joyous, and all for your love's sake. **Amen.**

Visit this place, O Lord, and drive far from it all the snares of the enemy; Let your holy angels dwell with us to preserve us in peace, and let your blessing be upon us always, through Jesus Christ our Lord. **Amen.**

All:

Guide us waking, O Lord, and guard us sleeping; that awake we may watch with Christ, and asleep we may rest in peace.

All:

Lord, you now have set your servant free to go in peace as you have promised;
for these eyes of mine have seen the Saviour, whom you have prepared for all the world to see: a Light to lighten the nations, and the glory of your people, Israel.
Glory to the Father, and to the Son, and to the Holy Spirit. As it was in the beginning, is now and will be forever. Amen. *(Song of Simeon. Luke 2:29-32)*

All: **Guide us waking, Lord, and guard us sleeping, that awake we may watch with Christ, and asleep we may rest in peace.**

Officiant: Let us bless the Lord.
People: **Thanks be to God.**

Officiant: The almighty and merciful Lord, Father, Son and Holy Spirit, bless us and keep us. **Amen**.

A Spiritual Companion
Spiritual Direction/Companionship

Spiritual direction is a fairly new term for me, and a new skill or practice in my life. It is similar, yet different, to mentoring or coaching. I have had a spiritual director for eight years now and have found it very beneficial on my spiritual journey. It has been such a gift to have someone listen to me and co-discern what is going on in my relationship with God and the various areas of my life. Spiritual direction asks questions more than it gives answers. It listens to what God is saying by His Spirit and brings peace and clarity to our lives. Spiritual direction is extremely effective to those who value their spiritual journey and the formation of Christ within.

"Spiritual Direction is the simple gift of offering to another the gentle but tenacious encouragement to open fully to God's loving presence and to co-discern God's activity in every aspect of life." – Steve & Jeff Imbach, SoulStream Ministries, Canada. (SoulStream has provided most of what you will be reading and receiving in this article.)

"Spiritual direction is not giving direction to someone of where to go spiritually; it is rather concerned with helping a person directly with his or her relationship with God. In Spiritual Direction the person is not encouraged so much *to understand* relationship with God, the lover, but to *engage* in relationship, to enter into dialogue. The focus is on what a person *listens* to and *responds* to; our self communicating with God who is the *initiator* of relationship with us." – *The Practice of Spiritual Direction*, by Barry and Connolly.

"In some ways, the art of spiritual direction lies in our uncovering the obvious in our lives and in realizing that everyday events are the means by which God tries to reach us." – *Holy Listening* by Guenther

"Spiritual Direction proposes to help people relate personally to God, to let God relate personally to them and to enable them to live

219

the consequences of that relationship." – *Inner Way* by Joseph Allen.

"The whole purpose of spiritual direction is to penetrate beneath the surface of a person's life, to get behind the façade of conventional gestures and attitudes which he presents to the world, and to bring out his inner spiritual freedom, his inmost truth, which is what we call the likeness of Christ in his soul ... A spiritual director is, then, one who helps another to recognize and to follow the inspirations of grace in his life, in order to arrive at the end to which God is leading him." – *Spiritual Direction*, by Thomas Merton.

"The radical re-orientation of the whole person, down to the roots of one's being ... to be suspicious of every aspect of the motivation, and to be willing to explore and reorient this motivation." – *Friend of the Bridegroom*, by Thomas Green.

I think these quotes have said very well what we are being invited to look at in this series of prayer exercises. Let us become more fully open to the Spirit who is the true Guide on the spiritual journey. I highly recommend the courses offered by SoulStream Ministries for a thorough in-depth teaching and practicum. The years I spent doing the course work and practice has truly changed my life and given me wisdom and understanding regarding so much of what I was experiencing and wondering about in my spiritual life.

People who will likely benefit from spiritual direction are those who have lived life and are becoming less afraid of its joys and pains and who have strong desires for something more in their relationship with God. "Transparent" is a good description of the attitude of openness that is invaluable to receiving and responding fully.

Spiritual direction will encourage discovery rather than teach, and this will lead to one's own experiences with God, rather than focusing on ideas or problems. It helps directees (those being directed) to be aware of their ability to notice things about themselves and their responses. Directing them to bring these things to God in prayer is an important role of a director.

A director will be humble, receiving, resonating, and have an ability to probe the encounters we face in our lives with those seeking care for their soul. A surplus of warmth is what fosters a loving committed relationship between directors and directees. Directors will also have love for people as they are, exhibit a commitment and willingness to help another, be unafraid of strong emotions, mysterious experiences and all that is human while at the same time trying to maintain a contemplative attitude—which allows the director to perceive how someone is experiencing the Lord and life. They will be self-confident, use discernment and be able to express their own feelings, thoughts and hopes to encourage the directee. They will always bear in mind that a director is entering on holy ground when entering the chamber of another's heart.

At every level of the Church we need to become companions to others, using our gifts of nature and grace through support systems— and *doing* the truth, not just *holding* the truth. We want to help others know their gifts. (How important it is to have another point out what is alive and growing in us!) We want to see healthy people who know what they feel, accept those feelings, and be able to choose how to act in the light of those feelings. Let us surrender unessential parts that are inside us, and discover new and deeper realities within.

Prayer Exercise 60

Spiritual Direction/Companionship

1 Ponder how you feel about your relationship with God and your spiritual journey. How have you sensed the Spirit in your life recently? How do you describe your openness/resistance to the Spirit?

2 What quality traits would you want in a spiritual companion? What gifts or character traits do you have to offer as a spiritual companion?

What strengths or weaknesses do you see in yourself when you move to care for someone? What area might need to be strengthened? How can you see using your strengths to be active in your community and in God's Kingdom?

I'm Listening to You – Or am I ?

Spiritual listening goes beyond simply hearing to a deep responsive attentiveness of the many ways God is speaking to us and to others who come to us for direction. You need to listen to the story being presented, listen "under" the story being presented, listen to your own inner responses, and listen to the Spirit of God within you.

Some things to listen for: What is missing? What seems to be the motivations and longings? Is there a persistent theme over time? What seems to be an invitation, an opening or a nudging? Do there seem to be any blocks to this kind of listening? Be open to explore your own attitudes and habits about how you listen and why. It is good to practice the skills of listening and to develop the art of subtle under-the-surface listening to God's "still small voice" (1 Kings 19:12) in your own heart, when listening for those who come for spiritual direction, or for the world at large. This is listening deeply and intentionally with our hearts to God and others.

PRAYER EXERCISE 61

I'M LISTENING TO YOU – OR AM I?   XX

1 Do you listen to others easily or is it challenging for you? Why might that be? What attitudes or habits might you have now or need to develop to do well at listening deeply with another?

2 Recall a time you really felt listened to. Why was this so meaningful?

3 Practice listening to another person for 15 minutes without interruption. What body language can you offer to show your attentiveness without using words? (For example: leaning forward, nodding, making eye contact.)

4 Listen to what the person is saying and what might be underneath the words.

"The New is Here!"

(2 Corinthians 5:17 TNIV)

Community – Conflict and Love

"'The glory of this present house will be greater than the glory
of the former house,' says the Lord. Almighty. 'And in this place
I will grant peace,' declares the Lord Almighty."
(Haggai 2:9 TNIV)
"All this comes from the God who settled the relationship
between us and him, and then called us to settle
our relationships with each other."
(2 Corinthians 5:18 MSG)

I have a strong sense that what is happening in my life just might
also be happening in yours at this time, or will in a time to come.
Perhaps this is a corporate move of God among us. I sense an increase in conflicting situations. I am experiencing shock at some
new things popping up in my life and the lives of those I love, and
frustration with and disappointment in some old things "coming
back for another round."

I sense the invitation to both hold the old ground that has already
been conquered, and to step up to the plate to take some new ground
that is being offered by the Lord, and yet for which the enemy will
highly contend. I stand facing so much while part of me really just
wants to crumble or give up. How's it going with you?

"When enemies come in like a flood,
the Spirit of the Lord will put them to flight."
(Isaiah 59:19 TNIV)

Here is a prayer exercise to help you process some of what the
Lord may be inviting you to learn regarding community or family
conflict. This has been helpful to me more times than I can count.

223

PRAYER EXERCISE 62

THE NEW IS HERE! COMMUNITY – CONFLICT AND LOVE 𝕏𝕏𝕏

What are the enemies that you are presently facing? (The evil one, unhealed parts of our hearts, your vulnerabilities, underdeveloped areas, family, friends, loved ones, difficult people, circumstances with jobs, vocations, finances, reputation, housing … whatever is presenting itself as an enemy.)

I like the way the King James Version states Isaiah 59:19: "The spirit of the Lord shall lift up a standard against him."

Enter into God's presence and power to heal.

1 Hold your ground in the midst of much conflict

Hold onto who you are and what God has already said or done, trusting that God is holding you.
Who has God shown or told you that you are?
What has God already been saying or doing in this area of your life, your present situation, or one like it?

2 Be still in the presence of God

Be aware of God holding you in the midst of whatever you are facing. How might this look to you? How does it feel? (If unable to settle on your own, find a praying friend to join you.)

3 Let the Spirit comfort you deeply and gently fill you with fresh love and power

"Abide in Me, and I in you" (John 15:4 NASB)
"Remain in me, and I will remain in you" (John 15:4 NIV)
"Live in me. Make your home in me just as I do in you" (John 15:4 The Message)
(Do not rush away. You will sense when the Spirit is done for now. Recognize that He will continue this good & transforming work within you through this day and continuing into night.)

"Being confident of this, that he who began a good work in you will carry it on to completion until the day of Christ Jesus" (Philippians 1:6 NIV)

4 **Move toward those in conflict with devoted love, faithful support, and encouragement in the truth**

This may even be in *silence* … yet being connected with God and led by the Spirit of Love and in the Holy Light of God.

"If I … have not love, I am nothing…. I gain nothing." (1 Corinthians 13:2, 3 NIV)

How does God want you to do this practically in your present situation?

Ask God for a plan or strategy that is wise and loving. Look at the virtues of Wisdom in Proverbs. Let Wisdom guide you.

Be sure that any goal does not depend on another person to make it happen. Goals are those that you can do on your own and with God's help and strength.

5 **Let us continue our actions toward unity in relationships by the Spirit**

(This is the opposite of contributing to division or rejection.)

Do not respond to lies. Notice Jesus' silence to anything not worthy of conversation.

Jesus does rise and speak truth with love; not to defend it, but to speak it.

What may you be invited to ignore or walk away from?

What may you be asked to speak simply and clearly?

Say what you mean and mean what you say and don't say it in a mean way.

Are you free to walk away from anger or abusive treatment?

Ask God for strength and courage.

6 **Recognize that you may be thinking that you always have full truth and perfect vision**

Be willing to adapt and be open to change. Yielding to another person is a valuable skill that may need to be learned.

"Love … is not self-seeking, is not easily angered, it keeps no record of wrongs".

(1 Corinthians 13:4, 5 NIV)

Ask God:

> Am I actually eating some bad fruit from the tree of the knowledge of good or evil?
> Do I actually believe (or subtly think) that I always know what is always right/wrong,
> good/bad, best/worst, etc?
> Do I allow Christ to be enthroned as Lord and Judge over all the Earth or might I be trying to take this place?

If we can stop our minds and obsessions from trying to figure out who is right and wrong in every situation and simply care for the hurt we have given to and received from each other, and look to Wisdom in this for our future living together, we will win!

Take some time to surrender whatever the Lord may be asking you for, and yield to the Spirit of God who likely wants to move in this situation for and with you.

7 Respond to God's invitation to eat from the Tree of Life for yourself and with others

"The tongue that brings healing is a tree of life."

(Proverbs 15:4 NIV)

Receive enlightened wisdom as you wait upon God to give it to you or someone in any given situation.

Rest while you receive by the Spirit all that He has for you now. In a sense, you are invited to eat and share the leaves of the tree for the healing of yourself and others.

Move towards reconciliation as much as God gives, and settle in peace.

Be encouraged by these powerful promises of God:

Revelation 2:7 NIV
"He who has an ear, let him hear what the Spirit says to the churches. To him who overcomes, I will give the right to eat from the tree of life, which is in the paradise of God."

Revelation 22:2 NIV
"On each side of the river stood the tree of life, bearing twelve crops of fruit, yielding its fruit every month. And the leaves of the tree are for the healing of the nations."

> *"And now these three remain: faith, hope and love.*
> *But the greatest of these is love."*
> (1 Corinthians 13:13 TNIV)

Crafted Prayer
God's Light and Voice

Spiritual Warfare and Strategic Prayers

"Be self-controlled and alert.
Your enemy the devil prowls around like a roaring lion
looking for someone to devour."
(1 Peter 5:8 NIV)

Sometimes when you are going about your ordinary life and, occasionally when praying, do you sense that you may have really entered a battle? I do at times. I much prefer to focus on the Lord than to confront the enemy in a way that gives him too much attention. But there is a time when we are called to battle the enemy with the power of the Lord. "In the name of the Lord I cut them down" (Psalm 118:11, 12 TNIV).

One time during prayer I sensed the enemy interfering, and the Lord gave me a prayer. I sensed an invitation to pray this strategic prayer as God led me. He told me it was my battle prayer. It is mine to pray and declare in His authority whenever He brings it to my mind. I call it *"God's Light and Voice."* As I share it you will see why this name is relevant. I love that God showed me how He wanted me to demolish the enemy without becoming focused or fixed on the enemy.

My main goal in sharing this prayer is to show that we can be open to receive and even to ask for strategic prayers in certain situations. Specially crafted prayers such as liturgical prayers have been prayerfully designed to hold powerful truths and heartfelt expressions that we, at times, may not be able to say or put into words as well as those who have written them.

This particular prayer is prayed with love for the person I'm praying for; it is not to be waved around like a weapon that is out of control, or a lucky charm, hoping it works. I simply keep it handy at my side, as it were, for the times when the Lord impresses me to use it. I sense the invitation to be mindful that no matter what is happening in my life or in the world around me that my first response should be to listen to the Lord and ask what He wants me to do or not do. Here we follow Jesus example: "But the world must learn that I love the Father and that I do exactly what my Father has commanded me" (John 14:31 NIV). My intention, like yours, is to do my best for the Lord, even though I fail miserably at times. My desire is to stay close to Christ and not go off on my own strength to battle. I sense God has great delight over my longings to do His will, even when I fall short.

Occasionally, I will discern that the evil one seems to be affecting my life or someone else's life. The Lord brings this prayer to my mind when I look to Him for guidance, or sometimes He simply reminds me of it just because He is way ahead of me and knows what is really going on.

PRAYER EXERCISE **63**

CRAFTED PRAYER – GOD'S LIGHT AND VOICE   **XX**

Please start at the top and move through it.

1 **Compassion:** Let me invite you first to compassion for the one who is under attack or in whose life the enemy seems to have a foothold. The compassion of Christ holds so much power. Without compassion for the hurting or the lost we may be operating out of our own needs or wishes. As you move toward the person requesting prayer be open to receive God's heart of love and compassion for them. In a sense, you are standing with them and entering into this prayer on their behalf.

2 **Look to the Lord:** I look to the Lord for permission to do this prayer of battle for them. I do not want to enter into a battle against demons that I have not been given permission to proceed with. Sometimes we will sense enemy involvement in lives or situations and God is only inviting us to join a group of intercessors to pray together. I will occasionally get a specific word or picture to pray for this particular person as we go through the prayer, but typically it will be basically what is written here.

I picture the person standing in their situation. Then I pray these three parts:

a.) **God**, I ask for Your Light to cover this person like a spotlight of mercy and grace flooding down over them from Heaven. I ask for your Light and Love to shine over them and expose any plans or strategy of the enemy that is not in agreement with You for them at this time. I ask for the enemy and his schemes to be cut off in the name of the Lord. I ask for Your Light to push back all darkness and I ask You to gather it unto Yourself and to take it to the Cross to stay. I ask for Your Light to continue to surround, flow over, and fill this person. I ask that they would know and feel Your presence with them now. (Pause)

I picture the Lord coming to the person's mind with His hand upon their forehead.

b.) **God**, I ask You to come to this person and if there are any thoughts, ideas, plans, belief systems, etc. that are not in full agreement with You for this time, that You would silence and still them. Even if some of the thoughts and plans are good, but not for now, I ask you to still and silence them so that Your voice can be heard more clearly. I ask for Your words of love, comfort, and direction to come flowing to them. May all that is from You flow into him/her.

I picture the person set free and having moved to a spacious place, being filled with joy. (In the original picture that I had I saw one of the people from our church who has a major disability rolling all over the floor in spilled chocolate milk, laughing their head off. To me this was a sign of freedom and merriment even though the spilled milk represented things not going as perfectly as I had pictured in my mind.)

c.) **God**, I ask that the joy of the Lord would be restored to this person. I ask for the restoration of great joy and laughter and pleasures forevermore that are theirs in Your presence. I ask for a large portion of joy and peace for them and their family/friends.

Amen

Isn't it incredible that after what perhaps was an intense battle, we are invited to celebrate and be reminded that Christ died and the Spirit fought for our joy and freedom? We now can live in the amazing grace of the resurrection life given to us.

PRAYER EXERCISE 64

CREATING A PRAYER   XX

1 Ask the Lord to guide you if you sense an invitation to make a specific prayer. Be open to hear God's voice, sense His heart, and to create something new and beautiful with Him.

2 Journal or write what God is making known to you as you listen and feel with both His and your heart. Articulate as simply and clearly as possible what God's message is and His invitation of what you are to pray.

3 Find one or two people who you trust, and who are grounded theologically, and go over the prayer with them. Adjust it as might be needed.

4 Pray as led by the Spirit of God.

" that many would be set free … That many would be healed…"

One of my favourite crafted prayers is called, "Painting the Dragon Red Prayer." Leanne Payne shares it in *Restoring the Christian Soul*.

She, and her team, have listened in how to pray for our "Beloved Enemies." Those who are close to us yet have become against us or the ministry we have been given. I highly recommend her entire chapter, The Gift of Battle, in *Restoring the Christian Soul*.

Her approach is to love our enemies being aware of our real enemy, Satan and his tactics. Her focus is on the Cross and on Christ, our Savior, rather than on the demonic. This is a strategic prayer that God gave her to deal with certain situations when our loved ones turn against us (or others), especially when it involves healing ministries. It seems to be one of the enemies' schemes to thwart or take us out.

Leanne says, "Often the enemy takes advantage of opposition that arises within our most intimate circles – our close relatives or friends in the Body of Christ – to stir up the most heart-rending kind of spiritual warfare. This especially occurs where an effective ground-breaking ministry is at stake. Always in such demonized warfare, there will be slander and lies. I've yet to see a case like this where a root sin of envy did not have to be exposed and reckoned with as well. Oddly enough, that dread vice is rarely recognized for what it is today."

The Table of the Lord
An Invitation to Justice

"So, my friends, when you come together to the Lord's Table,
be reverent and courteous with one another.
If you're so hungry that you can't wait to be served, go home and
get a sandwich. But by no means risk turning this Meal
into an eating and drinking binge or a family squabble.
It is a spiritual meal – a love feast."
(1 Corinthians 11:33-34 MSG)

It occurred to me that when we come to the Table of the Lord to receive the Eucharist that we come alone, yet we come together as one, one family of God. What a great picture of all of God's children coming to one Table for God's love, forgiveness, healing and great joy. Picture yourself there and all the family of God with you.

All are invited. Whoever desires to come to Christ is welcome. Yes, all are invited to join in God's love and be a part of this family. Then why are some people under the Table? And why are others on top of the Table? The picture I have is that those who are oppressed, demoralized, or exploited feel like they do not belong *at* the Table. They have a sense of being less than others or of not being worthy; perhaps there is isolation or loneliness, or it just simply may be hard to find the way to the Table in this present state.

Meanwhile, some people feel they are better than others; they are partial to people they like or think are the best. Perhaps they have been the ones oppressing or exploiting others. While fear, or ignorance, or inadequacy has caused some to crawl under the Table, pride and injustice causes others to parade on top. What a messy sight!

I sense the Lord wanting us to all simply come and eat *at* the Table together. How can this be? How can the people who are eating crumbs in loneliness, fear, and focused on their brokenness and challenging circumstances, but longing for more feasting, come to sit beside those who have been on top of the Table? The ones who have been on top, possibly feeling superior and focused on getting all they can without regard of others, but now they too, see The Way and follow Christ, and come to eat as an equal member and as one family.

I found it more difficult to pray for the people on top, but I sensed the Lord showing me that this was mistaken comfort as well. All are to be loved and embraced without prejudice. I wanted to knock the ones on top off or at least tell them off! But God bids that all must come. All are wounded and acting out of unmet needs, pain and wrong belief systems. All are invited to eat together.

Can I have the same mercy and grace that God has for me? Am I willing to eat with all at the Table? Let's do an exercise that will help to identify what may be going on in related circumstances in your life or places in your heart.

PRAYER EXERCISE **65**

THE TABLE OF THE LORD – AN INVITATION TO JUSTICE

Prayer for you:

1 Picture the Table of the Lord laden with bountiful blessings for all God's children.

2 Where do you think you are in this picture at this time?

3 Can you believe that Jesus is there with you? What would Jesus be doing?

4 What does Jesus want you to know or show you or perhaps give you?

5 Why does he want that for you? Can you receive it?

6 Respond to Jesus' love, actions and gifts. Pause here, receive, and rest.

7 Do you have a gift for Jesus? What do you have to offer?

8 How does Jesus respond to your gift? Enjoy a time of gratitude.

Prayer for others:

1 Ask the Lord to show you if there is anyone in your life who is under the Table at this time. Who is it? (Is it you?) Is it someone in the world?

2 What does Jesus want them to see or know? Let your prayer for them be intercession and an invitation to come.

3 How does Jesus want you to pray for them, their fears, their future, their wounds, etc?

4 Is there someone in your life at this time who is on top of the Table? Who?

5 What does Jesus want them to see or know? How does Jesus want to approach or touch them? Let your prayer for them be intercession and an invitation to come.

6 Give your intercession and burdens to the Lord, come to the Table, and enter in!

Can You Drink the Cup?
To the Dregs!

"Can we hold our life, lift our life, and drink it, as Jesus did?"
Henri Nouwen

By Eden Jersak

Lorie: Eden is a very special friend of mine. Eden and I teach and lead retreats together. It is an enormous gift to have her as a ministry companion as we travel to different places and journey through life together. I can truly say after years of doing life and ministry together that she is a valiant and devoted Jesus Lover and not scared to drink the cup of life together, the joys or the sorrows. Eden, thank you for writing this great article and being all of who you are. I drink to *you*!

Eden: I can't remember when I first read Henri Nouwen's book, *Can You Drink the Cup?*, but I can tell you that I have read it many times since. It is a wonderful little book that uses the analogy of the cup (Matthew 20:22-23), and all that it may hold, to draw us into a lovely encounter with God and ourselves.

Can you drink the cup? Can you empty it to the dregs? Can you taste all the sorrow and joys? Can you live your life to the full whatever it will bring?" These are the questions.

One of our greatest challenges as humans is just that, being human. We can get so frustrated by our limitations and we can spend too much time avoiding our humanity instead of embracing it. Henri Nouwen goes through several steps to show us how we can embrace our lives, with all that they hold, in order to embrace God with all of our lives. Here is a prayer exercise that I designed to invite us to The Cup.

PRAYER EXERCISE 66

CAN YOU DRINK THIS CUP?   ☒☒

To work through this encounter you may want to grab a wine glass and put it in front of you as you work through these steps. Just use it as a visual aid to keep you on track and aware of the process you're working through.

HOLDING the cup of life:

This is not going to be easy. Holding our cup is all about looking at what's in our life, what we've been consuming, maybe even looking at how it got there. But look at the cup, and ask yourself some very sincere questions:

> What sorrow is in my cup?
> What joy is in my cup?

LIFTING the cup of life:

When we lift the cup we are sending an invitation to those in our community to come and have a look. It's an act of trust that will ultimately create community as you are both accepted and accept others in their vulnerable sharing of the cup.

> How are you willing to lift your cup in order to create community?
> How have you brought life to others in lifting your cup?

DRINKING the cup of life:

Holding and lifting will never be enough. Drinking the contents of our life is what is required. As we drink the cup we become aware of who we really are, who we were made to be, and our unique potential and ways of moving through this world. Drinking the cup requires some disciplines in order to be able to fully accept all of the joys and sorrows that are ours. The following disciplines will help in your being able to fully drink to the bottom of your cup.

The discipline of silence: don't hide from your joys and sorrows by surrounding yourself with noise and busyness. Allow yourself the space for silence where you can look at the joys and sorrows directly. The result of not shrinking away is being able to embrace who you were made to be in Christ. Silence affords that opportunity. Try to locate some space for silence in your day.

> Ask Jesus what He would like to look at with you specifically today.

The discipline of word: silence is not enough, you need to share your cup and its contents with your community. That will require you to find trusted and committed friends to share with when the burdens are too heavy and the way too dark. Speaking out will create community; keeping silence will leave you in isolation.

> Do you have a community that you can share with?
> Is there anything that you have been keeping to yourself
> that would become lighter by sharing it with someone else?
> Look for the time and space to share that burden.

The discipline of action: this isn't action for the sake of moving and looking busy. This is a purposeful moving into our calling that comes from knowing what is in our cup and not being afraid to drink it. We can take these purposeful steps because we aren't afraid of encountering something bitter in our cup. Nor will we be craving the sugar high from the sweet things that we have encountered.

> Ask Jesus what steps He would like you to take today.
> What direction is He pointing and what path does He
> have for you to take?

A few years ago I bought each close friend in my community a nice wineglass. On each I had the words etched, "To Life." We each have one in our homes, and when we're together we toast to our lives, to the sorrow, and to the joy. We have learned to drink deep and love deep, and to drink to the dregs!

Do This In Remembrance Of Me
A Toast to the King!

By Eden Jersak

I grew up in a conservative church, and was baptized when I was 16. Until the time I was baptized, I had never been to a communion service. Our church always held communion services in the afternoon or evening, and only the baptized members of the church were invited and included. On the Sunday that I was baptized, I was invited to come to the afternoon communion service, and there at the front of the sanctuary was a solid wood table with the words carved in it, "Do this in remembrance of Me." The pastor handed out a tiny piece of blessed bread to each person present, and followed that with a thimble-sized cup of wine. Then we turned and kneeled on the floor with our hands crossed on the bench and we prayed, examined our hearts, and remembered what Christ had done for us. What had never really made sense to me was why we would remember Christ's sacrifice with such a small amount of bread and wine.

It was nearly 25 years after my baptism that I decided to lead a group of ladies from Fresh Wind in a communion service at the end of a retreat. In making the plans for this I expressed my frustration with the "smallness" of the elements, and how quick we seemed to rush through that part of our service. It was decided that we would do something about it.

We purchased a full size wineglass for each woman who would be attending, and for the service filled it full. We brought out full loaves of bread for the service as well. I was determined that we would not short-change our remembering of Christ at this service. Each woman received her wineglass and was encouraged to rip off a large piece of bread from the loaf.

That's when we shifted gears, and instead of being introspective and solemn, we asked the women to share how they had remembered Christ during this retreat. It was an incredibly holy time of women sharing their hearts, but also of us being reminded of ALL that Christ is. As each woman shared, she would propose a toast to Christ, and we would all toast with her. The toasting went on for a long time; we toasted "Christ the King," "Christ the Lover," "Christ the Friend," Christ the Good Shepherd," "Christ our Savior," and more. Each memory shared was hallowed and sweet, and I couldn't keep from thinking that we had really remembered Christ well in this service.

Since that service, I have enjoyed several more just like it, and there is something wonderful in refreshing our memories of Who Jesus is, how He is affecting our lives right now, and how He has been with us in the past. It brings the reality of why He died for us, and the sacrifice He made, very close.

I invite you to not short-change your remembering the next time you have communion. You might even want to try this at home with some of your close family and friends.

PRAYER EXERCISE 67

DO THIS IN REMEMBRANCE OF ME – A TOAST TO THE KING **XXX**

Fill a big wineglass, get some big pieces of bread, and don't stop remembering and toasting until it's all gone. Let the truth of Who Jesus is, and what He has done, linger on in your heart until the next time you come together to remember.

Prophetic Prayer Tunnel

"Encourage one another day after day,
as long as it is still called 'Today'...
We have become partakers of Christ,
if we hold fast the beginning of our assurance firm until the end."
(Hebrews 3:13-14 NASB)

We all lined up in two lines facing each other. We reached our hands to each other and, when joined, we formed a tunnel that we could all, in turn, walk through. We prayerfully entered the tunnel when it was our turn, and when it was someone else's turn, we prayerfully listened to the Lord for them for what He might want to say to them as they walked through the tunnel. We would then share what we saw or heard to the one we were praying for.

A similar exercise is called, "The Blessing Chair." A chair is placed in the center of a circle of chairs where we all sit together. We take turns sitting in The Blessing Chair as people listen, pray, and prophesy over us, bringing us encouraging words, scriptures, pictures, or thoughts.

Entering these types of prayer exercises can feel uncomfortable at first. Perhaps because the spotlight does shine on you for a few minutes, and maybe we aren't sure we want people to be listening to God for us.

I learned this at a prophetic school I attended for two years, Samuel's Mantle, in Abbotsford, B.C. <www.samuelsmantle.com>.

PRAYER EXERCISE **68**

PROPHETIC PRAYER TUNNEL **XXX**

1 Make a tunnel by standing in two lines that face each other. You can put your arms up and pray for this listening and blessing time together.

2 Each of you take a turn walking through the pathway, allowing people to speak words of encouragement, support and love to you, or to give you pictures or images. God will make these messages clear as the days unfold and other pieces of the puzzle that He is putting together in your life come together.

3 If possible, journal what was said to you and look at it later. Add to it anything that confirms this message or things that God shows you later to broaden or complete it.

4 Have a time for people to share what they were given. This will strengthen the words and increase faith and hope in Christ.

A STORY FROM THE JOURNEY...

One time when we were doing a Prayer Tunnel at a Christmas party for our prayer ministry teams and spouses, God spoke to me in an unusual way. My friend, Kevin shared with me the children's story of Jack and the Beanstalk. He wasn't sure why God showed him that, but suggested I look into it. I was curious, but as the busy Christmas season kept going I soon forgot about this word and picture he had given to me.

A few weeks later as I looked to God in prayer about something that I had been asked to pray for. Suddenly I had a picture come to mind of Jack climbing the beanstalk. I had totally forgotten about this prophetic message from Kevin until now. I had a sense that God invited me to be like Jack going up to the heights with my prayers and to take hold of what I sensed was God's will. A few days later I heard that this prayer was answered. I was filled with joy.

One simple word and picture given can bring encouragement and hope beyond many words. I think God enjoys connecting with us in so many ways, many that are just simple fun. I hope you will be open to receiving prophetic messages for one another in your family or community—and giving them, as well.

In the Presence of my Enemies

"You prepare a table before me in the presence of my enemies."
(Psalm 23:5 NASB)

Picture God inviting you to a delicious feast that has been prepared and set out on a beautiful table. Here God is bidding you to come and everything that is for you is so attractive. And then as you step forward to enter in you slowly notice some troubling things near this place. Your enemies! There they are, and they're watching what is going on. What's with that?

Now, are you still expected to participate with God and enjoy this time of dining together? Can you join in? Will you come close to smell, touch, eat, taste, drink, and enjoy what has been prepared for you? Surely God doesn't expect you to do that!

Is this the way of the Cross? Are you to keep living with our Mighty God while things assail your life, demons tempt you, and pain just won't go away? Can you do it?

I remember being at a gathering of people and in the room was a person who had deeply hurt me in a very public way. It was uncomfortable at best, and soon we were to be invited to worship together. I remember sitting there wondering how I would ever be able to worship God. How would I take my mind off of this person and the circumstances of our relationship?

Of course, I knew that the person wasn't the *real* enemy. "But I tell you, love your enemies and pray for those who persecute you, that you may be children of your Father in heaven. He causes his sun to rise on the evil and the good, and sends rain on the righteous and the unrighteous" (Matthew 5:44 TNIV). "For our struggle is not against flesh and blood, but against the rulers, against the authorities, against the powers of this dark world and against the spiritual forces of evil in the heavenly realms" (Ephesians 6:12 NIV).

It felt like this person was an enemy but they were also in God's family, sitting at God's table, and they weren't going away. The table was set for a time of worship. The saints were gathering and the worship team was prayerfully ready to begin our time together. It was looking like a feast for all of us. Could I enter in? Could I "taste and see that the Lord is good"? (Psalm 34:8 KJV)

I invite you to enter into Psalm 23 and the Table at which your "enemy" may be present. I trust God to bring you comfort, healing, and the strength to overcome, for God surely helped me.

PRAYER EXERCISE 69

IN THE PRESENCE OF MY ENEMIES   XX

1 Slowly read Psalm 23 until it becomes your prayer and place of communion with God. You may experience God as the Good Shepherd, who is attentive and loving.

2 Receive the Good Shepherd who is already there waiting for you. Visit in the green pastures and beside the quiet waters. What might this look like for you today?

3 Receive love, comfort and healing as God restores your soul. Trust the kind touch.

4 Follow the Wise Shepherd as you are guided in paths of righteousness. How does this feel? What do you notice?

5 Deeply sense that God is with you as you think of anything in your life that may feel like "the valley of the shadow of death." What might be dying? What might need to die, and what is to live? Be comforted with caring compassion.

6 Notice the table that's been prepared for you. It is stunning and loaded with everything possible from God's heart and kingdom. What has been prepared for you with profound love? What nourishes and satisfies you?

7 Recognize that your enemies are there. Are they quietly watching, mocking or perhaps taking painful stabs at you? Identify what your enemy/ies are at this time. What are the things that seem to be against you at this time?

8 How does God see your enemies? How does God see you? How do you see God?

9 Perhaps you wonder, *what is going on?* God steps toward you and anoints your head with oil. What does that say to you?

10 Then God fills your cup and it overflows. What is being poured into your cup?

God, help me to enter into being anointed and filled even in the presence of my enemies. Let me dine with You, celebrate You, and know and declare that surely Your goodness and love will follow me all the days of my life, and I will dwell in the house of the Lord forever. Amen

QUESTIONS FOR FURTHER REFLECTION:

Become aware that Jesus is with you as you slowly move through some of these questions or stay on a particular one that seems important to you.

- Do you sense a need to lie down for a while and rest from whatever you may be facing? Can you do that and let go of whatever is tiring you?

- Do you feel empty in some places?

- What would Jesus like to restore in you?

- What would you call the paths you may have been travelling on?

- Can you identify what one or more of your fears may be at this time?

- How does Jesus want to take care of your heart knowing how you feel?

- What does Jesus want to fill you with?

- Is there anything you are being asked to do practically to move in forgiveness or healing?

- How does it feel to know that the goodness and love of Jesus will follow you all the days of your life?

- Can your heart and mind rest in the knowledge that you will dwell in the house of the Lord forever? What does that feel like?

Thankfully, God helped me to enter into the joy of Jesus in that room that day. The joy of the Lord was my strength. "Go and enjoy choice food and sweet drinks, and send some to those who have nothing prepared. This day is sacred to our Lord. Do not grieve, for the joy of the Lord is your strength" (Nehemiah 8:10 NIV).

I enjoyed God's presence immensely and each instrument and voice that was praising. When I became mindful of the person who had hurt me I would lift them to the Lord in blessing and continue my worship to God. This was a wonderful time of freedom for me. It can be done!

We're on the Same Page!

"Therefore, since we are surrounded
by such a great cloud of witnesses,
let us throw off everything that hinders
and the sin that so easily entangles.
And let us run with perseverance the race marked out for us."
(Hebrews 12:1 TNIV)

While struggling to come to peace with some major challenges in community a few years ago, I received a picture that changed my life. All I wanted was for people to live together in harmony. Simple. Let's just be and live on the *SAME PAGE!* This would give us full "unity" forever on every issue, every prayer request, and blah, blah, blah... You can probably see where this is going. I merely wanted Heaven on Earth now and for all time. It is a good longing, but how realistic could it be?

The picture I got came when I was sitting in a prayer meeting delighting in how God made everyone in the circle very different. I was enjoying that we all thought different, prayed different, and we all certainly looked very different. I was loving the diversity in community. There had been some discord among us, but none of that seemed to matter in this beautiful moment of being one in Christ.

The picture was of a big book like The Book of Life in Heaven. It was full of many individual pages, yet just one big book. I felt God nudge my heart and say, "You each have your own page. I made one for each of you. I designed you each on your own page. I like this very much. I like your page. I want you to like it, too. I want you to enjoy it. I want you to be settled on it. I want you to be fully alive and moving in your destiny. It is you. It is your own personal page. It is your own personal map of your own personal life."

I was being invited to discover more of my true identity and live more authentically as my true self; to accept and love my own page or life as it was. God had a much more wonderful way for me to live and showed me the way. I was hearing, "You can visit other people's pages, but you must go back to your own and others can visit your page – but they must go back to theirs and you must let them." How clear and liberating this message was to my heart. I was filled with gratitude that I was an individual, yet part of a big family.

PRAYER EXERCISE 70

WE'RE ON THE SAME PAGE! 𝕏𝕏𝕏

For a time in solitude or a group activity at a retreat

Light 3 candles as a symbol of The Trinity being with you.
Be mindful that you are surrounded by the Trinity and the Great Cloud of Witnesses.

1 Get a piece of paper to represent "Your Page." As creatively as you care to be, put your name on the paper somewhere. Write or draw on your paper some words or pictures that tell who you are, character traits, and things about your life. There is no right or wrong way to do this – just be you!

2 When that is done look at your own "page." Enjoy it and ask God to help you to live your true identity; who He has made you to be and specifically who you are in Christ.

3 Perhaps you get "stuck" on someone else's page. Are you identified by others or by what you do? Let God "un-stick" you and your page from other people's pages. May God guide and teach you through the Holy Spirit how to love yourself and others.

4 Recognize that we are not islands. We are a "book" together, a body and a family. We have the joy and the privilege of doing life together. If you have a tendency to isolate, feel alone or be like an island, ask God to help you come close and receive a sense of belonging with others and with God. Be open to have the pathways of giving and receiving from others heal and be restored.

GROUP EXERCISE:

1 Go around the room and each person choose three words to describe their page.

Be disciplined with this; simply say the three words without elaboration.

2 Share a bit of your page with at least one other person in this group. Let them ask you questions.

3 Visit their page as they share with you for a few minutes as well. Ask them questions which honor them by showing that you are interested in them and getting to know them better by learning more of who they are.

The Recovery of Love

A superb resource for me on my healing journey has been *The Recovery of Love*, one of the books written by Jeff Imbach.

Here is one of the many valuable quotes from Jeff: "To reclaim oneself is to go to the very center and find one's 'is-ness' in the One who is bringing life to birth within. It is to return to the Source of intimacy in order to come back into the world able to experience intimacy with freedom from the ways we load love with our needs and dependencies. Anything less is just a new round of living out of the projections and needs that drove one out of oneself into dependent relationships in the first place. The mix may be different, but it is still only tinkering with the system. The real need is to discover one's true value and to live there."

Jeff has spent many years as a pastor and spiritual director. He was president of the Henri Nouwen Society in Canada. He is cofounder of SoulStream, a ministry that provides spiritual direction training, and retreats.

From Henri Nouwen: This book is a wise book. Its wisdom is

not a borrowed wisdom. It is a wisdom born of the personal struggles of its author, lived in the light of the Gospel of Jesus Christ and shaped by the great mystics of the church."

Following is a creative writing piece from my journal as I processed some deep inner healing and God's love:

If I go outside of that which I am to love,
And the way I am to love it,
Then the harmony of my heart is broken;
I ache.
If I enter into all that I am to love,
And delight in it,
And cherish all of it,
I find a deeper peace than I've ever known,
And a desire for the depth of all love holds.

Lorie Martin 2005

"Button, Button, Who Pushed my Button?"

"Why are you downcast, O my soul?
Why so disturbed within me?"
Psalm 43:5 NIV

Did you play this simple game when you were a child? It was a favorite at our birthday parties. The anticipation of someone secretly dropping a button into your nearly closed hands was so delightful. Then, if it wasn't you who received it, it was quite exciting to watch closely to see if you could figure out who had. Over and over, round and round the game would go until it lost its thrill and we were onto another game such as spinning ourselves around and around to either fall or try to keep our balance. These were some of the simple and easy ways to have fun together when we were young, back in the '60's.

Well, unfortunately in some ways, having fun together changes as we go through our teen years, young adulthood, and on through life. As we become more aware of ourselves, others, the interactions that occur in our lives, and what we may face in relationships, engaging with one another can sometimes be painful instead of pleasant. "Our buttons get pushed." Something unpleasant triggers a place within us and the resulting feelings can be pretty nasty. The reactions that rise up inside us can be equally as—or far more—undesirable than whatever set us off.

What gets to you? What hits that tender spot within you, perhaps even catching you off guard? What really bugs you or provokes deep emotions in you? All of a sudden, there it is: unexpected anger, sudden sorrow, unexplainable disappointment, unpredicted lust, overwhelming fear, deep loneliness, profound discouragement or despair, regret or powerlessness, or one of the many other emotional responses we experience. Some reactions are the opposite to these less desirable ones, such as a passionate sense of love, deep loyalty, zealous courage, tender kindness, genuine compassion, etc. Some of these reactions or feelings in us are predictable, while others seem to be unforeseen and can even shock us.

Brainstorm a minute. Think of a recent situation where you felt noticeably stirred. How did your heart and emotions move? These movements inside us can tell us a great deal about ourselves and God who lives within us. Catherine of Sienna describes the power and life of these emotions as "double knowledge" – knowledge of self and knowledge of God. I learned at a Marriage Encounter years ago that "feelings are neither right nor wrong." They just are what they are; they simply come upon us. It is very important to try to discern what your first heart movement is before it goes to your mind, where it can be interpreted incorrectly due to past experiences or ungodly or unhealthy belief systems, etc.

I used to think that experiencing some negative emotion was always the enemy tempting me; however, as I mature I realize that maybe it is, or maybe it is a deep subconscious place within me needing attention. Regardless, God uses the situation to uncover what I may need to know to become more complete in Christ.

I am so encouraged when I read John 11 and hear of all the different emotions that Jesus experienced; hope, trust, gladness, confidence, being deeply moved in spirit and troubled, sorrow causing weeping, being deeply moved again, thankfulness, and other emotions. He experienced great zeal when he flipped the tables of the moneychangers in the temple. He was moved with compassion many times. In Gethsemane Jesus said, "My soul is overwhelmed with sorrow to the point of death." He even fell to the ground praying, "My Father, if it is possible, may this cup be taken from me. Yet not as I will, but as you will" (Matthew 26:38-39 NIV). These stories and so many more observations of Christ in the gospels, give me permission to actually feel what is rising in my heart, rather than deny, ignore, stuff down, blame, regret, or apologize for having these emotions. I receive comfort realizing that it is a long journey to purity of heart, but that many have travelled before me, so I go on.

What I am also learning is that as Christ heals my mind of fears, unhealthy belief systems, incorrect thinking, etc., I then can engage more honestly with what I am really feeling and respond more purely and authentically in ways that give me true life, and give life to others as well. I am learning that as I become more aware of my present situation and any emotions that come to me I can respond from a place of more wholeness. I can progress and move forward as God gives me guidance and courage. I can not heal myself apart from the Spirit of the Living God who does His divine work within me. What a relief!

I have recognized that sometimes I am emotionally attached in unhealthy ways to things that I love deeply or to things that are important to me. In this state, if any buttons are loosely or tightly attached to me in unhealthy ways, I am far more likely to feel them should they get pushed. Jesus is so kind to continue to come to these places within me as I pray and detach and become freer from anything that has a hold on me or affects my life negatively.

Here are some good goals for our journey: to become aware of the movements of our heart, to learn to identify them, and to know how to interpret their significance and make necessary changes, and then do so. This is a three-step process: Awareness, Identification, and Healthy Action.

Here is a prayer exercise that may help you look at yourself and your emotions.

PRAYER EXERCISE ⁊**71**

BUTTON, BUTTON, WHO PUSHED MY BUTTON? ⌛

1 Sit comfortably in quietness, if possible, and become aware of God being with you. Listen to His voice of love and acceptance of you and His delight to be meeting with you.

2 Come to an awareness of a tender place in your heart that has recently been touched, or ask God to bring to your mind a reaction that you have a tendency to experience when something pushes one of your buttons.

3 Share the experience with God as you are listened to with kindness.

4 Be comforted in your pain and sorrow as God holds you.

5 Ask God why this experience hurt you and brought forth such strong emotions. Let God help you identify where this came from—whether it is a past experience that was never resolved or healed, or is it connected to something significant to your life, or is a justice issue, etc.

6 As you share what you are discovering with God receive loving assurance of God's presence with you, allow yourself to feel what is going on inside your heart and mind. Let the emotions rise and come before God. Let God feel with you, receive care for your heart, and any weight that you may be carrying that is connected to this situation.

7 Receive from God what you need in place of this desolation. Linger with the Spirit of God until you sense it is alright to come back to an awareness of your present place of sitting.

8 Move slowly and tenderly into your day, continuing to receive all that the Spirit of God has for you.

9 Be mindful of the next time this button gets pushed. Repeat this exercise to encounter God and allow Him to continue to heal the various parts of your heart.

10 Sooner or perhaps later, great joy will come when the button gets pushed again, and there is no longer any pain! Rejoice, be thankful, and share this encounter and process with someone else.

Whatever we may face, may we turn to Christ and join Julian of Norwich in saying, "I choose Jesus as my heaven."

"Why are you downcast, O my soul?
Why so disturbed within me?
Put your hope in God,
For I will yet praise him, my Savior and my God."
(Psalm 43:5 NIV)

Invited to Healing

O Spirit of God,

Set at rest the crowded, hurrying, anxious
Thoughts within our minds and hearts.
Let the peace and quiet of your presence
Take possession of us.
Help us to rest, to relax, to become open and receptive to you.

You know our inmost spirits,
The hidden unconscious life within us,
The forgotten memories of hurts and fears,
The frustrated desires,
The unresolved tensions and dilemmas.

Cleanse and sweeten the springs of our being,
That freedom, life and love may flow into both
Our conscious and hidden life.

Lord, we lie open before you,
Waiting for your peace,
Your healing
And your word.

George Appleton
Bishop of Jerusalem

Healing of Memories

"God has come to bind up the broken-hearted,
to proclaim freedom for the captives and release from darkness
for the prisoners,
to comfort all who mourn, and provide for those who grieve;
to bestow a crown of beauty instead of ashes,
the oil of joy instead of mourning,
and a garment of praise instead of a spirit of despair.
God will rebuild the ancient and ruined cities
and restore the places that have been devastated for generations.
As the soil makes the sprout come up
and a garden causes seeds to grow,
So God will make righteousness and praise spring up
before all nations."
(Based on Isaiah 61:1-4, 11 TNIV)

Our interior world, the places deep in our hearts and minds, can often be tight in bondage from incidents of the past. These may have been negative experiences, things that our family passed on to us knowingly, or unknowingly, or things we just picked up along our journey in life. When God's loving touch gives us inner healing we experience freedom from lies, release from fear, and forgiveness for sin; we learn truth, receive comfort, and God's Spirit moves wonderfully in our lives in many ways. This is "one of my favourite things"—watching God in action and being a part of deep healing in people's lives.

Some of the men and women that I have been deeply impacted by in this field are: Dr. Charles Ringma, Leanne Payne, Bradley Jersak, Trevor Walters, Karin Dart, Brian and Della Headley, Agnes Sandford, Mary Pytches, Mark Pearson, Gerald May, and Dennis, Sheila and Matthew Linn. These precious lives have brought much knowledge, understanding, training, trust, experience, and insights of the Spirit to the healing ministry of Jesus and I have been privileged to learn and participate in them. The different streams of the Christian faith that they flow from and their different approaches have come together to meet in a powerful river and precious pools of healing. I am most grateful to God for these people. Their books, writings, and experience far exceed mine and I have become wiser by learning from them.

I am also very thankful for my dear friend Jenn, who introduced me to Healing of Memories. Her kindness and tenacity have been huge gifts of life and training for me.

God, Jesus and the Holy Spirit are always present with us. They are with us in the past, in the present, and in the future. Our Father promises, "I will never leave you or forsake you" (Hebrews 13:5). This promise is given to us over and over. New mercies are ours every morning. When Jesus died, resurrected, and then physically left the earth, He sent the Holy Spirit to dwell as God within us and around us. He doesn't stop watching over us and being concerned about our state of being. Jesus is also a good lover as a Bridegroom to us, His Bride. Our Bridegroom's eyes are always toward us.

We can talk to Jesus about past, present and future things. Jesus wants to meet us in all the times of our lives. When we think about God being in our past or in our future it then becomes a 'present moment' for the time we are thinking of it. As we remember certain past experiences they often feel very real, very 'now.' In a way we are re-living them. How great God is to invite us to encounter the reality of being with us in our past by meeting us with our memories and providing truth, comfort, and God's loving presence that heals us.

The many practices of medicine, psychology, counselling, prayer, etc., as well as common sense, show us that unresolved conflicts of the past can adversely affect us today – so Jesus takes us to these conflicts to resolve and/or heal them. In our Christian development and spiritual journey it is important to know that sometimes the Lord brings us back to places in our development to receive what we missed and/or to leave some things behind that we mistakenly thought we'd need.

When certain things happened to us in the past (especially if they were traumatic or affected us deeply) we may have forgotten that God was with us, or perhaps we never knew that God was with us, or we may have been unable to connect with God at these times or places. A negative, debilitating memory can be held within us. It can be extremely hard to believe that our loving God could let those bad things happen to us. Our invitation at these times is to understand and believe that God will come to love, comfort, and rescue us from these terrible, worldly or evil traps. Otherwise we can become angry, resentful, or disillusioned with God and think that we don't matter.

This is a normal part of our spiritual formation. During this time on Earth, evil things are allowed to happen. Thankfully there is coming a time when it will end. This is not always easy to understand or accept, however, but as we trust the Holy One and get to know and trust who He really is, we are formed and transformed by this great Love. God does not always remove the challenges of life from us, or the consequences of our sin or other people's sin, but the promise stands for us to receive help through all of life.

Experiencing peace and freedom in these places of our heart and life is a process of love, care and healing with Christ, and with safe people. The Lord gives us journey mates to help us remember God is in the midst of life's joys and challenges and to help us turn and to wait on God in times of great pain and distress.

I have some nasty memories of some painful events that hurt me deeply. A part of my healing journey has been to look at them when they come to my mind and have Jesus care for me. I had been able to function for a while without dealing with many of these things, and I think this was God's grace and mercy to help me cope – keeping some things hidden or forgotten until I was able to look at them and deal with them in a safe place and with trusted people. Eventually it was better that these memories and feelings, with their resulting behaviours and attitudes, came to my mind to be taken care of rather than just managed or allowed to continue to affect me. The bleeding wounds or the poison inside of me needed attention – "heart sur-gery" might be a good word to use for this process.

The healing process is not always easy and is a little unsettling at times, but the good fruit that has been resulting in my life is what I have always longed for: peace, freedom, joy and health. Though these memories once came up from within us to torture us, there comes a time when they come up to have Jesus tenderly heal our pain, replace the lies, comfort our sorrows, and strengthen us so that we can become who we were created to be. We will recover what may have been lost, stolen, and broken.

We do not need to dig around in our heart and hope to find some-thing that needs healing since it is God's job to initiate all things in our lives and to let us know when something needs taking care of. We do not want to look at or think about painful things without the awareness of Jesus being with us. If something is unsettled or needs attention, I look at it with Jesus when I feel led to do so. It is impor-tant and necessary to know that if Jesus is inviting us to meet Him with an emotional or disturbing memory, or there is the potential for an emotional challenge, that is when I suggest we do inner healing prayer with trusted and skilled friends or trained prayer ministers.

Personal examples of God giving me inner healing range from relief from horrifying moments or deep unknown anxieties to tiny problems that didn't seem to impact me at the time – yet which had an affect upon me without me even realizing it; either that or the incident may have pushed a button connected to my deeper unmet needs or wounds. God longs to meet us and transform us in all the unresolved incidents and areas of our lives.

Childhood days for me included a group of little girls that lived around my neighbourhood. I remember one day two of them came out to play wearing skirts and said I couldn't join them unless I had a skirt on too. Wanting to be accepted and join the skirt party I rushed home and changed my clothing. I joyfully flew out the door only to be further rejected when they informed me that for some reason the skirt I had wasn't quite acceptable. I remember being very sad, confused, and devastated as hot tears rolled down my cheeks. I re-member my mother being kind and understanding, so I don't think my heart felt damaged by not being cared for; I had simply been mistreated by two seven-year-olds … no big deal.

Decades later, the same feelings arose when a similar set of cir-cumstances in my adult life touched my tender and sensitive heart. Feelings of shock, disappointment, sorrow, and rejection filled my senses. God used the present situation to lead me to deeper places in me where the memory of being rejected by those two girls served as a symbol of my often feeling like I try so hard to please but in-stead feeling unwanted or rejected. What a precious time I had as Jesus loved, healed and filled my wounded heart. Both the little girl part of my heart and the current adult were comforted, corrected, and healed – but most importantly, my relationship with God was strengthened as I experienced love in a real and profound way. This brought me deep peace and much freedom.

As a child, I saw things from one point of view, which was prob-ably a true view, but perhaps was not the whole picture or totally accurate. I very likely picked up lies, may have made inner vows (declarations that become debilitating), or likely assumed things in-correctly. However, what happened to me, real or perceived, could still be felt and could still affect my life today. Things done to me, my reactive sins, or things I have done to others – regardless of how righteous I felt they were – had turned unhealthy and harmful to me and others and needed attention. Forgiving myself for missing the mark has often been a key component to my inner freedom. Jesus loves to come bringing light, truth and freedom to clean and fill these memories even though we may have been unable or unwilling to receive this at that time.

Here is one of the ways inner healing is administered. These are some general steps that you can follow. However, keep in mind that Jesus leads the way, and we follow. Our approach is compassion and grace for our places of pain and wounding. Our focus is asking Jesus questions and letting Him answer the one seeking healing. We ask Jesus to direct our thoughts and memories and to come heal and restore us. Should deep emotional memories need to be cared for, I strongly encourage you to seek out the help of a trained prayer team if possible. A much more thorough and detailed way to administer this is found in *Can You Hear Me? By* Brad Jersak.

Below are the general steps we use to receive inner healing. The key is connecting and dialoguing with God. Find a quiet place. If possible, have a prayer partner or ministry team with you. Ask one of the intercessors to journal what Jesus may be saying and doing. Plan for a time of rest following this prayer exercise. Ministry procedures for Listening Prayer Sessions for Inner Healing can be found on page 301.

PRAYER EXERCISE ⌐72

HEALING OF MEMORIES   XXX

1 We always want to start our prayer times connecting with Jesus. Waiting upon Him and being centered in His love and presence is vital to healthy inner healing. We ask Jesus for what we need or what He may know we need. Usually we find a meeting place in which to engage with Him. A meeting place is a picture that comes to our mind of the reality of our connecting with Him in our heart. This "place" helps us focus if things get emotionally overwhelming or a bit swirly. (Meeting Place, pg.156.) Not all of us are as visual as others but you could have a keen sense of hearing or a strong knowing in your heart rather than a picture. We begin by putting our focus on God or Jesus, however that is expressed to us, and receive reassurance of God's presence, steadfast love, reminders of the promises or blessings that are for us, or something important that we may need to know before going on. Pausing at these times of intimacy with God is extremely important and delightful. It may be best to linger there at spots along the way to continue to receive what we are being given and to strengthen our relationship with God. If this is as far as we get with the listening prayer it is no small thing. We simply ask the Holy Spirit to continue the good work in us.

2 When there is a sense that it is time to move on, we ask Jesus to lead us. Pay attention to feelings that may surface along the way. They may be telling us much of what is going on inside. As we follow Jesus we will be shown, reminded, or brought to something deeper from our heart or mind that needs to be looked at together. It may be a memory from an event in our childhood, teen years, or something that happened last week. It could be a number of things that surface; words that were spoken over us, a belief system that we have been taught or picked up, a label or name we were given, lies that confuse us, or burdens for others that we've carried for a long time. These are some of what may be exposed.

3 As we continue to meet with Jesus we will follow and look to what is being made known to us about ourselves, others or about the issue. We will be attentive to Jesus being with us at the present moment, seeing also where He was with us in each situation that comes to our mind, and we will notice how Jesus sees us and feels toward us. Jesus will make known who He wants to be for us there, bring us truth, healing, direction, forgiveness, or whatever we need. If nothing more comes to mind then we enjoy our time with Jesus. Sometimes we just need to receive God's love and "simply" be together. Sometimes a memory is too painful to fully remember and we need not be re-traumatized. Jesus wants to heal these places in our lives and will often give us a snapshot of it, like a photograph in which we can talk to Him about and receive healing without having to fully re-live it. Sometimes we will need to re-visit this snapshot to receive deeper healing and greater understanding, but each time we do we are transformed in some way.

4 Receiving God's peace, truth, deliverance, freedom, comfort, forgiveness, cleansing, love, joy, kindness, etc… into the places that have been wounded is a most wonderful experience and is part of the transforming work of the Spirit in us.

Come, Holy Spirit, Come.

Questions for Jesus:

Where is a safe place to meet or connect with You in my heart? (The answer might be a symbolic picture, a sense of God's Spirit, or the present room. Our teams suggest having a Meeting Place. Where are You, Jesus? What are You doing? What do You want me to know or notice? What is the truth in this situation? How do You feel about this, Jesus? How do You see me? How do You feel about me? How do You see my enemies? What do You want to do with this situation? This person? What do you have for me instead of this? Help me receive what is from you.

Questions for you:

Can you let Jesus come close to help you? How does Jesus want to be with you? What might Jesus want you to know? What feelings are coming to the surface? What is this telling you? What does Jesus want to do to help you? Can Jesus take care of your enemies? What does He want to do for you or give you? What do you need from Him? Can you receive what He has for you? How does that feel? Is there anything Jesus wants you to do? (I.e. let go of something, forgive someone, forgive yourself, receive forgiveness, let go of a lie, break a vow, receive comfort, correction, direction – the gifts are endless.) Are you able to do what Jesus is asking? If not, ask for help. What does Jesus want you to have to replace the lie, the pain, the ungodly belief system, or the burden? Can you receive God's peace, the messages of Jesus' heart, the freedom or wholeness that is for you?

Thou art
Painfully parting
The fibres of my being
In order
To penetrate
To the very marrow of my substance
And bear me away within Yourself.

Based on a prayer by Teilhard de Chardin, S.J. (1881-1955)

Healing for Future Events
Why Wait?

By Eden Jersak

"For I know the thoughts that I think toward you,
saith the LORD,
thoughts of peace, and not of evil, to give you an expected end."
(Jeremiah 29:11 KJV)

Brad and I had been invited to bring our books and talk about them for a Christian TV show. As soon as I heard about the offer I began to worry about how on earth I was going to do this. And of course, we were given a few months notice, so I had plenty of time to stew about it.

During this waiting time, I joined in a Listening Prayer Seminar that was being held locally. They had decided they would lead everyone through healing of a memory.

We were given a few minutes to consider which memory we would like to have healed, and during this time I realized two things; one, I didn't seem to have a memory that I needed healing for at the moment, and two, I remembered this upcoming TV program and thought to myself, "I'll probably need healing for that when it's all said and done!"

At that point I wrestled with God for a short time, asking if it would be alright for me to look ahead to this "traumatic experience" in a months time. I felt a peace about doing this, and so without telling anyone else what was happening, I entered into what I was imagining that day to be like.

I entered into the studio and saw all the lights, the set, the cameras, and most especially where I would be sitting. I immediately asked Jesus where he would be, and then I saw the "Redemption

Swing" right there on the set. I would do the interview right there from the redemption swing, a safe place that Jesus has provided for me in my heart. Jesus sat down beside me on the swing, and I started to share my fears and concerns with him. And as I raised each one, he spoke to me and calmed my heart.

My biggest fear was just freezing there on camera, not having any clever or insightful response to a question, but Jesus promised to stay by my side, and to whisper in my ear when I wasn't sure how to proceed. After the workshop, I was at peace about the interview, and barely spent any time thinking or worrying about what was to come.

On the day we taped the shows, I saw just how amazing this exercise had been! We were slated for three interviews. Brad would take the first, we would do the second one together, and I would take the last one on my own. To add to the potential stress, once the cameras got rolling, they just kept rolling, there was no cutting and pasting on this show. The pressure was really on!

I watched Brad enter in and was thrilled to see how well he did. I was glad that we got to share the second interview together, and then it was my turn to be on my own. Just before the taping began, Brad came to me and said, "You don't have to do this alone, I can sit in with you if you like?" I just smiled and said I was fine to go alone.

Throughout the interview I felt myself there in the redemption swing, and I could feel Jesus there beside me, and I could hear him whispering helpful thoughts and comments in my ear. This moment that might have been extremely stressful, this experience that could have traumatized me, had now become a wonderful memory of Jesus being with me.

PRAYER EXERCISE '73

HEALING OF FUTURE EVENTS – WHY WAIT? ⧖

1 Breathe slowly and deeply a few times to become still in God's presence.

2 Ask God to bring to your mind any upcoming event or challenging life circumstance.

3 As you think about this situation allow yourself to experience the feelings you may have as you invite God to meet you there.

4 Pray, "God, what do you want to show me here? Where are you with me? What do I need to know? How do you see me? How do you want me to see you? How will you be with me? What can I do for you?" Interact with God as you feel led.

5 Notice your feelings and how your heart moves as God comes near you and your event. Let yourself be surrounded with God's loving presence and filled with the fruit of the Spirit.

6 You may want to journal what God is making known to you. This may be helpful in the days leading up to the event. God may continue to speak to you about this situation and your journaling may unfold more of what you are to know.

Draw near to God and He will draw near to you."
(James 4:8 NKJV)

GROUP PRAYER EXERCISE

1 Invite the participants to be mindful of the next day to come, or a typical day in their life. Ask them to write in detail each part of their day starting from the very beginning; even the mundane tasks, such as brushing teeth.

2 Invite the participants to ask God to highlight one particular piece or event of that day.

3 Take them through the above prayer encounter (steps 3 – 6), allowing time to connect their hearts and minds with God and what is being given to them.

A STORY FROM THE JOURNEY...

Bev's graduation party was to be held at my home. Our house lends itself well to holding large gatherings and I was delighted to have Bev's celebration fill our home. I was feeling a bit overwhelmed, however, with much to do over the coming few days; that's when God led me to an encounter I will never forget. Eden and I were at a retreat inviting people to ask Jesus to show each one of us a coming event where there was a possibility for some anxiety or a lack of peace within us. As we looked to the Lord, what came to my mind was the setting up for this gathering that was to happen that week. I saw myself anxiously preparing the main meeting room, pushing the furniture into place far too quickly, and knocking over a vase that smashed on the floor, giving me further work to do. I could feel the exasperation already and it hadn't even happened yet.

When we invited Jesus to meet us in the situation that He brought to our minds, we then asked Him to show us how He would like to be there for us. Quite quickly I sensed that, of course, He wanted to be with me and help me do what I needed to do. The image unfolded as I sensed He would even help me move the furniture, allowing me to move slowly and enjoy the setting up. He was joyful and I was so glad for His presence. I even felt great relief that if a vase did fall and break, I could clean it up peacefully and not get stressed out. What a relief!

I can clearly remember how I enjoyed setting up that afternoon as I was mindful of God being with me. A soft smile came across my face and my work seemed quite light. I was mindful of His hand upon me keeping me in peace, and his heart of love bringing me a fullness of joy that I'm sure I would not have experienced had we not stopped to do this exercise. Once again a prayer exercise turned into a prayer encounter.

A Story from the Journey...

Two memories come to mind of women we met in Wales, both of whom encountered God and His freedom when doing this exercise. As their faces filled with delight and their eyes were moved to tears we all sensed God touching them deeply.

One of the women who had travelled quite a distance to attend this women's retreat was to leave in a couple of hours. Having had such a beautiful time in worship and encountering God she was struggling to go back to her home town where her anxieties would return; she even dreaded the long trip back. Re-entry was always very difficult for her. Her husband did not share the same faith as her and life was often quite difficult.

As she looked to God, she saw that when she opened the door to go into her home, God would be there to greet her and warmly welcome her in with a hug, and fill her home with Divine presence and be with her. She told us that all anxiety about going home had lifted as she sat with God and let Him touch her in this area of her life.

One of the other women at the retreat had difficulty waking up every morning. For some reason it was not a pleasant time of day for her. As she offered this to God she was surprised to see a picture of Jesus, first thing in the morning, with a big smile popping out from behind the curtains of her bedroom window. This encounter caused her to break out into a big smile and filled her with delight. She could hardly wait for the next morning to come. I wonder what happened that morning ... and the next one ... and the next? I trust that God is "restoring her soul."

> The Holy One renews our strength
> and guides us along right paths.

Healing in Dreams and Nightmares

"We live within the shadow of the Almighty,
sheltered by the God who is above all gods.
This I declare, that he alone is my refuge, my place of safety;
He is my God, and I am trusting him.
For he rescues you from every trap....
Now you don't need to be afraid of the dark any more,
nor fear the dangers of the day;
nor dread the plagues of darkness, nor disasters in the morning.
For Jehovah is my refuge!"
(Psalm 91:1-3, 5, 9 TLB)

I used to panic when my kids woke up in the night with bad dreams. I felt so helpless, not knowing what to do other than to hold them. It was as if the fright of what they had seen or heard had power over us. The dream may have ended, but the unsettled thoughts and fears of the night often lingered and seemed to lay unanswered and in some way, to find a place to stay within my child's heart.

Knowing that Jesus never leaves nor forsakes us, I wondered where He was at times like this. I had experienced Jesus coming to my present dilemmas and healing my unwanted memories of the past so it wasn't a stretch to ask for help and what was going on with a dream or nightmare. I began to look to Jesus at these times for wisdom and freedom from the fear of the night terror or the confusion of an unsettled dream. I didn't realize the immensity of what we would experience as we came to these deep, tender places in us where dreams emerge. Some of our mental faculties are at a place of rest when we are asleep. When sleeping we are not fully aware of all our thoughts and emotions, therefore we are unable to manage, ignore or reject what might really be mattering to us. Hidden or sub-conscious thoughts or concerns can surface in our dream life.

Now I actually look forward to dealing with night terrors or dreams that have a strong emotional impact. Often when we are in a desperate state we are more ready to receive God as our refuge, and we can engage more easily with what is going on. At times I have needed trusted friends to help me when looking at a dream. Samuel's Mantle, a prophetic school in Abbotsford which I attended for two years, helped me develop my skills and learn to trust the Lord in this area.

Children are often very quick at receiving Jesus because their child-like faith can trust Him with a bad dream. He helps them with everything else, after all, and this is just another way to show His love and power to them. My daughter, Adriana, who is now fourteen, has a list of gifts that God gave her when she was younger that help her replace the lies and fears from bad dreams, with good things.

One night when Adriana was eight years old she woke up with great anxiety telling me that an enemy had just come to her and he had taken hold of her heel. She was noticeably upset and certainly wasn't able to "just go back to sleep."

I asked her if it was okay to ask Jesus to come and help us. I invite people to do this so that their will is engaged to receive from God if they are able. It is important to not use any force with people when inviting them to focus on or listen to Jesus. Sometimes they just don't seem able at that moment. Time and/or peace may be needed. Asking simple questions helps us engage with the Lord, so I asked Adri, "How would Jesus like to come to help you?" She knew that Jesus wanted to remove this enemy and take care of her. Jesus showed Himself to her in her night terror by taking the enemy away from her. It was a visual of what He wanted to do for her. She was visualizing the dream and now Jesus showed the truth of what He could do for her – and was, in fact, doing for her. As Jesus removed the enemy her fear and anxiety fell away. Peace filled her heart, mind and body as she sensed Jesus so near. She received His presence, the reassurance of His power over enemies, and she felt so loved. She saw in the dream that Jesus was giving her some gifts to comfort and strengthen her. She was free of the fear and gladly went back to sleep. She still remembers these encounters with Jesus and they give her courage and confidence in her daily living even today.

Adri helped teach this with me at a workshop (and at a local Bible College) this past year. Here is what she taught a room full of adults:

God is always there with us. Everywhere. In dreams it may seem like he isn't there. But if you look carefully, you can find him. It's like the book, "Where's Waldo?" You're going to have to search through all the ordinary day problems, or scenes, to find God. Even if you give up, he is always right beside you waiting to give you that gentle little push to keep you going. When you do find God, your hope cup fills up again, and you're ready to turn the page and keep going in your life, still searching, and knowing you'll find God.

She then shared Jeremiah 17:12 NCV: *"From the beginning our temple has been honoured as a glorious throne for God. Lord, you are the Hope of Israel. Those who leave you will be shamed. A person who quits following the Lord will be like a name written in the dust. That is because he has left the Lord. The Lord is the spring of living water."*

She went on to tell of a very significant dream that has strengthened and sustained our family for the past two years. In a dream she saw our family, Dwight and I, followed by our five children and son-in-law, being pulled through a dark room full of sticky black tar. In the morning I asked her where Jesus was in the situation. She saw Him at the front leading us out the rancid room. I asked where He was taking us. She sensed to a room of peace. She was not mentally aware of the horrible series of events that our family was passing through at the time, so her dream came to us as a great gift of hope. I am so thankful for her sensitivity to the Lord and how He shares His heart with her at times.

I occasionally get dreams that I sense are a warning or a form of guidance. Sometimes there is an issue in my life that I'm not sure how to handle or the situation is subtly affecting my subconscious.

Sometimes God makes known to me what to do when I'm reading Scripture, sometimes when I'm worshipping, and sometimes He uses a dream. A couple of years ago, I was considering going a certain direction in my life. It was quite foggy for me since I had so many things to think through in making this decision. I was so thankful for a dream that showed me some things about this situation. God used the dream to get my attention, to nudge me to sit and wait on His wisdom and direction. As some other things fell into place it became very clear and specific that I should move forward with my decision. I now had a peace about it.

One time I became very angry in a dream. I hadn't realized that I was holding in some pretty intense anger over something that had happened in my life. The feelings were very strong when I woke up. Again, as I sat with God, He showed me it would be best to surrender the anger, and I was strengthened to hand it to Him. In His kindness God helped me deal with it before it exploded in a place that could have hurt me and others.

A dream that is still so special to me began with Jesus coming to me on a white horse and then we rode off on many adventures. The dream continued over a few weeks where I would have a dream every once in a while that was connected to the first one. It was a series of encounters. I learned much of His love and His ways as we talked in and about these dreams during the days that followed.

Let us remember when we look at dreams and consider what God may be showing us or saying to us, that we are in good company with many men and women in the Bible and throughout history.

I was discussing this with my long-time friend, Herta, one morning while we were picking blackberries. Our chat reminded her of a dream that she had had about heaven. She said that she could not remember a lot of the details after she woke up, but she could remember that it was so very, very wonderful. It was a most wonderful place with so much peace. She felt it was a gift of reassurance of the amazing place that Heaven is. The gift kept giving as she felt the same peace from God as she had felt in the dream.

Positive dreams of God's presence can be as emotionally charged as the more disturbing ones. I simply love that God can use all things for good. "Do not be overcome by evil, but overcome evil with good" (Romans 12:21 NIV).

I recommend a book that explores dreams much more than I will in this exercise and it's titled, *If This Were a Dream, What Would it Mean?* It was written by Murray Dueck who leads Samuel's Mantle, the prophetic school I mentioned earlier. Murray and his wife, Kelly, teach and lead ministry teams in the lower mainland of British Columbia. They also have an online course that you may want to check out at <www.samuelsmantle.com>.

My friend, Rose, is a part of Samuel's Mantle and was preparing to help teach a class on Dream Interpretation. God surprised her with a very significant dream at that time and she realized that she was given a clear blueprint to use when teaching people and leading them through their dreams. She said I could share it with you, so here it is:

1. Write out the key points to the dream noting

   a.) the settings

   b.) the people

   c.) the objects

   d.) your feelings

   e.) the actions

2. Optional: She color-codes the key words according to the above categories for easy and thorough interpretation.

3. Beside each place, person, object, feeling and action in the dream note what that means or represents to you.

4. The message of the dream becomes clear as these components are looked at and understood in relation to the overall

dream and what may be going on in your life at the present time.

5. Rose encourages spending time with Jesus and asking Him where He is in the dream and what He wants you to show or bring you.

Use the above blueprint and the following questions and suggestions to bring clarity and value to what you are hearing and seeing in your dreams.

PRAYER EXERCISE 74
HEALING IN DREAMS AND NIGHTMARES   XX

After a dream that seems significant (these dreams usually have strong feelings, thoughts or wonderings attached to them) find some time to be with Jesus. Here are some good questions to ask Jesus and yourself:

1 Lord, which part of this dream do You want me to look at with You?

2 Can You show me that You are with me here, Lord?

3 What is happening and is there anything I need to know about this?

4 What do the different components of the dream symbolize?

5 What would You like to do here, Lord?

6 Does this mean something for my life right now?

7 Can I please hear Your words of love, life, truth, healing, freedom and peace?

Here are some additional things to do:

8 If you can, record what the Lord wants you to know.

9 Wait on the Lord until you feel He has finished showing you what He has for you in the dream.

10 Sometimes I ask a friend to pray with me while I do this. It helps me stay connected to the Lord and not go off with my emotions, fears, confusion, etc.

GROUP EXERCISE:

Helping someone with their dreams can be done in a group setting or breaking into small groups of 2–4. Insights coming from a mature group can be very helpful.

1 Listen to a person share their dream. If it is really long, ask them to only share the part that seems highlighted for now. It is helpful if someone can write out what is being said.

2 As led by the Spirit, the group can share thoughts or insights, being sensitive to the fact that this person is sharing a tender part of their heart.

3 Be sure to let the person that is sharing their dream connect with Jesus along each step or thought; also, help them to listen to God, not just to the group.

4 They will come to a place of peace, as it seems they have received what the Lord has for them for this time. Sometimes all the pieces of the dream may not be fully understood in one sitting. At times, the Lord wants to continue to bring the pieces together over the next few days through different ways.

5 Have a time of prayer for the person who shared the dream to bring closure to the group listening time, and invite the Spirit to continue His work in his or her heart through the day or night.

SUGGESTED READING:

If This Were a Dream What Would it Mean by Murray Dueck
Interpreting The Symbols and Types by Kevin J. Conner

Physical Healing Prayer

"Is any one of you sick?
Call the elders of the church to pray over you
and anoint you with oil in the name of the Lord.
And the prayer offered in faith will make you well;
If you have sinned, you will be forgiven."
(James 5:14-15 TNIV)

"He is the fire – we simply bring some wood, kindling, matches, and paper." You may want to ponder this a moment.

It was my turn to bring a prayer exercise to my classmates. Why did my name have to be at the top of the list? What do I bring? How might God want to meet with us?

One of my all time favourite books is *Prayer – Finding the Heart's True Home* by Richard Foster. I highly recommend this book if you want to gain insight and knowledge in the many areas of prayer. He teaches and explains about forty different types of prayer. I was working on an assignment using this book and as I turned through the pages I asked God if there was anything in this book that would be good to present to my class.

I kept looking over the many types of prayer and when my eyes saw Healing Prayer on page 203, I suddenly felt mysteriously drawn into it. I went with it as my eyes scanned the first few sentences. When I read, "God cares as much about the body as he does the soul," it dawned on me that he was talking about *Physical* Healing Prayer.

I had become very comfortable, even confident, in God's healing work in our soul, will, mind, and emotions ... but physical healing! That one was on the back burner of my life. "Difficult," "fearful," "beyond me," these were words I would use to describe this type of healing.

As I read on, Foster taught me that healing prayer "is part of the normal Christian life. It is not to be elevated above any other ministry in the community of faith, nor is it to be undervalued." I was hooked. I had to know more, I wanted to be a part of all of the ways God heals.

God cares as much about our bodies as our souls, and as much about our emotions as He does our spirits. This was a truth that shook me up. Really? Could it be? I had come to believe that my heart was far more precious to God than my body. After all, it would soon be "passing away" (2 Corinthians 4:16). Coming alive to me was the fact that my redemption from Jesus is total, involving all the aspects of my life – body, soul, will, mind, emotions, and spirit.

I was thrilled to see Foster encourage us to celebrate the growing army of women, men and children who are learning how to bring the healing power of Christ to others for the glory of God and the good of all concerned. I really liked his strong belief in healing by faith and by medicine, and that both should be pursued at the same time and with equal vigour, for both are gifts from God.

The question that pops into all our minds still remains: "Why, then, are some not healed?" The most straightforward answer to this perplexing question, says Foster, is " I don't know." "We desperately wish that every single person who sought healing prayer were instantaneously and totally healed, but it simply does not happen that way. Some are, and we thank God. Many others evidence substantial improvement, though not total healing. But others show no change whatsoever. Even people who have effective healing ministries are themselves sometimes crippled by some persistent physical ailment. Jesus is the only one of whom it can be said, "He cured all of them" (Matthew 12:15).

Foster says, "In one sense healing prayer is incredibly simple, like a child asking her father for help. In another sense it is incredibly complex involving the tangled interplay between the human and the divine, between the mind and the body, between the soul and the spirit, between the demonic and the angelic. There is much that we do not understand."

Diagnosis of the problem and knowing what to pray for is important. Physical healing may not be the real need; it may be for emotional healing. Here we see the value of practicing His presence and learning to listen to what the Father is saying and what Jesus is showing us to do.

Like anything, when praying for healing, knowing what to do is important and so is knowing what not to do. You should never say to those receiving prayer that it is their fault if they are not healed or that they lack faith, or that there must be sin in their life. It has been painful enough for them to seek us out. Remember that Jesus' disciples asked Him, "Rabbi, who sinned, this man or his parents, that he was born blind?" (John 9:1-3) I love Foster's response: "Jesus dismissed their speculations as irrelevant."

One thing I've seen that is of utmost importance and must be remembered is that what we are to do is show compassion. Always! Jesus looked at the leper and he was moved with compassion. The Hebrew and Aramaic roots of 'compassion' are 'inward parts,' what the old King James Version used to call 'bowels of mercy.' It comes from the same source as the word 'womb,' and so we could speak of the womblike heart of Jesus, which brought healing mercy to the leper. And yes, touching a leper means putting our own life in jeopardy. Is getting dirty part of it? I think so.

There is such value in the different streams of the Christian Church. When they come together we have a mighty river. We can see that the traditional, charismatic, orthodox, and evangelical steams of the Church have all made room for physical healing.

Some of the components that we all bring are love and compassion, faith in what God says and does, laying on of hands, anointing with oil (James 5:14), the gifts of the Spirit, and so much more. Through one another, the community of faith, God imparts to us what we desire or need, or what God in His infinite wisdom knows is best for us. Our simple obedience quickens our faith and gives

God the opportunity to impart healing. It sometimes is accompanied with a gentle flow of energy. We cannot make the flow of heavenly life happen, but we can be open to receive it.

Let me recommend a wonderful book on healing, *Christian Healing – A Practical and Comprehensive Guide* by Mark A. Pearson who says that God makes His healing power available to us through the prayers of Christians, through the spiritual gifts God has given the Church, through the rites, clergy and sacraments of the Church, and through skill and science – doctors and therapists.

I have been moving in the ministry of inner healing and have seen the healing of Jesus come to many. I have often prayed for people's bodies as I've felt led but, I have noticed my courage to "go there" is weak and my faith needs enlarging and exercising to move there more confidently and wisely. I seem to have more faith for God to heal my friend's camera than her headache, although she has had headaches leave after we have prayed.

This exercise is not meant to be a step by step guide to physical healing. Not at all. Rather, it is a path that we follow Jesus on as He leads us to care for another.

PRAYER EXERCISE 75

PHYSICAL HEALING PRAYER XXX

1 **First**, we **listen**. This is the step of **discernment**.

We listen to people, and we listen to God. We ask Him to show us the key to the problem. Ask the Lord to show what He wants to do and where in the person's body. Experience or ask for His compassion.

2 **Second**, we **ask**. This is the step of **faith**.

We invite God's healing to come. We speak a definite, straight-forward declaration of what we sense that the Lord wants to happen. Move and pray with Him as He leads into healing. (We can visualize Jesus coming into the wound, pain or body part and doing what He wants to do there.) This is a good time for laying on of hands and anointing with oil.

3 **Third**, we **believe**. This is the step of **assurance**.

We believe with the whole person: our body, mind, and our spirit. We echo the father of the demonized child in Scripture who cried out, "I believe; help my unbelief!" (Mark 9:24) Regardless of whether we feel strong or weak, we remember that our assurance is not based upon our ability to conjure up some special feeling. Rather it is built upon a confident assurance in the faithfulness of God and His steadfast love.

4 **Fourth**, we give **thanks**. This is the step of **gratitude**.

With the eyes of faith look ahead a bit – a few weeks or months or years – and give thanks for what can be, what the Lord seems to want, what will be by the mercy of God.

Perhaps we can join Foster in saying, "My Lord and my God, I have a thousand arguments against Healing Prayer. You are the one argument for it … You win. Help me to be a conduit through which your healing love can flow to others. For Jesus' sake. Amen."

GROUP EXERCISE:

Break into small groups to pray for someone requesting healing. Here is a shortened version of what is above to take into each group to help lead the prayer time.

1 **Listen** to the person & **Listen** to God:

(What are the keys to the problem?) (What does God want to do?) (How is God inviting you to pray?)

2 Ask in faith: Invite God's healing and declare what we believe God wants.

Move with the compassion of Jesus as He shows and leads you into healing prayer.

3 Believe with confident assurance in the faithfulness of God and God's steadfast love.

4 Give thanks: Look ahead to what God may make known to you, see with the eyes of faith to what will be by the mercy of God.

I can give a healing report from our class time with this exercise. We met in our small group and listened for my long-time friend, Diane. She had been having sharp pains in her shoulder for a few weeks. In normal living she didn't notice it, but when she was in the car with her grandchildren she would sometimes put her arm backwards to give them something, or to try to help them, and then it would hurt.

She felt led to ask for prayer for physical healing. Diane sensed quite quickly that God was making it known to her that it was connected to an unhealed emotional wound that had been caused by a series of hurtful events. When she looked back at what had happened to her, she wondered many things, and her heart ached.

We anointed her with oil and laid our hands on her shoulder, which we realized symbolized the pain she had when she looked back. We prayed for a few things as they were revealed. We prayed for her shoulder and for the difficulty she had when looking back. This also led for us to pray for the root wounds and for Jesus to touch the places deep inside her heart where she had been wounded. She was so thankful to be loved, prayed for, AND when I checked in with her a few days later her arm was much better. When she moved it backward to help her grandchildren in the car once in a while, she felt no pain. The Lord used her body pain to lead her to an emotional pain that needed attention. Here we are reminded again that we are whole persons, body, soul, mind, and spirit. And each part of us affects the other.

Our bodies will often hold the pain from negative things that have happened to us. When we pray for inner healing with an individual we will often be led to pray for the place in their body that has held this pain and either they will know where it is or the Lord will make it known to them. These are no small healings, even if we do not see everything that is going on inside a person. Thankfully, we will have ten thousand years after ten thousand years in heaven to hear of all the marvellous things that the Lord has done. It will be time to celebrate for sure!

A STORY FROM THE JOURNEY...

At a women's retreat in Alaska with my good friend, Sylvia, and team, we sensed to ask for physical healing for a woman. She was healed right before our eyes. She had an excruciating backache and could barely stay in the room. We all listened to God and prayed as we sensed God lead us. Many hands were laid on her and oil was applied. This time in prayer, although it was for physical healing, gave room for many interesting words of knowledge, scripture and insights. As we prayed and spoke out what the Lord was making known to us, her pain level went from a 10 to a 0 and she came on a 3 ½ km hike over fairly tough Alaskan terrain that same afternoon. Another miraculous sign of her healing was that she was able to join us as we traveled over a river via a pulley, rope and muscle, which she had been too fearful to do months earlier. It was a wonderful gift to her and our team as we were preparing to go to China the following October.

A STORY FROM THE JOURNEY...

We got to take this healing gift with us to China months later. While praying for inner healing with a lady who was sent to do mission work in China the Lord took her to some fearful memories and some deep abandonment wounds. After spending about an hour with her she left filled with peace as God's loving presence had touched her so profoundly. She came running up to me a couple of hours later proclaiming that God had healed her ankle during our prayer session. Her ankle had been troubling her every day since she had been emotionally and physically wounded, but she could no longer feel any pain in it. I can hardly wait to see her again, if only in Heaven, to hear the rest of the tales of God's love for her.

Remember the saying I quoted at the beginning of this lesson? "He is the fire – we simply bring some wood, kindling, matches, and paper." To me the fire is God and the components invite the Fire. Perhaps the wood is the humility and the victory of the Cross, the kindling is the faithfulness of God to us in the past, the matches are our coming together in Our Most High God's name, and the paper is the words of God given to us for healing. May it be so. Lord, have mercy.

Healing for Wish-dreams
Embracing Reality

"Finally, brothers and sisters, whatever is true,
whatever is noble, whatever is right,
whatever is pure, whatever is lovely, whatever is admirable
if anything is excellent or praiseworthy
think about such things.
Whatever you have learned or received or heard from me,
or seen in me put it into practice.
And the God of peace will be with you."
(Philippians 4:8, 9 TNIV)

"And the God of peace will be with you." What if this is true? Well, it is.

As for the phrase, "think about such things," I like how the New American Standard Bible translates it, saying, "dwell on these things." To dwell reminds me of being in a home. We are invited to make these attributes our home and have them be at home in us. Finally, "put it into practice" is a vital part of our Christian walk as it relates to wish-dreams. You will see why as we go along.

Some time ago, I needed to learn some extremely important life skills. Some of my character weaknesses were getting the best of me. My life seemed to have far too much disappointment, worry, misunderstanding and loneliness. Desolation was an apt word to describe my state. My times of consolation were very sweet, but I sensed a need to know how to live more and more from a place of peace, especially when challenges or difficulties came.

Do you ever long to be part of a community where everyone lives in the utmost harmony, where you all agree, conflict is non-existent, love and unity are flowing, and peace reigns over all?

I long for God's kingdom to come, for His will to be done on earth as it is in heaven, where Jesus is Lord and we all get along. This is a good longing, right? The only problem is that I want it now, and all the time. I want to have all people healed and reconciled now. Even though I am fully redeemed because of Christ, at times I am not very satisfied to live in the hope of our "eventual redemption" when all will be made right. There are other things that I yearn for as well, some perhaps not quite so noble. Perhaps you have some deep longings or prayer requests that you would like to have, or ways you really want to live and it would be nice if they could be a reality right now!

Dietrich Bonhoeffer addresses this issue in his book, *Life Together*. He calls us to be careful that what we long for isn't actually a "wish-dream." Wish-dreams are desires or longings for good things, often based on a God-given dream or promise of what He wants for us, but we may have developed an assumed or set idea in our minds of how these are to look, to be, or to play out in life. Wish-dreams can stem from a Biblical view, a prophetic word or picture given to us, or a misdirected teaching or understanding. They may have become an agenda or a goal which we now feel a personal responsibility to produce, and can be very subtle and hard to detect. These "supposed to be" realities can go unchecked in our minds for a long time. We can justify or believe that all of what we have construed the wish-dream to be is true and from God. How we may have imagined it to be can be very debilitating and destructive in our lives and relationships. In fact, we could likely be destroying the very thing we long for. What we have already been given and presently have, may in time blossom into what we long for.

The reality is that what we desire usually doesn't happen fully or look exactly how we imagined it to be. We try so hard to fix or change what we have so that it will match our preconceived picture. Wish-dreams need to be surrendered to the Lord. As we relinquish our agenda and move in thankfulness for the community, home, family, job, etc. that we have been given. Our present reality is more apt to be and/or mature into our original longing in a pure and holy form. We are unable to embrace that which God has already given us while holding onto unrealistic ideals.

As we let go of the unrealistic wish-dream it makes room for us to pursue what God originally intended for us to have with love, grace and patience. We receive fresh energy to move forward with new insights, realistic strategies, and revived prayer, for what we may now see much more clearly. We can engage with what we have and pursue what we consider God is *truly* asking us to believe is from His heart for us.

As I wrestled with my desires for what I thought was good, pure, lovely, and even Scriptural, it became clear to me that even though I wanted good, even godly things, they would most likely not look the way my mind had envisioned them. A more accurate reality was that I was being invited to have what I *really* wanted. My holy longings had been given by God to bless me, but I had to let Him grow and cultivate them rather than me trying to make them happen my way.

I had set up very lovely wish-dreams in many of my relationships with my church community, with my vocation, and in my family. Perhaps we all have in some way. I had a picture or a belief system concerning what a good Christian family should be. It had formed over time from my personal situations, from my inner longings, from some teaching I had received, and from seeing what other "model" families had or how they functioned.

When my family was functioning in these ways I was very happy, fulfilled, and hoping we had finally "arrived." When conflicts, confusion or chaos would show us we didn't measure up to this ideal family, I would become very discouraged, despairing, resentful, and confused. I wanted a good family based on the Bible, yet why did I seem so far from having this at times?

My wish-dream had to go! As I let it go with sorrow and grieving, a new reality of what I had already been given seemed to come into a more clear view. I embraced what I had and loved my family, just as they were. I let go of my desire to control how things should look or be. Jesus showed me how I was destroying my relationships with my children because they weren't cooperating with my wish-dream. As I continue to love what I've been given it is now the wonderful family I have desired and it is evolving into the likeness of Christ as we grow together. Everything is not perfect, by any means, but we are happy and working out the conflicts as they come along. My friend, Sue, says "Living in Reality and not in wish-dreams allows God to build character, perseverance and non-judgemental ways into us." I have found this true.

One wonderful thing God taught me was to stay present to those that were in conflict with me. I was not to exit from the situation, nor was I to send them away from me. Rather, if I was able, I was to take a step closer and pursue a loving connection and reconciliation.

Let me share this scripture that is my reality as my wish-dreams fall away:

> *"The glory of this present house will be greater*
> *than the glory of the former house,'*
> *says the Lord Almighty.*
> *'And in this place I will grant peace,'*
> *declares the Lord Almighty"*
> (Haggai 2:9 NIV).

PRAYER EXERCISE 76

HEALING FOR WISH-DREAMS   XX

You may want to interact with the Lord in an established Meeting Place in your heart. (See Meeting Places, pg.156)

1 Come to a place of quiet and stillness. Be attentive to God's presence with you. Do you discern that you may have a wish-dream set up in your life? Be open to God showing and helping you if you do. If so, what does it look like?

2 What is the bad fruit coming from this fantasy?

3 What are the good parts that you can keep?

4 Ask God to help you let go of the wish-dream you have constructed. You may feel led to ask for forgiveness for holding onto this and contributing to any unhealthy ways. If so, receive the forgiveness of God to the depths of your soul.

5 Be open to embrace the reality you live, even if it is less than you desire.

6 Receive the comfort and compassion of God for any losses and sorrows you face.

7 When you are able or ready, ask the God what steps you are to take to live well in the actual place you are now in.

8 Embrace the actual, real situations in your life and ask God to guide and strengthen you with wisdom, strength and hope.

Following is a chart comparing some characteristics of consolation and desolation that may help you identify where you are in any given moment. It also shows you what you are invited to. I received this from SoulStream Ministries in Abbotsford, B.C.

CONSOLATION		DESOLATION
Inspiration & Holy Spirit led, life giving	vs.	Panic & Anxiety – "needing to", not life giving
A sense of being drawn, invited	vs.	A sense of being driven, pressured or stifled
Focus is turned outside & beyond self	vs.	Focus is turned in on ourselves
True freedom	vs.	Deeper bondage
A sense of being connected to God	vs.	Spiral down into our own negative feelings
Peace & joy that is not conditional Increase in faith, hope, & love	vs.	Confused, upset, lacking faith, hope, love
Deep appreciation	vs.	Contentious
Light-hearted, lifted	vs.	A shrinking and sinking heart
Bonded more closely with community Expanding to contain others	vs.	Separated from community
Generates new inspiration, ideas, energy	vs.	Drains us of energy
Restores balance and refreshes our way of seeing – from God's view	vs.	Takes over our consciousness and crowds our distant vision – we forget God

CONSOLATION		DESOLATION
Shows us where God is active & leading	vs.	We forget the times when we felt God was alive & helping us
Can include a sense of sorrow for sin, a sting of remorse, awareness of how feeble and compromised our responses to God's unwavering love can be	vs.	We feel guilty, blamed, hopeless, stuck Focus on self and how bad we feel
What is coming to us feels like water gently falling, saturating a sponge	vs.	What comes to us feels like splattering and clattering onto stone

When we are in consolation it is good to plan a strategy for how to conduct ourselves in the time of desolation. We need accurate knowledge of the patterns of our own specific consolation and desolation in order to do this well. (I.e. I feel guilty when I get angry and then I feel depressed. Therefore, when I feel angry I will meet with Jesus to discern what needs to happen; in so doing, I will be avoiding guilt and depression and moving into truth and healing.)

A spirit of humility is needed in the midst of consolation. Remember (for the sake of self and others) how dark it can be. Enjoy God's grace rather than self exaltation. Avoid being over-zealous. Practice gratefulness to God.

Have patience and trust in the Lord and work diligently against the desolation – not against yourself.

When upset or in turmoil (desolation) it is not a good time to make decisions. Avoid secretiveness – talk honestly and get desolation out in the open.

 Invited to Action

Your prayers will lead you to Action, but hear this:

"To work without love is slavery."

Mother Teresa

Listening Prayer Ministry
Healing Prayer Sessions

"The Spirit of the Sovereign Lord is upon me, because the Lord
has appointed me to bring good news to the poor. He has sent me
to comfort the brokenhearted and to announce that captives will
be released and prisoners will be freed."
(Isaiah 61:1, 2 NLT)

There seems to be a natural outflow from us when we receive the love and healing of Christ in our lives. The good fruit of the Spirit that grows in us nourishes and feeds us, those closely connected to us, and often flows out from our lives to others. After receiving healing prayer ministry and being blessed by God through it, some are called to serve in this ministry in more ongoing ways. I'd personally love to see a trained listening prayer minister in every family and care group, on each leadership team, and at every altar prayer time. It is a very powerful prayer instrument in the "tool belt" of our spiritual skills.

We have many trained prayer ministers (or prayer counsellors, as they are also called) at my home church, Fresh Wind Christian Fellowship. This is the ministry of inner healing, healing of memories, and listening prayer. I am especially thankful for two of our faithful pastors, Bill and Jamie Pegg, who led approximately 500 sessions last year! What a dedicated and anointed team they are. Altogether last year our teams offered well over a thousand sessions serving people from our church family, the people and communities that come to us for prayer, or wherever we may be invited. And that is in just one small piece of God's Kingdom! I say all of this to make an important point; it is no small thing when people are transformed in ways that are thorough, deep and lasting.

We also have intercessors who, when possible, pray from their homes for the prayer ministers during the prayer sessions. These are booked ahead of time and we encourage the off-site intercessors to share anything they saw or heard while praying – if they feel it is to be shared. This can be very helpful to the ministers and very encouraging to the one who received prayer. This is a wonderful ministry for people who would rather pray from home.

We have regular prayer ministry and teams available every Sunday, but if someone needs more than ten minutes of prayer, especially regarding an important area of their life, or if the prayer teams detect that there could be some root issues that need some attention, they will suggest the person call for a listening prayer session. They can then meet with a team of two ministers for usually one-two hours per session. We will discern together whether it is a one-time session, or if ongoing ministry would be advised. Here is what works for our group. Others do it differently, of course.

Requesting Prayer:

1. Someone calls the person who coordinates the teams for ministry and shares in brief why they want listening prayer ministry and if they have any preferences as to who they would like to pray for them.

2. Some of our team members then meet to pray and listen regarding who would be a good team to pray with this person.

3. The contact person for the ministry calls the prayer ministers and they call the person from there to set it up.

4. We try to arrange for off-site intercessors to be praying from their home for each session.

5. We meet for either a set number of prayer sessions or leave it open-ended. We strongly encourage people from other communities to bring a prayer partner with them, because it is good to have someone in their life remind them of what Jesus has said, and someone with whom they continue their spiritual journey.

SUGGESTED READING:

Can You Hear Me? – Brad Jersak, Freshwind Press
Set My People Free – Mary Pytches
Restoring the Christian Soul – Leanne Payne
Christian Healing – Mark Pearson
Developing Your Prophetic Gifting – Graham Cooke

Inner Healing Teams

"Instead of your shame you shall have a double portion,
Instead of dishonor you shall rejoice in your lot;
Therefore in your land you shall possess a double portion:
Yours shall be everlasting joy."
(Isaiah 61:7 RSV)

"I simply remember my favourite things." I can hear Julie Andrews sing it now. It's like a theme song for me when it comes to inner healing. When the dog bites, when the bee stings, when I'm feeling down... I simply remember one of my favourite things, which is meeting with Jesus and a healing team.

I have been a part of healing teams for almost a decade and could write an entire book on the many encounters men and women have had with Jesus in the depths of their souls. I've seen a lot of good fruit that came from such encounters and tasted much myself.

As leaders involved in inner healing, it is vitally important that we are open to the Spirit of God and that we have the compassion of Christ for the person we are ministering to.

When meeting as a team we always have a leader who leads the listening session and an intercessor who, unless asked, remains quiet and who writes down what Jesus is saying or giving to the person. We give the person receiving ministry the notes to take home following the session. We encourage a prayer partner to accompany the person receiving prayer, if possible or desired, who would also remain silent unless asked or until it is time to speak at the end. They will serve as a support in the session and an encouragement on the journey once the session is completed. Having friends to remind us of what God has said or done is invaluable. Friends sing back to us the songs we may have forgotten.

Listening Prayer for inner healing in a team setting is a three-way conversation between God, the person we are praying for, and our self. Usually we address our questions and communication with Jesus, however, sometimes people connect better when using a different name for God, such as Father, Friend, or the Good Shepherd. We ask Jesus the questions and help the person meet Jesus, stay connected to Him, listen for His words, and encounter His truth for themselves. We quietly allow space and time for Jesus and the person to interact. We also confirm His truth, character, and love along the way. A great resource for a much more detailed teaching on this is *Restoring the Christian Soul* by Leanne Payne.

When someone is in the midst of a memory it is not the time to share our own stories, to give advice, to ask questions of our own curiosity, or to judge that person in any way. We do best to listen to them, be with them, and encourage that they are on a good path with Jesus leading the way. We may get scriptures, words, pictures, etc. along the way. Usually it is best to keep these until the end of the prayer session and then share them as a confirmation of what they have experienced in their encounter. Sometimes we may be given something to teach or counsel them along the way, but almost always it should be kept and said at the end. Not everything we sense needs to be shared.

This is a wonderful way to connect hearts in a community. A picture of this ministry of our healing teams is of little paths taken to each others' hearts in the garden of our lives and communities. Once we have trodden a path to each other we are connected with love and care.

We have been given the privilege of learning and practicing with "The Listening Prayer Community" in Mission, B.C. We have also had the privilege of teaching others at workshops to help them learn this valuable tool. It is a key to healing and intimacy with God. My life has been enriched beyond words in giving and receiving the ministry of inner healing.

Come, Holy Spirit, come!

Prayer Team Ministers:

1. Sense a call from the Lord to this ministry.

2. Discuss your interest with the leader of the ministry.

3. Be receiving healing prayer for yourself.

4. Become an intercessor and scribe for a few different teams, if possible, to support the lead prayer minister and to learn from various people and experiences.

5. Ask a prayer partner (or people) in your community to be praying for you in general and in particular during the prayer sessions you are giving.

6. If possible, receive training from Listening Prayer Community, Mission, B.C. <www.listeningprayer.ca>.

7. Connect with prayer ministry team monthly for encouragement, ongoing training, and personal prayer.

Here is an Information Sheet we ask our team members to fill out to help us know them and their giftings and availability:

Name:

Address:

Phone/email/cell:

Family:

Job:

Personal Healing Journey:

Past Prayer Ministry Experience:

Your Passions:

Your Spiritual Gifts:

Your Strengths: Weaknesses:

What areas of prayer ministry do you enjoy? Lead or assist?

What prayer ministry do you sense Jesus is inviting you to at this time?

Pre-service prayer	From home intercession
Inner healing sessions	Sunday Service Prayer
Healing of memories	Communion Station Server/Prayer
Visiting the sick	Listening with dreams

How often are you available for ministry?

Weekly, bi-weekly, or monthly

What days of the week work for you?

What times? Morning Afternoon Evening

Would you like to receive more training?

If so, in what area?

What do you feel you offer to others in prayer ministry?

A True Story
Of God's Healing in Listening Prayer

By Fiona Calder

"So spacious is he, so roomy, that everything of God
finds its proper place in Him without crowding.
Not only that,
but all the broken and dislocated pieces of the universe
people and things, animals and atoms –
get properly fixed and fit together in vibrant harmonies,
all because of his death, his blood poured down from the Cross."
(Colossians 1:19, 20 MSG)

My friend Fiona, like myself and many others, has received significant, life-changing healing through listening prayer ministry for inner healing. I have been with Fi as she walked with Jesus on some of her healing journeys and it brings the words of an old hymn to mind: "How marvellous! How wonderful! And my song shall ever be: How marvellous! How wonderful! Is my Saviour's love for us!" (*My Saviour's Love* by Charles H. Gabriel.) It is with great joy that I invite you to her story and the prayer exercise that follows.

I (Fi) had always been fascinated by the encounters with God that men and women of the Old Testament had. They literally had conversations with Him. It was a frustration to me that, living in times *since* Christ's arrival, I had a relationship with God that was largely limited to head knowledge and my dogged determination to believe in Him. I knew that God had so much more for me, but I was somehow unable to tap into it. Over and over I felt the sadness of observing Jesus work His miracles in other people's lives, while He seemed to pass me by. I had been a believer since I was a small child, and a 'committed Christian' since my late teens. It was only in my forties that God gave me my own story and how our relationship began to spill from my head to my heart, from my longings to my experience.

In 2003 I immigrated to Canada from Britain with my husband and our two young sons. We joined a local church and I quickly discovered that they taught and practiced encounters with God as a lifestyle from which no one need be excluded.

This community of believers became the safe place God provided in order for me to dare to venture beyond the limitations of what I had known. The vehicle for the journey was a prayer form called 'Listening Prayer' through which I was permitted to trust that God really could speak with me by any means He chose, including all of my senses and even my imagination. At my request, a team of two prayer ministers were assigned to me and periodically they met and prayed with me using Listening Prayer. During those prayer times we would ask Jesus to lead us, and I would listen for whatever He wanted to tell me. The prayer ministers were there to support me and help me if I got stuck.

I am a particularly sensitive person, and during my growing up years there had been much to traumatize and wound me. As an adult I was painfully conscious that elements of my childhood thinking still clung to me and, at times, even controlled my responses. I remained immature in many aspects of my personality but, try as I might, there seemed to be nothing I could do about it. Over the years, with the assistance of a number of different counsellors, I had tried repentance, submitting my will, deliverance and continually feeding myself a hefty diet of Scripture, but there had been very little fruit.

Discovering that I really could hear from God myself opened up a whole new world for me. My new church taught me how to test what I was hearing in light of the Scriptures, and how to weigh it in the balance of the wisdom and listening of my mentors and believing friends. The more I practiced listening to the voice of my Shepherd, the more accurate my hearing seemed to become.

Using Listening Prayer, the Holy Spirit taught me not only how to tune into the voice of God, but also how to listen for the voices of my own heart. I was most surprised to find that I had been suppressing many of the messages my heart was trying to give me; I'd dismissed and rejected them because I believed them to be my 'flesh' (my self-pity, my fears, etc.) and unacceptable parts of me – or even the voice of a passing demon. But with the Holy Spirit's help, I came to realise that I needed to get to know not only Him, but also myself. As I cautiously took steps towards this, God brought images of children to my mind to accompany the voice or message I was hearing. These children were all parts of me, and I called them my Little Fi's. They were of various ages and it seemed that they were trapped in the distressing emotions, traumas and double-binds of my childhood.

During my Listening Prayer encounters, I began to watch how Jesus related to my Little Ones. I can't say I exactly 'saw' Jesus but I often had a strong sense of where He was, what He was thinking or saying, and what He was doing. He would invite me, in my imagination, to a 'safe place,' and there He would meet with me and one of my Little Ones. He would explain to me things I needed to know about her; the root of her pain, her deepest needs, her unhealthy beliefs, the keys for her healing, etc.

Jesus grew in my estimation through those years. I had never before seen such kindness, such patience, such tenderness. I could hardly believe the depths of His love for me, nor His tenacity and good humour. Watching Jesus and responding to His invitations taught me how to love Him and how to care for myself and others. Finally, I was able to start maturing.

Encountering God through Listening Prayer is beautiful because Jesus is the One in charge of the details and the order of the journey, although Jesus required that I work with Him in the process of mending my battered and disfigured heart. All I had to do was follow Him, like a little sheep trotting behind her Shepherd. My job was to listen to Him, to keep myself in a teachable attitude, and to say 'Yes' to what He asked me to do. His job was to lead me and to supply the divine energy which enabled transformation. Isn't it true that everything about Him effects change? – His words, His gaze, His touch, His presence. When we listen and allow Him to be close, He is the One who produces the good fruit in our lives. It's a miracle really, a mysterious harmony between God and His beloved kids, and the result is that something new can grow out of our ashes.

Perhaps you would permit me to share a brief encounter I had with the Living Christ back in 2004. This took place in a prayer ministry time. Previously, Jesus had built a special home in my heart where all my Little Fi's could live under His care and authority, and where He could help and heal them over the course of time. I had visualised this house as a big white mansion with many bedrooms and nurseries, playrooms and gardens for the children to enjoy. There was one particular room which we called the Kindness Room. This was like the living room of the house, and it had a large wood-burning fireplace, armchairs and couches, and vases of yellow flowers in the windows. This is where I could go (in my imagination) and visit with Him and any of my Little Fi's that He wanted to meet with.

On this day, I sat with Jesus on the sofa, and He reassured me (as was His custom every time we met) that He loved me and I need not be anxious since He had something good for me today. He waited until I felt safe and ready, after one of His wonderful hugs, and then He had a little toddler Fi come in and join us. She must have been about two or three years old and she clutched a teddy bear to her chest. She looked normal enough as she stood quietly in front of Jesus. I wondered what was going to happen.

Jesus didn't speak at first; he just looked at her. I could tell that He loved her and that just resting His eyes on her made His heart very soft. I think she knew this too but it also seemed that He was still a stranger to her. Perhaps He was waiting for her to calm, and to come to realise that He would do her no harm.

After a little while I sensed that her name was 'Hidden One', and that her personality was hidden in a secret place inside of her. Next, with the eye of my imagination, I 'saw' that this child had a prison in her chest; its walls were tall, grey and impenetrable. I even got to hear the name of her walls: 'self preservation.' And it was behind these walls that her personality was hiding.

With this knowledge I asked aloud, "What do You want to do Jesus?"

He responded, "I want to give you a key," but it was not to me that He spoke, it was to the little girl. Instantly I knew the name of the key. It was 'unconditional love.'

The prayer minister praying with me then asked, "Can a trade be made of Your unconditional love for this Little One's self-preservation?"

Jesus and I looked questioningly at the child, waiting for her response. This was going to be her choice, and she hesitated for what seemed like a long time. To make the exchange would take great courage on her part and would mean that she would no longer be able to keep the same strong defences of self-preservation. Finally, she handed Jesus her teddy bear, thus baring her heart to Him. Now I could see there was a secret door in the grey wall. Jesus put His key into its lock and turned it. It didn't seem to hurt her at all.

The prayer minister then asked, "Is there anything You want to show us behind that door, Jesus?"

I, the Big Fi, started to feel an awful dread at the thought of what ghastly sight might await us behind the door of this Little Fi's heart. I wondered what horrible darkness I'd have to share with my prayer ministers and I didn't want to look. But I knew that I was committed to this healing journey, and that no matter how hard it might be to face things along the way, I was determined to follow wherever Jesus led me. So, with a deep breath I agreed to look behind that door.

In just a moment my dread turned to surprise. Indeed, there was lots of stuff behind that door, so much that it was all backed up and starting to spill out – great big mounds of gold dust. It was tumbling out of the Little Fi's heart and collecting in piles all around her on the floor. She really liked it. She squatted down to run it through her fingers, drawing pictures in it and playing with it. And all the time it just kept on pouring out of her. I knew what the gold dust was too. It was all the love in my heart which I'd been too afraid to give for fear of rejection and because of all the bad names it might be called. This Little Fi held not only my fear of expressing love to others, but she also held my capacity to love. It had been stored up in there, backed up to overflowing.

I fell in love with this child. Who wouldn't? She was made to love, and she was a natural at it. I opened my arms to her, and she climbed up onto my lap and then into my heart. It was a sweet reunion. Embracing this part of myself, now healed by Jesus, and Little Fi being able to function as intended by her Creator, has enriched my adult life enormously. Such a simple little encounter with the Living Christ has opened up a world of loving relationship to me! I can walk through life now, with that gold dust still tumbling out of my heart, wherever I go, to whomever I meet. And it's all possible because of Jesus' unconditional love exchanged for my coping defence of self-preservation.

Jesus woos our broken hearts. He draws us into His kindness and as we grow secure in Him, He heals us. He invites us to exchange our unhealthy beliefs for His life-giving Truth, not by beating it out of us or by tearing it from our thoughts, but by helping us to be ready to let go and to move on to better things.

As the years have gone by, Listening Prayer has become an integral part of my waking and my sleeping. Jesus' loving companionship and conversation are with me moment by moment, even when I'm not thinking about Him. He continues to bring to my attention issues relating to my heart. Some He has settled with His healing and redemption, others are a work in progress. Bit by bit He is adjusting and rebuilding my foundations. Gradually He is changing my perspectives. Slowly I am growing up! It's a humbling experience to walk in step with Almighty God, but truly it's the best journey ever. And as one of my dearest friends often reminds me, no matter what life's circumstances or other people's choices are, walking with Jesus will enable me to grow healthier and more whole every single day.

Questions for Jesus

1. Jesus, how do You see my heart? If it were a place that You live and walk in, what would it look like?

2. Jesus, how can I care for my heart better?

3. Are there any immature parts of me that You'd like to teach me about?

4. What is Your message to my heart today?

Listening Prayer Ministry
at Church Services

"I pray that the eyes of your heart may be enlightened in order
that you may know the hope to which he has called you, the
riches of his glorious inheritance in his people, and his incompa-
rably great power for us who believe."
(Ephesians 1:18, 19 TNIV)

At Church Gatherings – such as at a Sunday morning service

The goal of this kind of prayer ministry (some call it altar ministry) is to bring hope and comfort to the person and the situation they are bringing up for prayer. We want to focus on what God is already showing them or bringing to their attention and to bless what He wants to do for them. Usually there is a limited amount of time to spend with each person, possibly 10 minutes; however, much can happen in this short time as the Spirit moves upon a heart open to receive. If a prayer minister discerns that the situation requires more prayer or a healing of a memory or root wound is needed then the prayer ministers may suggest they call to book a 1- or 2-hour prayer session with trained listening prayer ministers (see below). They are not to use this space or time of vulnerability to go digging into the issues in someone's heart and life.

To implement listening prayer in ten minutes it is recommended that the person be familiar with listening prayer, have an established meeting place (pg.156) or be open to Jesus speaking directly to them with the assistance of the prayer team. We prefer to use listening prayer if at all possible because then the person will hear from God themselves rather than through us. Since we value each person hearing God and always want to encourage an intimate relationship with Him, we try this method first. If it seems best not to introduce this idea or to take time for it on a Sunday morning, then we will use a simple format of the burden-bearing questions (pg.202) so they can connect with God in this way; or we will pray what we are feeling led to pray for them, with their consent.

Words can often take away from what Jesus is saying or doing so use words sparingly. Become comfortable with silence as it is often in these moments where God is heard or known. Recognize that God's healing power shows us something about who God is. This ministry is one of the ways that we get the help from God we really need. God wants to make His people whole. We need the direct intervention of God for healing. We encourage the gift of medical care and the gift of prayer as God leads each person. Here are the steps we aim to use when doing listening prayer at church:

PRAYER EXERCISE 77

LISTENING PRAYER AT CHURCH (ALTAR PRAYER) 𝕏

1 Listen to the person as they share why they've come for prayer. What does God seem to be highlighting to them and what is He already doing? Ask a few simple questions.

2 Listen to God to hear what He may be saying or making known to you.

3 Identify the issue or the burden they may be carrying and perhaps where they may be carrying it on their body as well.

4 Invite them to respond to Jesus' invitation to come.

5 Encourage them to give the burden to Jesus, or to let Jesus take it from them. Wait with them until they feel it lift or ask Jesus to help them let it go. This will be a moment of surrender and God's transforming power. We do not push them here as there may be very good reasons why they are unable to relinquish it that need to be explored further for deeper and longer-lasting healing. Treat any blocks they may have to meeting God like this as well.

6 Ask the Lord what He would like to give them to replace this burden. Invite the person to receive the gift, promise, blessing, etc. that God has for them.

7 If there seems to be a block then we invite God to hold them and the burden and encourage them to continue to look to the Lord, trust in Him; we may also book a prayer session with a team for another time when it can be cared for more fully. Sense if the person has come to a place of peace, and pray a blessing on what God did for them. Before the person leaves ask them if they are okay and if they have a sense of God being with them and caring for them.

Actual Questions You Can Use at Altar Prayer Time:

1 What is God doing in your heart? (What is the reason you are asking for prayer)

2 Would it be okay if we brought that to Jesus?

3 Would you like to meet Jesus at the Cross or another Meeting Place? (If it seems hard for them to connect, then it is okay to be directive and lead them to an image or an inner knowing of Jesus at the Cross or to a Psalm where Jesus will minister to them.)

4 Do you see or sense Jesus? As you feel led by God ask what they are feeling, anything is coming to mind, etc. to keep in touch with them, Jesus and the healing journey.

5 If yes, we can now direct the questions to Jesus; is there anything You want to say to this person or situation? What do You want for them? Bless what Jesus wants to do.

6 Pray a simple prayer of blessing for them. Short prophetic words or pictures that may have come to you can be offered, although it's good to ask if it is okay for you to share them first. Allow for times of silence to listen or connect with God.

7 Invite them to stay in God's presence as they move to the worship service or a quiet place where interacting with God can continue. Dismiss yourself, but encourage the continuation of the blessing or ministry of Jesus.

Physical Healing: See page 283

The Prayer Tent

Prayer is a very important component of community and connecting with the Lord and is always to have front and centre importance when we gather. We do not use the front and centre stage for this ministry, however; we have a "prayer tent." It is a special place set apart for those who want a prayer team to listen with them and to pray for them. We have the prayer tent open and available for the entire time we gather. Some come before entering the service, others feel led to come during the worship, and others come for prayer before they leave.

My friends, Lyle and Catherine, were given the vision for this and implemented it at Fresh Wind. They listened on how God wanted this tent to look and they added symbols and colors to represent various components of God's love and faithfulness to His people. We have had profound encounters with God through this ministry. Thanks, Lyle and Catherine for your insight and overseeing this holy place and the teams that meet there! Here is what they share:

Why we have the Prayer Tent: Adapted from Exodus 33:7-18; 40:34 (paraphrased)

> Moses used to take a tent and set it up. He called it the "Meeting Tent" and anyone who wanted to ask the Lord about something would go into the Meeting Tent. When Moses went into the Tent, the Pillar of Cloud would always come down and stay at the entrance of the Tent while the Lord spoke with him. The Lord spoke to Moses face to face as a man would speak with his friend.

Moses said to the Lord, "You have said to me, "I know you very well. Show me Your plans so that I may know You."

The Lord answered, "I will do what you ask, because I know you very well and I am pleased with you. I myself will go with you and I will give you victory. Then Moses said, " Now, please show me Your glory."

Then the Cloud covered the Tent and the Glory of the Lord, filled the Meeting Tent.

The Prayer Tent is a physical manifestation of the meeting place (pg.156). It is a place where people come to meet with Jesus and receive comfort, love, and encouragement through the ministry of Listening Prayer. It is a place that gives a sense of privacy and safety for those receiving prayer. It is a place where the heart is met and change happens.

Listening Questions for your church or ministry:

1 Jesus, how do You see our present prayer ministry?

2 Is there anything You want us to let go of? Hold on to? Be open to receive?

3 Can You give us a picture or strategy of Your heart for this area of our church?

Listening in Community

"Where two or three come together in my name,
there am I with them."
(Matthew 18:20 NIV)

By Eden Jersak

Eden Jersak loves to spend time and energy in her home and garden and with her family. Now that their three sons are growing and starting to leave home, she has more space in her schedule and is often called to lead, teach, and care for others. She and Brad planted Fresh Wind Christian Fellowship in 1998. Their call and obedience have been used in what God has created in this unique church family where the disabled, the poor, and the wounded come for refreshing, love, and healing. Eden is now the team leader as Brad has been called to further his education, and continues to write, travel and speak itinerantly.

Here Eden will share how listening to God is so valuable in community.

Eden: We have been created to live in community, and it's important to know how to listen to God in that setting.

We began doing this early in our little church's history. Fresh Wind is a small church that doesn't really make it onto any maps, but we have something very sweet that has been poured into our foundation, and has helped to set solidly who we are as a community. From the start we have been firm on the fact that Jesus is our pastor, and it is Him that we follow, and it is Him that we listen to. And this is how we keep that true.

Initially, we called a small group of people who would listen as a team, "The Posse," and in spite of the name, this became a very vibrant facet of our church. We would call a meeting and have a question we would pose to the group that we wanted each of them to listen to God on. These questions usually stemmed from a situation or concern that the church was facing and that we wanted to have God's thoughts on.

The questions were never asked ahead of time, or given out before the meeting to allow people to prepare. We weren't asking folks to come with their guns loaded and ready to shoot. What we wanted to do was create space within community where we could corporately listen to Jesus and share what each of us heard. The results were dynamic and amazing at times.

I remember one particular meeting. It was a larger group that had met (16+) and we were asking about finances. We were a small church with no outside financial covering and we wanted to have a little breathing space in the budget. We had heard about a particular opportunity to qualify for some funding, but we weren't sure about it. We did actually spend time chatting about it before we went to listen, something that we normally tried to avoid. The majority of the folks were leaning toward accepting the funding, while a small cluster felt uncomfortable about it. We came to a point where we said it really was time to ask Jesus how He felt about this.

We stopped and quietly listened and wrote out what we were sensing Jesus saying. Some folks saw pictures, some heard words, and others just had a sense. But as we had each person share and as we went around the room an astonishing thing happened. We had ALL come to common ground; we had all heard the same thing. We were not to accept this funding, but heard that God wanted to be our provider. There was no lobbying required, no vote was taken, just some quiet moments were spent listening to our pastor.

Now in this instance, we were looking for a particular direction to take. But that isn't always the case when listening in community. Recently we met with a group of about 20 to ask the question, "Jesus, what is Your heart for worship at Fresh Wind?" The responses after listening were diverse, except that they called us to worship, to be open to new expressions of worship, and to be stepping into worship with purpose. It was so fun to watch everyone listen to the other's responses. As they listened they would recognize a thread from that thought in their own hearing, and would respond with, "That goes with what I heard!" What resulted from listening to Jesus on this question was that a thick layer of trust, community, and a desire to worship authentically was laid.

We have also fostered listening on a Sunday morning, and incorporate it right into the morning service. (If you have control issues about who uses the microphone and what they say, this may be a challenge for you.) A common part of many church services is the pastoral prayer. It's generally the time when the pastor prays about and through almost everything. But what if you took those few minutes and asked Jesus or the Father what was on His heart to pray for that morning? What if the entire congregation was invited to listen and ask Jesus what was breaking His heart this morning? Or what was the Father thrilled with today? And from there you invited those who wanted to share what they heard to come to the mike, and not only share it, but pray for that very thing? Now you have people who have made a connection with Jesus, have heard his heart, and have been moved by what moves Him, praying out of that passion! There is something very powerful that happens in that exchange.

PRAYER EXERCISE 78

LISTENING IN COMMUNITY

1 Start small and allow folks to get used to the idea of being silent in a group. This can be a stretch for some.

2 If you are leading a group, listen ahead of time for an appropriate question. You want it to be an open question (not answered by a yes or no answer), and something that isn't biased or directive.

3 Remind folks that we all "hear" differently. We tune into God's voice from our own channel and some may hear a still small voice, while others see a picture, and still others have a knowing or a sense of His presence. One way is not better than the next, and all are valuable and critical in getting the whole picture of what is in God's heart.

4 Ask everyone to write out what they "heard." This helps in finding the threads that run through the answers, and it's always good to document these times so that you can look back and draw on the things that were said in the past.

5 Provide a safe environment for this to happen in. You may want to have a bit of worship before you start, and prayer to invite God to speak.

6 Share together what God is making known. There may be a felt need to elaborate on what one saw or heard. But just a reminder that it stays the purest when we each just share what was actually seen, heard, and felt.

Listening Prayer Ministry
at Retreats, Conferences, and Workshops

"Jesus went through all the towns and villages,
teaching in their synagogues,
preaching the good news of the kingdom
and healing every disease and sickness.
When he saw the crowds, he had compassion on them, because
they were harassed and helpless, like sheep without a shepherd."
(Matthew 9: 35, 36 NIV)

A few ways to multiply healing and wholeness in community is through larger group connecting times; such as retreats, conferences and workshops. I once sat through an entire church growth video presentation that lasted two days. It was encouraging, but the one thing that still stands out in my mind and has had the most profound effect upon the communities and ministries that I have been a part of was this: Going on a few day retreat with a group of people will take your relationships from simply seeing each other on Sundays, to what you would grow with each other in 5 years.

I had experienced this myself at many women's retreats that our team; Diane, Deb, Bev, Jodi, and myself had hosted. In fact we could see the relational growth in the numbers of women that came each year. The first retreat we did had 24 women at it. We had to pay for most of them to come and many were quite disconnected from each other and from their hearts. In five years when we celebrated our fifth retreat we had 130 women with 24 small group leaders! As love, healing, and wholeness grew among and within us, so did the number of people wanting to join in. Our strength was in relationships full of love, prayer, and healing.

I've noticed that at retreat settings we have time to focus on the things in our life that really matter or take a break from them to notice other components of our hearts and lives. When we are in community and sharing a few days or meals together and experiencing what God is making known to us then trust and belonging has a place to grow deep and strong. Much healing comes from encountering God in worship and in prayer exercises, but much is also received from simply being loved and accepted by a community.

Prayer Exercises at Retreats:

Retreat settings have mainly been created to spend time on our relationship with God, receive needed emotional and mental restoration, and physical rest. It is good to offer some teaching throughout a retreat, but we try to keep it to a very small component as we would much rather people have time to connect with God and to hear what He is saying rather than us. We facilitate this through worship and offering prayer exercises such as is in this book with time to journal, ask questions, and hear from God. Retreats are very effective with leadership teams, women's or men's groups, prayer teams, etc. We have enjoyed offering a contemplative focus with groups around Easter, Hearing God, or other themes. Having space to be with God is the key component, and offering material or guidance if that is wanted.

It is very effective to offer mini-retreats, or day retreats, as well. These are much easier to administer, less costly, but highly effective for refreshing, learning, and team building.

Silent Retreats:

Silence is the love of God. When I heard this I fell even more deeply in love with silence. Truly it is the space for God's love, voice and touch. I enjoy silent retreats immensely, although it was a bit uncomfortable at first. Silence has opened up a gift of becoming more deeply rooted in God. My friend, Cathy Hardy, has enjoyed eight day retreats where much of her intimacy with God has been deepened and from where many of her inspired songs have emerged <www.cathyajhardy.com>. Cathy offers a 3-day Silent Retreat each November at the MARK Centre in Abbotsford <www.markcentre.org>.

My first 24 hour silent retreat was part of a course requirement. I was apprehensive but optimistic about this time in quiet with God. I asked Steve my instructor if there was anything I should focus on or have an awareness of during this time. He said, "For you, Lorie, just go, I suggest you take nothing, not even your Bible or journal." I was surprised by this comment, but intrigued at not having anything to distract me from God with lots of time together. I really was in for a surprise as I had never done this before and relied heavily upon my Bible and my journal for my times of connecting with God.

It began with a time of spiritual direction offered by one of the Grey Nuns at this retreat centre. This was helpful to help me speak and unload where I was at. We met again at the end to debrief and pray together.

I was so happy to have everything out of the way for the Lord, and to have Him and I fill those hours. Well, I slept for many of the hours as I had been so tired from the fullness of life and once I relaxed into these hours I longed for sleep. I had very special times of listening to God, even though I had no paper to write them down; I treasured them in my heart. I was hooked! I could hardly wait for my next silent retreat and whatever it would hold for me and God.

I participated in one of Cathy's 3-day retreats and thoroughly enjoyed the days and nights with God as I read, slept, worked through issues, worshipped, sketched, went for walks, ate in silence with the group, and had an hour of spiritual direction (pg.219) each day where I could finally talk. The sounds I heard, the things I had time to notice, and the taste of the meals was so powerful and satisfying. All senses are awakened to God being with us. I have also thoroughly enjoyed being a spiritual director at this event as hearts are so open and turned toward God during times such as this and I love to be a part of what He is doing in peoples lives.

I highly recommend silent retreats. Especially if they have a labyrinth – Oh my goodness!!! Labyrinth: a path made of stone or brick that spirals into a meandering but purposeful path to a centre and then back out again. We walk it as a metaphor for life's journey.

It is an ancient symbol that relates to wholeness. It is a meditation and prayer tool that you walk; it takes you on a journey with God—a journey into your deepest self and back out into the world with a broadened understanding of who you are, and God with you. Each time I have walked a labyrinth it had a slightly different invitation or focus, but has always been very meaningful and encouraging.

Prayer Ministry at Conferences:

Conferences are typically a different format than retreat settings, however usually along with the speakers, worship, and possible workshops there may be available a place or time of prayer ministry that is offered as well. It is such a gift to offer listening prayer after the services if there is a call to the altar or prayer room.

We highly recommend having some openings throughout the conference where people can sign up for a listening prayer session with a trained prayer team. Often these are the most meaningful times for people as they have a chance to share and listen to God with whatever is presenting itself in their life or is coming up as a result of the messages, etc.

We see great value in the person requesting prayer ministry bringing a friend or prayer partner with them for support. It is important, if possible, for each person to wear a name tag.

Remember that we do not confront, counsel, argue, or give advice; we simply help people come to Jesus. We do discern together and must be honest if asked questions. A good response to use when sensing that what someone is hearing does not seem to be from God could be something like, "I think you may need to listen on that part further. I'm not in full agreement with that." Be open to recommend people to see others for care such as a counsellor, pastor, or prayer counsellor. It is a good idea to make it clear that all that is said is held in strictest confidence; however, we should inform them that if we need help with something we may need to go to the person who is supervising or overseeing us. People are generally understanding of this process.

We like to use the Burden Bearing prayer exercise written here below, or a shorter version (pg.202) for these times. This way the conference leaders and participants know what we are offering and how people will be prayed for. This has been most successful and the fruit so very sweet.

How rewarding it is to help people connect with God as they listen themselves rather than only hear our words.

PRAYER EXERCISE 79

CONFERENCE PRAYER EXERCISE

Matthew 11:28-30
"Come to me, all you who are weary and burdened
and I will give you rest.....
for I am gentle and humble in heart" (NIV).
"I won't lay anything heavy or ill-fitting on you.
Keep company with me
and you'll learn to live freely and lightly" (MSG).
For My yoke is wholesome (useful, good) – not harsh, hard,
sharp, or pressing, but comfortable, gracious, and pleasant, and
My burden is light and easy to be borne" (AMP).

Let us Meet with Jesus

1 Connect with Jesus. Have a sense or picture of His presence, His love, and His care with you. Take a minute to see, hear, or sense Him: at the cross, at Psalm 23, or at some other safe place.

2 Identify the Burden: What is the burden you sense or feel to bring to the Lord?

3 If the burden were an object, what would it feel like? Where might you carry that on your body?

4 What is the cost to continue carrying the burden?

5 Why might you think you need to keep this? Is there a payoff, a reason, to keep it?

6 What does Jesus want to do with that burden? If it's too heavy to give let Him come and take it from you. Be attentive to what He does with the burden.

7 Invite Him to touch you physically anywhere the burden has been carried in your body.

8 What does the Lord want to give you to replace that burden – a blessing or gift? What would He rather you carry in your heart, body and life?

9 Receive what He has for you by His Spirit.

10 Receive Scriptures, words, pictures, etc. from a prayer minister or prayer partner.

11 Rest and continue to let the Lord's presence touch, settle, and heal you.

Prayer and Prophetic Ministry Afternoons:

Breathe in, breathe out; a natural flow and movement in our life. This is how we see our contemplative and active lives play out in ministry. We breathe in God's love and all He has for us, then we breathe out in service to others. On and on it goes. Based on this picture we set up a regular Breathing Out Ministry Afternoon. It is a highlight to our congregation and to the prophetic and prayer ministers as we all come together. This time of ministry is open to our church family, friends, family members, other ministry teams, anyone in the city or visiting!

We have four "stations" set up in the building.

1. **Soaking worship area** – an open area where people can sit, soak in God's presence, rest awhile, or wait for their ministry times. Live worship is preferred, but we have used CD's at times. Slow, gentle, inspirational music (words not needed.)

2. **Prophetic team ministry** – Drop-in for 15 min. of prophetic ministry with a team of two. They will listen to God with the person requesting ministry and offer anything that they sense to share. One person will write what God is showing so they can take home a reminder. Having a prayer partner, spouse, or friend along works really well.

3. **Listening prayer inner healing sessions** – pre-booked if possible, 1 hour with a team of two. One person will lead the session; the other will intercede and take notes to give to the person receiving prayer when they leave.

4. **Drop-in prayer ministry** – teams of two are available to pray for whoever comes for prayer. Usually 15 minute each.

Ministry teams meet a half hour early to pray and prepare. Each team takes paper, pen, and a box of tissue, and possibly a bottle of healing oil, to their location. We typically have it going for two hours. We gather at the end to debrief about how things went and to pray for those doing ministry to wash off any burdens that have been picked up, and ask for God's refreshing for them. Often we allow a longer period of time to offer these ministries to each other. Many lives and families have been touched by these simple Sunday afternoon times of prayer in community.

Teaching and Training at Workshops:

Being a part of these listening prayer methods and offering them to others and their communities is such a rich experience. Seeing the gifts that God has given us being multiplied in the world is again an organic outgrowth from the Spirit of God. These times of sharing and training are very rewarding for both our teams who assist and those coming to learn and practice with us. Hearing about this ministry is one thing, watching a demonstration of it is another, but the best is entering into it for yourself and being touched by our Living God.

We have been blessed to have been taught ourselves by our church leaders, Brad and Eden Jersak and Fresh Wind leadership and prayer teams, Brian and Della Headly of Listening Prayer Community in Mission, B.C., our friends and colleagues at St. Matthews Anglican Church in Abbotsford, and other sources and teachers as well.

Anchored in Your Community
Ministry Trips

As we go out into the world carrying the Light of Christ that He has given us, that which has been imparted to us by the Holy Spirit, it is of utmost importance to have a sense of belonging and being held. We need to be firmly anchored to our communities at home, with family, and the others who also love and pray for us.

Henri Nouwen's book, *The Inner Voice of Love*, has a powerful message that has been extremely life-giving to me and my community. The Lord brings me back to it occasionally, helping me stay on course.

> "When your call to be a compassionate healer gets mixed up with your need to be accepted, the people you want to heal will end up pulling you into their world and robbing you of your healing gift. But when, out of fear of becoming a person who suffers, you fail to get close to such people, you cannot reach them and restore them to health. You feel deeply the loneliness, alienation, and spiritual poverty of your contemporaries. You want to offer them a truly healing response that comes from your faith in the Gospel.

> "It is important to remain as much in touch as possible with those who know you, love you, and protect your vocation. If you visit people with great needs and deep struggles that you can easily recognize in your own heart, remain anchored in your home community. Think about your community as holding a long line that girds your waist. Wherever you are, it holds that line. Thus you can be very close to people in need of your healing without losing touch with those who protect your vocation. Your community can pull you back when its members see that you are forgetting why you were sent out.

"When you feel a burgeoning need for sympathy, support, affection, and care from those to whom you are being sent, remember that there is a place where you can receive those gifts in a safe and responsible way. Do not let yourself be seduced by the dark powers that imprison those you want to set free. Keep returning to those to whom you belong and who keep you in the light. It is that light that you desire to bring into the darkness. You do not have to fear anyone as long as you remain safely anchored in your community. Then you can carry the light far and wide."

PRAYER EXERCISE 8O

ANCHORED IN YOUR COMMUNITY   XX

1 What images or words come to mind when you think of an anchor?

2 What images or feelings come to you with the image of being held by a long line that girds your waist?

3 Do you sense that you have this established or operating in your life? If so, how does it look for you? If not, why might that be?

4 As you sit with God be open to receive wisdom regarding your relationship with the communities you've been given. Be attentive to what you are given to look at.

5 Make a list of those who surround and pray for you, and those whom you surround and hold as well.

6 Do you have an effective and/or established way of communicating with these people? If not, what might improve that?

7 Imagine a line holding you and the anchor of Christ and your community being there for you always. Give thanks to them and God.

One of our favourite songs at church is 'the Thank You song' we call it. It was written by one of our worship leaders, Jon Paul Vooys, who is very gifted and kind. I hope as you read these words you can receive a sense of the true anointing of God on his life. I'd like to share it with you and offer it as a gift of gratitude to God for all we have been given.

Thank You
© 2005 Jon Paul Vooys

I'm grateful for the things You've done
I'm grateful for the things You'll do

Thank You, thank You

For how You've always been to me
An ever present help in need

Thank You, thank You

Chorus:
Thank you Father that my life is in Your hand
That You never let me go
I will think of You before I lay my head down
And when I start the day I'll thank You

Thank You, thank You

You're always active in my mind
You help me leave my sin behind

Thank You, thank You

Topical Guide

Recommended Books & Ministries

Aron, Elaine	*The Highly Sensitive Child*
Aron, Elaine	*The Highly Sensitive Person*
Barry, Wm	*Spiritual Direction and the Encounter with God*
Brown, Carol	*The Mystery of Spiritual Sensitivity*
Cooke, Graham	*Developing Your Prophetic Gifting*
D'Elbee, Jean	*I Believe in Love – St. Therese of Lisieux*
Dueck, Murray	*If This Were a Dream, What Would it Mean?*
Foster, Richard	*Prayer, Finding the Heart's True Home*
Foster, Richard	*Devotional Classics* (Foster and Bryan Smith)
Green, Thomas H.	*When the Well Runs Dry*
Imbach, Steve	*The Recovery of Love*
Jersak, Brad	*Can You Hear Me?*
Jersak, Eden	*Rivers from Eden*
Lawrence, Brother	*The Practice of the Presence of God*
May, Gerald	*Dark Night of the Soul*
Murray, Andrew	*Waiting Upon God*
Nouwen, Henri	*Can You Drink This Cup?*
Nouwen, Henri	*The Inner Voice of Love*
Payne, Leanne	*Restoring the Christian Soul*
Zeff, Ted	*The Highly Sensitive Persons Survival Guide*

5 & 2 Ministries | Ward Draper — Street Ministry
  the5and2@hotmail.com
Brad & Eden Jersak | Authors/Speakers
  www.bradjersak.com
Brian Doerksen | Recording Artist
  www.briandoerksen.com
Cathy Hardy | Recording Artist/Retreat Leader
  www.cathyajhardy.com
David & Irene Gifford-Cole | The Well and The Hermitage
  thewell@island.net
Freshwind Press | Publisher
  www.freshwindpress.com

Herta Klassen | Watercolor Artist
www.hertaklassen.myartchannel.com
Jon Paul Vooys | Music Artist
www.vooys.ca
Kevin Boese | Recording artist
www.kevinboese.com
Listening Prayer Community | Brian & Della Headley
www.listeningprayer.ca
Lorie Martin | Author/Retreat Leader/Spiritual Director
invitedin@telus.net
MARK Centre | Steve & Evy Klassen — Retreat Leaders/Speakers
www.markcentre.org
MBMSI | Trek Missions and Training
www.mbmsi.org/trek/overview/
Samuel's Mantel | Murray & Kelly Dueck
www.samuelsmantle.com
SoulStream Ministries | Steve & Jeff Imbach
www.soulstream.org
Taize CD's | Gemma & Co. Cathy Hardy & Karin Dart MCC SSCS
1-800-622-5455

"The Lord bless you, and keep you,
The Lord make His face to shine upon you,
And be gracious unto you,
The Lord lift up His countenance upon you,
And give you peace."
Numbers 6:24-26

May all that is done be done in the name of Jesus Christ, our Lord,
to the Glory of God,
and for the healing and joy of God's children and kingdom.
Amen.

Commendations

"Lorie has gifted us with an extensive guide to a livable practice of prayer. Grounded authentically in her own life, her creative, personal prayer exercises open the door to deeper intimacy with God."
- **Steve Imbach,** Director of SoulStream, Spiritual Director/Supervisor

Invited: Invited is a verb – living, active, something that I move into. In reading your book I feel invited to participate in it, I'm moved by the words, I'm drawn into it. It is so full of life and action.
- **Herta Klassen,** Teacher and Artist

"Lorie is a modern day mystic, prophet, friend Jesus, and one of the most down to earth women I know. She has graced us with nuggets right out of her own journal, heart and spiritual journey. Read with caution because I can assure you that if you begin to practice what you find in these pages you are in for a real adventure. If you are looking for spiritual direction, inspiration, spiritual growth or have been wondering exactly what it means to have a "personal relationship with Jesus" you will not be disappointed...read on!"
- **Jodi Krahn** MC

"Those who enter into these encounters with Christ will inevitably see how extremely vital contemplative prayer is for a healthy Christian community. These exercises will equip and develop the spiritual eyes and ears of anyone who partakes, rather than leaving the depths of spirituality to vocational 'Super Christians.' The simplicity of what Lorie presents allows even the newest and youngest believers to enter in."
- **Eden and Brad Jersak,** Fresh Wind Christian Fellowship, Authors and Itinerant Speakers

"This book is a deep pool to drink from, to dive into and discover the depths of Father's love and kindness towards us in Jesus. There are many pearls and precious gems scattered across its pages, glistening with the light of heaven, leading you into encounter after encounter with the heart of God."
- **Deb Chapman,** Team Leader, Antioch Church and Ministries, Wales, U.K.

"My wife and I know Lorie as a friend who listens well. Her longing for listening and hearing God mark her life's journey. As you read you can feel Lorie's hunger to walk through life with God present and active in all of her joys and struggles. The wide variety of prayer exercises in this book speak to Lorie's energy to experience God fully. These may be used exactly as they are or to develop your own for a particular situation. I will personally use this book when I am preparing to lead people into encounters with God and need some direction for specific challenging situations."
- **Steve Klassen,** Steve directs the MARK Centre in Abbotsford, B.C. with his wife, Evy.

Its truly outstanding, and I believe it'll find its niche in the sacred corners of many churches and homes. Its turns out your bag lunch really will feed 5,000 and most likely many more!

- **Fiona Calder,** Intercessor Team Leader, Prayer Minister

"God bless you for writing this book so that others, by using your prayer exercises, can deepen their relationship with God - hallelujah!!"

- **Sue Vander Woude,** SoulStream facilitator, spiritual director/supervisor.

"This book is a treasure! *Invited* is both a manual for the Journey and a companion for the quiet places. Here is a guide for praying with the Scriptures, for healing, for retreating, and for living in community. It is a great help in discerning and listening to the voice of Jesus, and is a valuable handbook for retreat leaders. *Invited* is a joy to read and an invaluable and practical handbook for the disciple of Jesus."

- **The Rev. Dr. Irene Gifford-Cole,** Anglican priest, clinical psychologist, retreat leader, and spiritual director.

I am amazed at the depth and breadth of content here. It is a huge resource that will be very helpful to many. You have done a lot of research and pulled things together in a beautiful way.

- **Cathy Hardy,** Recording Artist, Retreat Leader, Music Teacher

"*Invited* is a book I have been waiting for, to help myself and others go further and deeper in encountering God. Lorie has brought together a feast of treasures old and new in a fresh expression of the 'hospitality of the pen'. *Invited*, as a well thumbed companion to many personal adventures in faith and in community, is likely to become a devotional classic."

- **Karen Lowe,** Senior Co-leader of Antioch Church, Llanelli, Wales